"Not only is this book expertly presented with amazing cake recipes for any mood or occasion (I see Hummingbird Cake!) and technique tutorials to ensure the home baker's success, but it's a true love letter to cake. Zoë's personality and passion for baking and life will have you cranking up the music and smiling while you dance and bake, as if she were in the kitchen with you!"

—**BRIAN HART HOFFMAN**, editor in chief of *Bake from Scratch*

"There are few I trust as much as Zoë François to deliver recipes for astonishingly beautiful cakes. She has the knack of demystifying complicated methods as well as imparting her amazing knowledge in ways that will have you rushing for your whisk. From the simple to the sensational, *Zoë Bakes Cakes* will inspire novices and experts alike. Generous, warm, and instructive, Zoë's family favorites will undoubtedly become yours too. A joyous and delicious celebration of cake!"

—**HELEN GOH**, recipe columnist and co-author of *Sweet*

"Zoë François's book on cake is a must-have for every kitchen. Through her recipes and instruction, she is able to take intricate, complex cake creations and present them in ways that are straightforward and accessible to everyone—new bakers with much to learn, as well as experienced bakers with years of recipes under their belts."

—**SARAH KIEFFER**, cookbook author, baker, and writer at The Vanilla Bean Blog

ZOË
BAKES
cakes

everything you need to know to make
your favorite layers, bundts, loaves, and more

ZOË
BAKES
cakes

Zoë François

How-to and author photos by Sarah Kieffer

TEN SPEED PRESS
California | New York

TO

All the women who raised me (there are many), shaped my view of the world, baked me cakes, and supported me in all my creative endeavors

CONTENTS

INTRODUCTION

My obsession with cake started in an unexpected way—with the humble Twinkie. It was tucked inside a Charlie Brown lunch box, unfortunately not mine, and that little cake opened up a whole new world. A lifelong love affair with all things cake was ignited on my very first day of kindergarten. Perhaps the average kid wouldn't even have blinked at that iconic tube of sponge cake, with its freakishly white and delicious filling squished inside, as if by magic. But, I wasn't average.

I grew up with my parents on a series of communes, which absolutely had its benefits. In 1969, I could toddle sans clothes around the Woodstock Festival with a backdrop of screaming guitars, as if it were any other day; in fact, I did just that. I have visceral memories of sitting in my dad's vast garden with the smell of tomato plants vining around me, mixed with dirt, pine trees, and wood smoke. The counterculture to which my parents adhered included a back-to-the-land philosophy on food. We lived in the Northeast Kingdom of Vermont, on a dirt road that was impassable by anything other than foot for long stretches of the year, due to mud or snow. Geography compelled our self-reliance. So, growing our own food was a necessity, not merely a fashionable trend, and we raised chickens for eggs and meat, a rather nasty-tempered collection of rams and sheep, and a cow for milk and the resulting cream that also became our butter.

My first kitchen memory as a wobbly toddler was standing inside the "Big House." This was the only permanent structure on the land and where everyone on the commune gathered for cooking and a respite from the winter. The room was filled with singing and music while sharing the chore of churning cream into butter. That is probably why, to this day, I find music (and butter) essential parts of baking. If you know my Instagram baking tutorials, you're familiar with the soundtracks that often start with Joni Mitchell and bring it all home with the dance beat of Drake by the end of the recipe.

Along with tending the gardens, my dad kept bees. The beeswax was transformed into ornate candles in a makeshift factory we had within a geodesic dome built out of VW car hoods (because it isn't really a commune without a geodesic dome). We sold the candles at the local co-op, along with homemade granola and bread that my Aunt Melissa baked.

There was also sap collected from the maple trees on our eighty-plus acres of land. We brought the sloshing pails to a neighbor's sugarhouse, where it was processed into syrup. Honey and maple syrup were the only two sweeteners I ever knew, and I was quite fine with that. Until that Twinkie. . . .

Today, those cylindrical cakes with the mystery creme on the inside are synonymous with junk food; but to a sugar-deprived flower child, they were a revelation—a parting of the seas, as it were, and the source of a newly born passion. I must have given my folks an earful about the deception they'd been pulling on me all those years. Carob was the actual lie—and decidedly *not* chocolate—despite all their lip service to the contrary. Grapes were fruit, period. Drying grapes in the sun to shrivel into raisins does not change them into candy. I fought *that* injustice with all the fervor and dedication those wonderful hippies had instilled in me.

The baking began soon after, tossing ingredients and a handful of hope in a bowl and expecting some sort of alchemy to return as cake. I was eight or nine years old before a miracle occurred by way of a Dutch Baby recipe, courtesy of my friend, and fellow commune-dweller, Sasha. That glorious mix of flour, eggs, and milk puffed to the point of exploding in the oven. We wolfed it down with maple syrup and slices of McIntosh apples from our yard. It was an auspicious beginning.

A parade of knowledge marched into my kitchen after that. First came the Time Life books on French cooking, which still hold space on my stuffed cookbook shelves. Through them, an attempt at a chocolate mousse was a gritty disaster, because I didn't know that adding coffee didn't mean Folgers coffee grounds. Lesson learned: mousse should be velvety, not chewy. The next batch was spot-on. Soon I had baked my way through Lee Bailey's *Country Kitchen*, *Baking with Julia*, and Martha Stewart's everything; Ina Garten's brownies were on high rotation. Over the years, my affection for sugar only deepened, along with a determination to figure out its transformational powers.

IN PURSUIT OF SUGAR

When I was in college, I launched a cookie company after writing a business plan for a fictitious company as an assignment for my accounting class. I could not have cared less about the profit and loss calculations. In fact, I was never much of a student in the sense of academics. If it hadn't been for home-economics classes in middle school, I would have had very little to wrap my head around in a school building. Growing up as the daughter of wandering hippies, I ended up going to sixteen different schools by the time I graduated from college. Each time I started at a new school, I'd reinvent myself, and by the time my folks were on to the next ashram, commune, cult, or concert, I was ready to leave too. I was bored in a school classroom, compared to the journey I was on with my parents.

College was no better, and that business class at the University of Vermont (UVM) had me wishing I could move again. Instead of sitting in class listening to business theory, I immersed myself in an actual business, taking a semester off from UVM to open Zoë's Cookies. I ran the "company" out of my boyfriend's (now my husband) tiny apartment kitchen. He even built me a beautiful rolling cart to launch my cookie-baking empire on the streets of Burlington, Vermont. The company was successful enough that I didn't lose money, but soon it became evident that more school was probably a wise move.

Back at work on a fine arts degree, I haunted the art department looking for my medium. There was never a doubt that artists were my people. And yet . . . neither paint, clay, nor soldering was my love language; none of those things moved me to create in a way that left me satisfied. But I was getting closer.

Taking a part-time job at a Ben & Jerry's ice-cream shop, I was put in charge of decorating ice-cream cakes. Filling that pastry bag with cream, as simple as it seems now, was the first time I'd ever felt serenity in a task. I didn't experience time, and I would have decorated those cakes even if they hadn't been paying me—it felt like my art. Time seemed to melt away as I twirled swirls and shapes onto frozen sheets of cake. You might think that implies I was good at it, and that would be the wrong impression to go away with. I had fifteen minutes of training and no video tutorials to rely on, so I had to learn by trial and error. I think back now on some of those cakes and how rough they must have been, but I loved making them, even with their imperfections. I was too young at the time to realize that I was where I was meant to be. There were miles still to go.

FINDING MY BLISS

After graduation, I plodded along, working in advertising because it was supposed to be where creatives created. These were the 1980s, long before the Food Network made kitchens seem like a legitimate job, and blogging was decades from existing. Yet the work stifled me, and I found myself coming home at night and pouring my frustrations into a stand mixer. It wasn't until I was married and settling into Minneapolis that my husband, after patiently listening to me whine about the cubicle I'd found myself working in, suggested I attend culinary school. Brilliant! I packed up and headed off to the prestigious Culinary Institute of America (CIA) in upstate New York. Once again, I found myself with a piping bag in my hand, and I immediately felt at home. I never looked back.

While I was at the CIA, I got a job; over the phone, sight unseen. It was with a Minneapolis chef named Andrew Zimmern, who was in need of a pastry chef assistant. Steeling my nerves, I took a giant leap of faith, left school unfinished, and landed spectacularly. Within six months, I was his executive pastry chef, and a lifelong friendship was born.

For a decade, I worked in professional kitchens—high-end catering and fine-dining restaurants. It wasn't unusual to bake a thousand cupcakes or an ornate wedding cake while at the catering facility. The experience was invaluable because I had to do the same task over and over, piping buttercream rosettes on all those before-mentioned cupcakes; this honed my skills in a way that you just don't get at culinary school or baking cookies at home, one recipe at a time. The pace and pressure were intense, and I loved every crazy minute of it.

CAKE IS (STILL MY) LOVE

Even though I have baked professionally for decades, I never tire of it. And my favorite thing to bake, after all these years, is cake. It is my medium, how I express my art and my love. It's what I give to people for special events and how I busy my hands and mind when I am stressed or sad. A cake can turn a Tuesday into an occasion. There is no day that can't be made better with a little slice. Cake is the way I tell my friends and family that I love them. When my son Charlie celebrated his birthday during his freshman year of college, I sent him a homemade cake. It was the best way I could think of to have a part of me with him. He and his dorm-mates made fast work of it and started requesting that cakes be sent regularly. I happily obliged!

I also profoundly enjoy the process of building a cake, finding the just-right recipe that a specific moment calls for. Old recipes are revisited like friends and often nudged into the perfect fit for a new era. I find fulfillment and delight in the process of creating, baking, and blowtorching (whenever I can find an excuse for busting out a flamethrower).

Part of the magic of cake is that what makes a great cake is somewhat subjective and emotional. There are cakes that are touted as the best in the world; I have tried many of these, and they left me yearning for something, someone, anything. They tasted as if they had been made perfectly but without the crucial ingredient—love. I don't care if you make a cake from a box mix and scoop frosting out of a can; if you are enjoying the process and making that cake for someone you love, that cake will taste better than one made by a disgruntled professional. One of my favorite cakes of all time was made by a friend for my birthday, from a box, during a snowstorm. Was it the most delicious cake I've ever eaten? Hell no (sorry, Todd), but I was touched that he had so much fun making it for me; and as a professional pastry chef, people rarely want to bake for me. I am sending him a copy of this book, so that the next time we're together on my birthday, he can bake me a delicious, homemade cake. And now that you have this book, you can make one too.

ABOUT THIS BOOK

This book began to take shape during an epic forty-five-mile cake-eating walk across Manhattan. I grabbed my best friend and we boarded a plane to New York City. The pace was ambitious: one mile, one slice. But we did it, forty-five cakes in all!

Because cake is always better enjoyed with others, and because two people eating forty-five pieces of cake is excessive, I pulled in some friends to share the bounty. I reconnected with people whom I hadn't seen since high school; and over the course of three days, we shared slices such as a light-as-air sponge cake at Lady M's on the Upper West Side and a Greek phyllo orange "cake" in Tribeca, with stops for Funfetti, carrot, chocolate, hummingbird, and a raspberry-stuffed charlotte along the way.

More cake walks followed through Los Angeles, Birmingham, Brooklyn, Madison, Minneapolis, and Philadelphia in the United States; Dublin, Ireland; and elsewhere. I ate phenomenal cakes that I couldn't wait to re-create, along with some that were meh (and that's being kind), both equally as inspiring and instructive to this book. I tasted cake triumphs and mistakes and I can now guide you to cake perfection every time.

In culinary school, I also studied the whys and hows of baking. There is a science to it, a bit of alchemy, and some hope that translates into lots of practice and process. Finally, when I made a cake, it would rise tall instead of collapsing. I unlocked the mysteries of textures. I mastered the tricks to prevent caramel from crystallizing in the pot. Soon I knew how to fix just about anything, including buttercream that had turned to soup in the mixer. Basically, I learned how NOT to panic. Instead, I enjoyed the process of baking so much that even my failures—which were many—added up to a level of confidence and competence that allowed me to become an award-winning baker, cookbook author, and baking instructor.

I have been teaching since my early days in the kitchen with Andrew Zimmern. He recognized my ability to explain complicated concepts to people who had very little, if any, experience baking. This was a time way before Instagram or Facebook—hell, this was before the internet—so he signed me up to teach at a local cooking school. I never stopped, and now I have more than twenty-five years of teaching experience to share with you.

This book spans all my favorite cakes, from family recipes such as Anna's Hazelnut–Brown Butter Cake (page 149) to cakes from my years in professional kitchens, like Chocolate Devil's Food Cake (page 125), and some new ones discovered during my cake-walk odysseys, like Hummingbird Cake (page 135). The recipes get progressively more involved in each chapter. Some of the cakes you can toss together in a single bowl using nothing more than a spoon; but from there, I add techniques to create classic pound cakes, which are leavened with nothing more than air whipped into butter, or light-as-air cakes, made with egg whites that are super-delicate and delicious. Some cakes are simple, old worldly, and rustic, while others are sensational and adorned with flourishes that look complicated but are really easy to make when you know the secrets. The final cake in the book is a three-tier wedding cake, which is a gasp-inducing showstopper.

I want you to feel comfortable baking anything in this book. Some people will want to dive right in to the recipes and bake a special cake for a loved one's birthday or for an after-school snack. Other bakers will want to know a little more about the whys and hows of baking the perfect cake. This book is for both the novice and the more experienced baker; there is truly something for everyone.

I created the Cake Academy section so you can jump to more information about the techniques I'm using. For those who share my enthusiasm, I geek out on things such as the science behind why egg whites whip up to perfection. But even if you aren't interested in these details, you'll still sail through the recipes. However, I recommend reading the chapter carefully if you want to be able to play with a recipe and give it your own spin. It's remarkable how a touch of cake science and technique can be such a useful tool if your cakes aren't coming out as you'd hoped. I will guide you through why that might be as well as put a note in every recipe if there is a lesson to be learned in the Cake Academy. I have the tricks to help you get your baking just where you want it to be. My first tip is to crank up your favorite music, any tunes that move you, then tie on your apron and get to baking cake!

INGREDIENTS

It is often said that a recipe is only as good as the ingredients used. I agree, so I recommend you buy all of your favorite brands when baking these cakes. When I have a particular recommendation for a brand, I will call it out. I do so only when I've tested with several and decided that one produced a cake that is superior to all the others. I try to bake with organic ingredients when possible, but I know they aren't always an option. In some cases, the natural and/or organic products don't create the cake I want. For instance, naturally derived food coloring is not as vivid as those made with artificial color. Organic cake flour is not as pure white as its nonorganic counterpart. They will all work, but just be aware that the results may be slightly different. Sometimes what you are eating is your priority, and sometimes you want it to look *just so*. No judging; you decide.

This is where I am going to get down on my knees and beg you to make ingredient substitutions in your cakes very carefully. There are times when I suggest you play with the type of fruit, spices, or varieties of chocolate called for in the recipe. Those substitutions are fun and will make a cake to fit your mood and occasion. However, swapping out gentle cake flour with equal amounts of a hearty whole-wheat flour will throw off the chemical balance of the recipes. You could accidentally end up with something you love, but chances are more likely it will be a dense and disappointing experiment. I spent a long time testing these recipes and I suggest you give them a go as I wrote them, before putting your creative spin on them.

CHOCOLATE

Chocolate is the grande dame of cake ingredients, representative of devotion and love. People have been eating some form of cocoa for thousands of years. It has caused wars—it's just that powerful. The chocolate that we consume today is made from the cacao tree in the form of cocoa powder, bar chocolate, chunks, or chips. They're all an essential part of many cakes, imparting richness and deep flavor. You will notice a big improvement in the taste of your cakes if you use the highest-quality chocolate you can afford.

Cocoa Powder Cocoa powder is the result of drying and grinding cocoa solids (see following). My favorite unsweetened cocoa powder is Valrhona, for the depth of flavor and deep color. The cocoa is Dutch-processed, which means it has been alkali-treated, so it is less acidic and darker as a result. All of my recipes were tested

WHITE CHOCOLATE—
THE MISNOMER

The only part of the cocoa bean that appears in white chocolate is cocoa butter. This is why white chocolate (cocoa butter blended with sugar and milk solids) is white or ivory in color. It also makes white chocolate behave differently than other chocolates, so you can't substitute it for them in recipes. Be sure that your white chocolate contains cocoa butter, otherwise it isn't really related to chocolate at all. Coating chocolate of any color should be avoided for the purposes of this book.

CHOCOLATE SHAVINGS

To make chocolate shavings, scrape a large bar of chocolate with a sharp chef's knife. The harder you press down as you scrape the chocolate, the thicker the shavings will be. (Trader Joe's sells a 17-oz / 480g bar of bittersweet chocolate that is flat on one side; which works perfectly for this.)

with Dutch-processed cocoa. Droste, Guittard, or other brands will also work but may vary in color from black to red, so the color of your cake may vary depending on the cocoa. Natural cocoa is more acidic and may change the way a cake rises, and the color won't be as dark.

Solid Chocolate ■ Cocoa beans grow in large pods on cacao trees. Those beans are fermented, dried, and ground into a paste before being melted into cocoa liquor that is then separated into cocoa butter and cocoa solids.

Cocoa butter gives chocolate its smooth melting mouthfeel and makes chocolate more glorious when made into ganache or a cake. You want to look for chocolate made with cocoa butter and not with other types of fats.

Cocoa solids give chocolate its distinctive flavor and color. The percentage number you see on a chocolate refers to the combined amount of cocoa butter and solids in the bar. If the chocolate says 70 percent, it means that 30 percent of that bar is some combination of sugar, milk solids, or other non-cocoa ingredient. In this book, I use bittersweet chocolate (about 70 percent cocoa), but you can replace it with semisweet (about 60 percent cocoa). Milk chocolate is a different beast and will make your recipes too sweet; it also doesn't behave the same way as do higher-percentage chocolates. For bittersweet bar chocolate, Valrhona is my favorite, but Callebaut, Scharffen Berger, Guittard, and other premium brands also work quite well. If premium chocolate is unavailable, try the recipes with your favorite brands of solid chocolate or chips.

DAIRY

There are many forms of dairy products that are essential to baking cakes. Depending on which one called for, they can add moisture, flavor, fat, acid, body, or all of the above.

Buttermilk ■ I use buttermilk to add liquid and acid to a recipe, both for flavor and to aid in the rising power when mixed with baking soda. Either whole milk or low-fat buttermilk work well in the recipes.

Cream Cheese ■ Cream cheese is a soft, fresh, mild-flavored cheese, and I use it to whip up into my family's favorite icing (see page 209). Philadelphia Original is my first choice for baking because it has a wonderful texture and lightly tangy flavor. If you can't find that brand, just avoid the low-fat or no-fat varieties and make sure the cream cheese isn't full of unnecessary gums, which don't have as nice a texture or flavor.

Heavy Whipping Cream ■ Whipping cream is a staple in my cake baking and making. I use it in cake batters, as a glorious filling between layers, or served whipped on top of a cake. In some cake batters, the cream is used as a liquid to add richness and moisten the crumb. In other cakes, I whip the cream first and then fold it into the batter, which means there is air trapped in the cream to help leaven the rich cake. The trick to perfectly whipped cream is to whip it low and slow (see page 227).

Always look for cream that is highest in fat content; it will make the most stable and delicious whipped cream.

Mascarpone ▦ Mascarpone is a super-soft cheese, like a cross between heavy cream, sour cream, and cream cheese. Whipped up, mascarpone gives the perfect balance to the chocolate in my Whipped Milk Chocolate Mascarpone (page 237).

Milk ▦ I typically use whole milk in these recipes; its added fat lends a richness to the cake that helps flavor and texture. Lower-fat milks will also work, but the recipe will come out slightly different. You can also substitute nondairy milk in any of the recipes (rice, almond, coconut, or soy). If you do use a nondairy substitution, I recommend going with a non-sweetened variety, since the added sweetness might make the final cake taste too cloying.

Sour Cream ▦ The tanginess of sour cream helps to temper the sweetness of some recipes. It is also super-rich, which gives the cake a wonderful texture without adding any greasiness from additional butter or oil. The fat and acid in sour cream act as tenderizers; the acid interacts with baking soda in a recipe to aid in the rise. If you can't find sour cream, you can replace it with crème fraîche, which is a younger, mellower version of this set cream, or use plain Greek-style yogurt. Avoid low-fat or no-fat sour cream for the best results.

Yogurt ▦ I love plain, Greek-style whole yogurt for its rich tangy flavor in cakes. Full-fat plain yogurt can also be used; it's just a touch thinner in flavor and consistency. Yogurt can be used in place of sour cream, which is sometimes a challenge to find around the world.

DRIED FRUIT

I make recommendations, based on tradition, for the type of dried fruit to use in your cakes, but they are just suggestions and you should use whatever pleases you. My eldest son won't touch anything with raisins, so they are avoided at all costs (mostly), and I totally understand that someone's palate takes precedence over tradition. I typically go for unsweetened dried fruit, since the recipes already have all the sugar I desire. Sometimes I want bright colorful fruit, like apricots, in a recipe, and this means fruit processed with sulfites. It is a preservative that keeps the fruit from turning brown, but some people are sensitive to sulfites and should stick to the unsulfured fruit.

EGGS

As everyone knows, eggs have two parts. There are the whites, which are mostly protein and offer strength and, when whipped, the rising power in a recipe. The yolks are mostly fat and help to emulsify a mixture, adding color and flavor. Eggs are where the wizardry comes in for most cake recipes.

How you use eggs in a recipe will give you wildly different results. Whole eggs can create a dense, smooth crumb when added slowly to a pound cake. On the other

INGREDIENTS

hand, egg whites can be whipped into ethereal pillows of meringue that lighten a cake. (For more on meringue, see page 37.)

All of the recipes in this book were tested with fresh large eggs. Check the date on your eggs; they will get thinner and lose some of their stretch and strength as they get past two weeks old. The most important thing to know about eggs is that they should be at room temperature when mixed into your batter, unless otherwise stated in a recipe. (For more information about proper temperature of ingredients, see page 33.)

Separating eggs is much easier when they are chilled, since the eggs are firmer; however, you then need to let them sit at room temperature for about an hour to warm up. If you forget to remove the eggs from the refrigerator before you start to bake, you can warm them in the shell in a bowl of hot water for about 5 minutes and then carefully separate. How you separate an egg was probably taught to you by your folks when you were young. There is no right or wrong way, as long as the yolks don't break and the whites separate cleanly and completely. That said, here are two methods.

→ Tap the egg on the counter until just cracked, face the crack to the sky, gently poke both your thumbs into the crack, and ease the shell apart. The white will start to spill out, so do this over a bowl. Rock the egg yolk back and forth between the two halves of the shell, allowing the sharp edge of the shell to cut off the egg white from the yolk.

→ Carefully crack all of the eggs into a bowl. Gently pick up the yolks with your fingertips and pinch off the whites, then put the yolks in a separate bowl. I've also seen this done by squeezing a plastic water bottle with a wide mouth to create suction and placing it directly over the yolk to gently suck it into the bottle.

Both egg whites and yolks can be stored if you find yourself with extras after making your cake. Egg whites can be refrigerated for a couple of weeks or frozen for months, without any preparation; just put them in an airtight container. Yolks don't last nearly as long, just a few days in the refrigerator and about a month in the freezer. To store yolks, you'll want to stir them with a pinch of sugar to prevent them from developing a skin in the refrigerator or from being too viscous when thawed from the freezer.

As for pasteurized or frozen egg whites, I've found that they don't whip up as well as egg whites from fresh eggs. I'd recommend using them only if you are in a bind.

EXTRACTS, FOOD COLORING, AND SPICES

Flavor extracts, food coloring, and spice are the little extras that make a cake sing. Sometimes the effects are subtle, and other times they are bold. I use vanilla extract in just about every recipe, so I consider it foundational. Food coloring can turn a simple cake absolutely spectacular. Spices are key to the personality in certain cakes, but you are free to play around to suit your tastes.

Extracts ▦ Pure extracts are made with the natural essences of almond, coconut, orange, mint, or anything else you want to flavor your cakes. I recommend using pure extracts whenever you can; I even go so far as to make my own vanilla, which is really quite easy (see page 12). If you use imitation or artificial flavorings, you may introduce a chemical aftertaste to the recipes. If you want a flavor in your cake or frosting that demands using an artificial flavor, just add a tiny bit at a time and taste it, since these extracts tend to be very strong.

Vanilla extract appears in nearly every recipe in this book and if you find one without it, I probably just forgot it. Vanilla is like salt, meaning it heightens the flavors around it. Most of the time it is just like background music, meant to allow the apples, chocolate, spices, or whatever is the star of the recipe to shine. On the occasion I really want vanilla to step forward, I will suggest using actual vanilla bean seeds, plus vanilla extract.

Food Coloring ▦ Sometimes I want to add whimsy or drama to a cake by using food coloring, but most of the time I go au naturel. When I do tint a cake, I try to use a natural food coloring because the colors tend to be less garish and because they're derived from natural fruits, vegetables, or spices. Having said this, there are times that the natural colors don't achieve the intensity I want. I tried to use a natural food color for my Red Velvet Cake (page 128) but it kept turning purple or brown, so I went with the chemically derived color. If you are dedicated to going all natural, you'll need to add quite a bit of acid to the recipes to keep the colors clean. You can add acid in the form of cream of tartar, but how much will be an experiment and may affect the flavor quite a bit.

I almost always use gel paste food color versus liquid, since the color is more intense and so you don't have to add as much to achieve the color you want. When adding food color to a cake mix, do it in the beginning, along with the butter and sugar. This way, you give the color time to combine thoroughly without over-mixing the batter. The exception to this is if you are adding it to an angel food cake or other egg-foam cake. Then you need to add it after you've established the foam, so you don't interrupt the strength of the eggs as they whip.

When adding food color to a frosting or icing, do it after all the mixing is done. Sometimes you'll want to divide the frosting into separate bowls, so you can tint it many colors. (To learn how I get a multicolored flower, see my piped rose technique on page 56.)

Ground Spices ▦ Once ground, spices can lose their flavors and aromas quickly, so it is best to grind your own whole spices as you need them. The easiest way to do this is in a spice or coffee grinder. A mortar and pestle also work and is a rather relaxing exercise.

Making your own vanilla extract is really so easy and delicious. I started my current batch in 2012, and I just keep adding more vanilla beans and vodka once it gets halfway down the bottle. The extract will keep indefinitely; and over the months, it just keeps getting better. The type of vanilla bean you use does not matter, and you can combine the various beans from Mexico, Madagascar, Tahiti, Indonesia, and beyond. They range in flavor and cost, so try many and pick your favorite. The amount needed will depend on the size of the container you use, but you want a bunch to get the best flavor. The beans can be expensive, so you may start with less and then add leftover pods after you have scraped out the seeds for another recipe. This will take longer, because you aren't adding the flavorful pulp, but it is a great way to use up scraped pods. (Don't use vanilla beans if they have been cooked in a recipe, such as custard. They'll contaminate your bottle and make the vanilla murky.)

You'll need a glass bottle with a stopper (I recommend 750ml, but the size doesn't matter; you can make a larger or smaller amount). If you prefer a nonalcoholic version, simply scrape the seeds into food-grade glycerin instead of vodka.

homemade vanilla extract

Makes about 3 cups / 750ml

12 vanilla beans

About 3 cups / 750ml vodka (enough to cover the beans in the bottle you choose)

1   Clean the bottle and dry it well.

2   Cut the vanilla beans down their length and then scrape out the seeds; this helps to better disperse the flavor in the alcohol. Put the pods and scraped seed pulp into the bottle.

3   Fill the bottle with the vodka, close the stopper, and shake to distribute the seeds. The vodka will remain clear for the first few days but darken over time. Shake the bottle every couple of days to break up the pulp and get the seeds distributed in the vodka. After a week, the extract will start to get darker and develop some flavor. After two weeks, you can use the extract but the flavor will be very subtle. At Week 3, the color should be amber and the aroma richer, but waiting for Week 4 and beyond is when it gets really exciting.

4   Use in any recipe that calls for vanilla extract. If you are using it in buttercream, you may want to strain out any pulp. You'll still have the seeds in your recipe, but the stringy bits from the pod will be removed.

FATS

Fat is fundamental to most of the cakes in this book. Not only does it make for a luxurious texture, creating a smooth, rich, and soft crumb, but it also carries flavor, so it heightens the taste of vanilla, spices, or any other flavors in the recipe.

Butter ▦ Butter is delicious, period. But it plays an even bigger role than taste alone and is foundational in many a cake recipe. Butter is a dairy product usually made from cows' milk. It is created by churning cream until it separates into fat (butter) and a remaining liquid (buttermilk). European butters tend to have a higher fat content than butters found in the United States, unless the US butter is labeled "European-style." I tested all the recipes with American butter, so using a butter from Europe, or one of that style, may make for a cake that has a slightly oily feel. But the flavor will be incredible!

When creamed to a light, airy texture, butter will help your cake rise and give it a beautiful crumb. The temperature of your butter is often the key to proper mixing. If your butter is too cold, it won't whip up light enough; but if it's too soft, it can't hold enough air to leaven a cake. I always call for unsalted butter, so you can control the saltiness of your recipes. It's best not to refrigerate butter cakes, since the butter hardens when cold and makes the texture of the crumb too dense. (For tips on perfect butter, see page 33.)

Oil ▦ Unless otherwise specified, I tend to use a mild oil that has little flavor, such as vegetable, canola, corn, or safflower, so that it isn't competing with the other flavors in the cake. There are exceptions, like Olive Oil–Chiffon Cake (page 153), where the oil is meant to be the star. Oil can make for a super-moist and tender cake that stays that way even when refrigerated. Oil lacks the deliciousness of butter, but sometimes you want the texture it provides. In some recipes, I add oil, to create a tender crumb, *and* butter, for its wonderful flavor, so I have the benefits of both.

FLOURS

This is a cake book, so, of course, flour is an important ingredient. Flour gives cake structure and is a key element in the texture of a cake. Conventional flours are made from wheat. When the proteins in wheat (glutenin and gliadin) are mixed with liquids, they form gluten, which is highly elastic and strong. Gluten development is desirable when you want a nice chewy bread. But for cake, we are going for something more delicate, so we need to keep the gluten development at bay. The flours described here have varying degrees of gluten based on what texture you want in the final cake.

All-Purpose Flour ▦ All-purpose flour is a staple ingredient for many of the recipes in this book. All-purpose flour is made from hard wheat and has a medium protein content. Why does that matter? Some recipes require a bit of gluten for structure to hold up to a heavy ingredient, like mashed bananas or grated zucchini.

BROWN BUTTER

Brown butter is simply butter that has been cooked until the solids start to caramelize, adding a toasty flavor to the butter that is exquisite in a cake batter. It is super-easy to make (see page 147); and I call for it in several recipes, so I typically just make a big batch and store it in the refrigerator. When the butter is done cooking, it will have no water or milk solids (the browned bits don't count), so it is oilier than regular butter and should be used only when suggested in the book. Brown butter will last in the refrigerator for a couple of weeks.

To strain or not to strain? I like the toasty bits that settle on the bottom of the pot and use the butter without straining. If you like a cleaner-looking cake, without the browned milk solids specked in your batter, then strain the butter through a fine-mesh sieve.

We just don't want to get the gluten too worked up, or the cake can be tough. This is easily avoided by mixing as little as possible once the flour is added to the wet batter. (For more on mixing, see pages 35 and 36.)

Each brand of all-purpose flour has a different protein content, so if your cakes seem dry or tough, you may want to explore the protein content in your flour. The more protein, the more water the flour will absorb and create gluten. I tested all of the recipes with Gold Medal flour, which has a protein content of about 10.5 percent. King Arthur has closer to 11.7 percent, so if you're finding your cakes are too dry with King Arthur flour, try decreasing the amount of flour by a couple of tablespoons.

Bleached and unbleached flours behave the same, but they may taste different and will have a slightly different color to them. The chemical process of bleaching the flour also changes the flavor slightly, and some people describe it as having a chemical aftertaste. I think this is pretty subtle and, when combined with other ingredients and baked, is imperceptible to anyone who isn't a supertaster (yes, that's a real thing; and my husband and youngest son are both supertasters, so they perceive flavors that I can't). Some people really like the pure-white color of bleached flour for cakes. Other people will prefer the flavor of unbleached flour; it's your call.

Cake Flour ▦ Cake flour is made from soft wheat and has a really low protein content, so it won't develop as much gluten as all-purpose flour when added to a liquid. It is wonderful for cakes that have a delicate, tender crumb, which is precisely why the flour is named after them. Generally, cake flour is bleached and very white, which may be desirable for some recipes, especially White Cake (page 119). You can also source unbleached cake flour; but in certain parts of the country, it's harder to come by. Unbleached will be a creamy color, not pure white; similar to all-purpose flour, it's a preference based on what you want in flavor or color for the final cake.

Gluten-Free Flour ▦ Some of the recipes in this book are flourless, so they are naturally gluten-free, but this book was not tested with gluten-free flours. If you have a flour blend you've used happily in place of all-purpose wheat flour in cakes, it is worth a try.

Nut Flour ▦ Nut flour comprises nuts that are so finely ground they resemble all-purpose flour, and it is used to create a wonderful flavor and texture in some cakes. But they are not a substitute for wheat flour. You can make your own by pulverizing whole nuts in a food processor until they are powdery, but be careful not to go too far or you'll end up with nut butter. Almond is probably the most common nut flour. It is the one that I use most, because it has a subtle flavor and it doesn't overpower a recipe. Hazelnut and pistachio flours are excellent as well and can be used in place of almond flour to change up a recipe. (*See also* Nut Meal, page 17.)

Semolina Flour ▦ Semolina is used in some southern European and Middle Eastern cakes, where it lends a beautiful yellow color and slightly winey-sweet flavor. The best semolina for cakes is the finely ground "durum" flour. If you can't find semolina, you can use whole-wheat flour instead, but the flavor will end up nuttier and less sweet.

Starches ▪ Starches are very finely ground (powdery) grains and roots. They have no protein, so they will make a slurry when added to liquid instead of forming stretchy gluten. They act as a very effective thickener, but only when cooked with a liquid. Starch is also effective in minimizing the gluten in a delicate cake batter when mixed with flour. I tend to use cornstarch when thickening a custard or fruit sauce. If you desire, you can also use tapioca, agar-agar, or arrowroot instead of the more common cornstarch.

Whole-Wheat Flour ▪ Whole-wheat flour contains the germ and bran of the wheat, both of which are healthful and tasty. Together they add a slightly nutty flavor, which I love, but it can also make a dense and heavy cake. I often mix whole-wheat flour with some all-purpose or cake flour to achieve a lighter texture, while still getting the flavor and healthful bits of the whole wheat. White whole-wheat flour is still 100 percent whole wheat, just milled from white wheat berries, so use it interchangeably. All-purpose and whole-wheat flours absorb liquid differently; swap them in recipes at your own peril, since it will really change the cake.

LEAVENERS

Most of the cakes in this book get their rise and airy texture with the help of a chemical leavener. Baking powder and baking soda are the two chemical leaveners used to create the rise in cakes, sometimes used together and sometimes used separately. But they are not interchangeable, as they work differently to help cakes become airy.

Baking Powder ▪ Baking powder contains both an alkali and an acid, so it is a self-contained carbon dioxide machine and needs only liquid and heat to react. On its own, it's not as powerful as baking soda, since it is made of baking soda plus a powdered acid. Sometimes a particularly acidic or heavy cake batter will call for both baking powder and baking soda to achieve a nice rise and the best taste. Baking powder loses its rising power over time, so be sure to check the expiration date. One of my testers learned this fact the hard way, when her cake failed to rise in the oven. It turned out her baking powder had expired the previous year.

You can make your own baking powder by combining one part baking soda (alkali), two parts cream of tartar (acid), and a pinch of cornstarch (to keep it from clumping; this is optional).

Baking Soda ▪ Baking soda is an alkali (base) and needs to be in an acidic environment to create carbon dioxide, which causes a cake to rise. Buttermilk, sour cream, cocoa powder, and brown sugar (because of the molasses) are acidic and react with baking soda. Baking soda alone is more powerful than baking powder, so it is used in smaller amounts. It can also impart a bitter, soapy flavor if overdone, so it is often used with baking powder to achieve the best rise and flavor. If your cakes are rising like crazy with big bubbles and then falling at the end of baking, it is a sign that there is too much leavener.

Cream of Tartar ▪ Cream of tartar is an acid produced by the process of making wine. It is used to create a stronger protein web when whipping egg whites. It can replace corn syrup when making caramel because it prevents the sugar from crystallizing.

NUTS

Nuts add richness, flavor, and texture to some cakes. Freeze nuts if you are storing for longer than a month or if you live in a warm climate, since the oils can go rancid and affect their flavor.

Some recipes call for toasting the nuts before using them. You can buy them toasted or easily do it yourself by spreading them out on a baking sheet and baking at 350°F / 175°C for a short time. The timing will depend on the size and type of nut (almonds are hard and require more time, while walnuts are soft and fatty requiring less time), so keep a close eye on them.

Almond Paste and Marzipan Both almond paste and marzipan are made from pulverized almonds and sugar. They differ only in the amount of sugar added (almond paste has less), so you can really use either one in the recipes. For Grandma Ellen's Trinidad Rum Cake (page 103), the marzipan is rolled thin and draped over the cake like rolled fondant.

Coconut Flakes I like to use Baker's Angel Sweet Coconut, because it is sweet and has a great texture straight out of the bag. It can be thrown into a recipe or used to decorate a cake. If you use the unsweetened version, it is dry and has a harder texture, so it's not great for decorating but can be used in a batter, such as for Ultimate Carrot Cake (page 136).

Nut Butter and Seed Spreads Peanut butter and Nutella are great for flavoring buttercream; because they are powerful flavors and thick, they don't mess with the consistency. Tahini, almond butter, hazelnut paste, and any other nut or seed spread are great to play with in your icings.

Nut Meal Meal is ground nuts that have been pulverized to the point of looking like flour. It adds richness and texture, but doesn't develop any gluten, so you can't replace nut meal with the other flours called for in a recipe. Nut meal comes blanched (skins off) or natural (skins on). You choose, but know that the natural (skin on) version will have dark flecks in it that may show in your cake. Because nuts have so much oil, it is best to store these meals in the freezer, so they don't go rancid.

SALT

Salt is just as key in creating the perfect balance of flavor in a cake as it is in savory dishes. Too much salt and the cake is obviously off, but the lack of salt can also make a cake taste flat and boring. I use kosher salt in my recipes. When a cake requires sifting, this can be a challenge, so I whisk the salt together with the flour after the flour has been sifted. I use sea salt to finalize a recipe if it needs a perk of flavor after cooking or baking.

SWEETENERS

Sweetness is the essential quality of a cake. You want just enough to make the cake pleasing but not so much that it's cloying. I try to strike that balance. The sugar also plays a role in the structure of a cake, making it more tender, so decreasing or increasing the amount will also affect the texture of your cake.

Granulated Sugars

The recipes in my book may call for brown, confectioners' (powdered), superfine (caster), and white sugars. You can use standard or organic brands for any of the recipes. All sugars obviously add sweetness to a recipe, but they are also hygroscopic; that is, they attract and retain moisture, helping to keep a cake moist longer.

Brown Sugar Like white sugar, brown sugar is made from sugarcane or sugar beets, but it has trace amounts of molasses in it to give it its distinctive brown color and caramel flavor. Brown sugar can be light or dark, and it doesn't matter which one you pick for these recipes. The color of the brown sugar is determined by how much molasses is added back to the white sugar before packaging. If you bake with cup measures, you will want to be sure to gently pack the brown sugar into the cup to get the accurate amount. Demerara, muscovado, and turbinado are three types of raw brown sugar; all have a larger grain than regular brown sugar and won't work well in the cake recipes unless called for.

Confectioners' (Powdered) Sugar Confectioners' sugar is granulated sugar that is processed ten times until it becomes a powder. (It is called 10X sugar in most professional kitchens.) In most cases, it has a small percentage of starch (usually cornstarch) added to prevent it from clumping in the bag. When used in a cake batter, it will produce a fine crumb. But confectioners' sugar CANNOT be used as a substitution for granulated sugar in the recipes, so only use when called for. Its fine texture is perfect for making icing or dusting over a cake as decoration.

Superfine (Caster) Sugar Superfine sugar is granulated sugar that is processed to be finer crystals. In Europe, it is known as caster sugar; and in the United States, it is often labeled as baker's sugar. I call for it in recipes when the sugar needs to dissolve quickly into the solution of the cake batter or egg foam, such as in French Meringue (see page 38). You can easily make your own superfine sugar by putting a few cups of granulated sugar into a food processor and pulverizing it until it is quite fine; you will know it is fine enough when it puffs out of your food processor like white smoke.

White Granulated Sugar Granulated is the most common sugar, and we're all familiar with its pure sweetness, which doesn't conflict or compete with other flavors of a cake. The recipes work equally well with cane and beet sugars, the two main types of granulated sugar found in the United States. The one exception to this is the Candied Hazelnuts on page 247, as I've found that cane sugar makes a more stable candy and is less likely to break or wilt. You can assume that all granulated sugar in the grocery store is beet sugar unless the bag is marked as Pure Cane Sugar. I didn't test coconut sugar or other sugar sources for these recipes, so you will need to experiment with their sweetness intensity.

Liquid Sweeteners

Some of the recipes in this book call for honey, molasses, or syrups. In most cases, the liquid is added in small amounts for their unique flavors. Liquid sweeteners behave differently than sugar crystals, so I don't recommend substituting them in the recipes as they tend to make a denser cake.

Corn Syrup I only use corn syrup in this book for its invert sugar properties; that is just a fancy way of saying that it prevents crystallizing when melting or caramelizing sugar. By adding a bit of corn syrup to sugar while it is cooking, it is much less likely to turn to rock candy. I always use light corn syrup, which is clear and doesn't add any color to the recipe.

Honey Honey is more intensely sweet than sugar, so you need less of it to achieve the right balance of sweet in a cake. Honey's flavor is determined by the type of plant nectar that the honeybees collect. Some honey has super-intense flavor, such as buckwheat honey, while others are quite mild, such as clover honey. You'll get great results with all kinds of honey, so experiment with different types and see which you prefer. Honey should only be used in the recipes where it is called for; it cannot directly be swapped out for sugar. Honey has a higher moisture content and can make recipes too dense. It is also more hygroscopic (it attracts and retains moisture) than sugar, so the cakes that call for honey will stay moist longer.

Maple Syrup The common pancake topping is made from boiling down the sap of maple trees. This is not to be confused with "maple-flavored" or "imitation" syrup, which is corn syrup, artificial flavor, and coloring. All pure maple syrup is now labeled Grade A, but there are different colors and flavors. Golden, which is the lightest in color and mildest in flavor, is the most common and popular. Many consider it the more desirable color, but I prefer to use the darker maple syrup, which is made later in the production season and has a stronger flavor. It is great for baking because the flavor stands up to the other ingredients, but either syrup will work nicely in my recipes.

Molasses Molasses is an unrefined sweetener derived from boiling sugarcane to concentrate the nutrients and iron. It is used in recipes to add color and rich flavor. Blackstrap molasses has the deepest flavor and can be used in place of "original" molasses, but it's not for the faint of heart.

Sugar-Free Substitutes

Stevia, Swerve, or many other sugar-free substitutes have been touted as a replacement for sugar. I only mention these because I have not tested them with the recipes in this book and therefore can't recommend using them for my cakes.

EQUIPMENT

You can bake a lovely cake without any fancy equipment, but there are some basics that make the process a whole lot easier. Here are some of the items that I think are helpful in creating a beautiful cake.

CAKE STAND

A stand is always lovely for displaying and showing off a cake. Find a decorative cake stand that is tall; just be sure it is sturdy enough to hold the cake.

CAKE TURNER

If you decorate a lot of cakes, a cake turner is one tool that will make your life a lot easier. It is useful when trimming and cutting cake layers, for frosting a cake, and for decorating. I suggest you invest in as sturdy a cake turner as fits your budget. A sturdy base will keep the cake steady as the top spins and you are decorating.

CARDBOARD CAKE ROUNDS

Cake rounds are one of those simple things that can make your life a lot less complicated. If you build your cake on cardboard, it is easier to decorate and lift onto a cake stand, especially if you are traveling with the cake. One note of caution is that there will be a cardboard round exposed when you cut into the cake. Unless I am baking a cake for a photoshoot, this doesn't bother me. I suggest you buy coated cardboard rounds because they don't absorb moisture from the cake and stay more stable.

COOLING RACKS

Cooling racks are very helpful in preventing a soggy bottom on your cake, and they help let a cake cool quickly, so it doesn't continue baking and dry out.

DECORATING SPATULAS

Metal spatulas come in many sizes and are either offset or straight. Offset spatulas are great for spreading batter smooth in the pan and for applying frosting. Some people are more comfortable smoothing frosting with a straight spatula. There isn't a right or wrong, just a matter of comfort. I also use a sturdy spatula to help transfer a cake from the turner to the serving platter.

ICING COMB

An icing comb is a tool used to smooth the sides of a cake. They come in a variety of sizes and textures. You can get flat ones if you want a perfectly smooth cake, or ones with "teeth" to create a texture in the frosting. For a flat finish, you can also use a bench scraper, which is a flat, rectangular piece of metal or plastic used to sweep ingredients off a cutting board or work surface into a bowl or pan.

KNIVES

A knife with a long serrated blade (I prefer a rounded versus pointed serrate) does a great job of cutting through cake without tearing, compressing, or kicking up too many crumbs. It's also the best tool I've found for chopping blocks of chocolate. For serving a cake, I use a super-thin delicate knife (serrated again is helpful but not a must) that won't compress the layers too much. I usually dip the knife in hot water first so it will melt through any layer of buttercream or icing without making a mess.

LINERS

I almost always line my pans with parchment paper when baking a cake in order to add insurance that the cake will flip out of the pan with ease. The exception is when I'm serving a cake in the pan. For some cakes and garnishes made in a baking sheet, I employ a reusable silicone mat. Sometimes when I am working on my counter, and I want to create a nonstick surface, I line the counter with vinyl.

Parchment Paper ▦ Parchment paper is something I call for when preparing pans for baking. I think it is a worthwhile piece of insurance when it comes to getting a cake out of the pan after being baked. You can buy precut parchment cake circles if you bake lots of cake and don't want to cut out paper for each use. As opposed to wax paper or butcher paper, parchment paper is coated with a super-thin layer of silicone, so it is nonstick-ish (you'll still want to grease it) and can withstand the heat of the oven. Wax and butcher papers are coated with paraffin and, therefore, not intended to be used in a hot situation, because the wax will melt if baked.

Silicone Mats ▨ Nonstick, flexible, silicone baking mats can used in place of parchment paper when lining a flat baking sheet and are particularly useful when creating candied carrot peel or chocolate bark. They are convenient and can be reused thousands of times. They are also beneficial as an insulator if your cakes tend to come out too dark on the bottom. Line a baking sheet with the silicone mat and place your cake pan on top of it before putting in the oven.

Vinyl ▨ I use thin sheets of vinyl to roll out fondant. Because vinyl is smooth and flexible, it creates a super-smooth and shiny finish on the fondant without having to use cornstarch to prevent sticking. It is also easy to move, which helps place the fondant on the cake. You can find large sheets of vinyl online and at fabric and craft stores. Run it under very hot water to smooth any creases.

MEASURERS

There are two ways to measure dry ingredients: either in dry measuring cups or on a scale. I prefer you use a scale, but if you don't have one, *yet*, you can make all of these recipes using measuring cups. Pick the kind that tend to be metal or plastic and come in 1 cup, ½ cup, ⅓ cup, and ¼ cup sizes. The large glass measuring cups are reserved for liquids only.

Dry Measuring Cups ▨ If you remain unconvinced about using a scale, invest in dry measuring cups. Just be sure to use the spoon-and-sweep method, which should collect 120g of all-purpose flour per 1 cup. This means you will fill the measuring cup with spoonfuls of flour and, once it is full to overflowing, use the flat blade of a knife to level off the top. (For more on measuring, see page 30.)

Scale ▨ If you buy *anything* for baking, it should be a scale. I love to weigh ingredients rather than use measuring cups, for several compelling reasons. First and most important, it's more accurate than volume measures. A cup of flour can vary wildly, depending on how you scoop up the flour, but 120g of all-purpose flour is always 120g, no matter what you do. Using a scale is also faster, and it cuts down on the amount of dishes you have to wash. Over the past decade, more recipes have appeared with both volume and weight measurements because it is common to use a scale in the rest of the world, and Americans are jumping in. Scales are particularly useful for novice bakers, because it takes the guesswork out of measuring; you can be sure each time that you have just the right amount of your ingredients.

There are many digital scales to choose from and they range in price, but my recommendation for a good starter scale at mid-price is the MyWeigh.

MIXERS

Some recipes really benefit from having a mixer to emulsify (blend) ingredients that don't want to mix together. Sometimes you can get away with a simple spoon or Danish dough whisk. Other times you need something with a bit more force, like a handheld mixer or a stand mixer.

Danish Dough Whisk ▧ A Danish dough whisk is my favorite kitchen tool; and I even travel with one, just in case. (It's a real conversation piece at airport security; they always let it through). The whisk is a single, heavy-gauged metal wire twisted into an artsy circular design and attached to a wooden handle. It is perfect for mixing one-bowl cake recipes. For any of my recipes that call for stirring with nothing more than a spoon, this tool is perfect. And it's just super-cool looking.

Handheld Mixer ▧ I have to admit that handheld mixers have never made much sense to me, but, because they are so popular, I know I am late to the party. I am sure you can accomplish everything you need with one, but it does require you to hold it the whole time. If you do use one, just be sure to pair with a glass or stainless-steel bowl, not plastic. I've had real issues whipping egg whites or cream in plastic bowls, and I've also had similar feedback on my website as well.

Stand Mixer ▧ My stand mixer is the second most-used piece of equipment in my kitchen, after my scale. It makes baking so much easier, especially when I need to whip eggs for ten minutes or beat butter into a soft, billowy mixture. If you bake a lot of cakes and have the space and budget, I highly recommend investing in a second whip/whisk attachment and bowl. There are many cake recipes that call for creaming butter and then adding whipped cream or foamed eggs; this requires emptying the bowl, washing it, and then carrying on with the next step. That second bowl allows you to do everything with less hassle.

PANS

Cake pans are not all created equal, so having the right ones can make baking a lot more successful and easier. When I was a kid, all cake pans had sloped sides, which made them easy to stack on the shelf, but it meant the cakes didn't have straight sides; and boy was it a challenge to put on the frosting without having the cake poke through in rings around the edge. Also, the pan's material make a difference in how a cake bakes. The following are my favorite pans, but if you have your grandmother's old pans and can't part with them, I get it. And you'll still bake delicious cake, you will just want to trim them straight (see page 47) for decorating.

Baking Sheets, Jelly-Roll Pans, and Cookie Sheets ▧ The highest-quality baking sheets are made of super-heavyweight aluminum and have short rims all the way around (sometimes called jelly-roll pans). When lined with parchment paper or, in some cases, a silicone mat, they are my preferred baking surface.

An "air-insulated" baking sheet can add a bit of protection since it promises a more even bake so that your cake won't get too dark—you can also achieve this by stacking two baking sheets together. Thin-rimmed cookie sheets can be used, but they are more likely to warp and may also scorch bottom crusts due to their uneven heat delivery.

Bundt Pans ▧ A Bundt pan is such a terrific and easy way to make a simple cake seem spectacular. There are so many fun shapes to bake in. Make sure the Bundt is the right volume for the recipe, since they come in many sizes. The key to success for baking in a Bundt is to butter it really well (see page 32).

What a pan is made of will have a huge effect on the way a cake bakes. Thickness of the materials and even the color will all change the outcome, and possibly the baking times.

Metal pans: These pans come in several colors, and they produce different results. The darker the pan, the darker a crust will be because the surface conducts more heat to the cake. If you want a paler crust, try a light-metal pan. Golden pans in the middle of the color range produce a crust that is caramelized but not as dark as a black pan.

Silicone pans: Even though they are made of a nonstick material, silicone pans also work well; but greasing them is essential. I always place silicone pans on a baking sheet when putting them in the oven, since they aren't as stable as metal pans.

Cake Pans ▦ The best pans for cakes are light in color and have straight sides. The light color produces a lighter crust on the cake, so there's less to trim off. The straight sides also minimize how much trimming you'll have to do to make your cakes straight. (For more on trimming, see page 47.) I use pans that are 2 or 3 inches / 5 or 7.5cm tall. These pans have plenty of space for cake to rise and produce a beautiful shape. If you don't have tall pans, you will want to bake in a larger pan than specified; for instance, if a recipe calls for an 8 by 3-inch / 20 by 8cm pan, you can bake in a shorter 9-inch / 24cm pan. The cake may bake a bit faster since it's not as deep.

Loaf Pans ▦ I sometimes bake cakes in loaf pans, especially the extra-tall and straight-sided Pullman pans (which have a lid). I just leave the top off, so the cake can rise beyond the rim.

Springform Pans ▦ There are a few recipes included in this book that bake best in a springform pan for easy removal. Make sure your pan has a tight seal, so the batter won't leak out. I always set a springform pan on a baking sheet just in case anything escapes the seam.

PASTRY BAGS AND DECORATING TIPS

For environmental reasons, it is good to purchase reusable cloth pastry bags. I suggest you get the "featherweight" bags that are made of thinner material, since they are not as stiff and are easier to use. Buy a variety of sizes so you have bags that will fit small and large projects. Flip the bag inside out and wash them with hot water and dish soap after every use and then hang to dry.

There are large decorating tips available that fit directly into a pastry bag, and small ones that require a coupler to fit into the bag. If you are decorating a cake and will stay with one tip, it is fine to use the large ones. If you think you will be switching from a round tip to a rose tip, then use the smaller tips that have a coupler, which will make the task of switching tips simple and clean.

THERMOMETERS

In most recipes, you can assess how something looks or feels to know if it is finished baking. But in some cases, you'll need to be super-accurate and use a thermometer.

Candy Thermometer ▦ You will need a candy thermometer for making certain recipes that require cooking sugar to a particular temperature. I like the Taylor thermometer that hangs flat against the pot I'm using. You can also use an instant-read thermometer if you don't mind repeatedly cleaning it as you take it out of the pot.

Oven Thermometer ▦ Home ovens are often off by up to 75°F / 25°C, so an oven thermometer is an important item. An inexpensive option will help you get predictable results in your cake. For best results, place your oven thermometer right on the rack on which your cake sits. If your oven runs significantly hot or cool, you may want to have it recalibrated by a professional. Otherwise, just compensate by adjusting your heat setting.

ZESTER

Many cake recipes call for citrus zest. Depending on how strong you want the flavor, you can use a Microplane zester/grater, which produces a fine zest without getting much of the bitter pith, or a coarser zester when you want an assertive citrus flavor. I tend to use a finer zester, but you decide which suits your taste.

CAKE ACADEMY

I'm putting all the super-helpful, kinda-geeky cake techniques and just a bit of food science right here in case you want to refer to it while you're baking your cakes. The hows and whys of cake baking are the kind of stuff I learned at culinary school and in professional kitchens, things that can make baking so much easier and more successful. I'm a visual learner, so having pictures of the process goes a long way in my understanding, and I hope yours too. I had the help of my friend, and fellow baker, Sarah Kieffer to take these pictures, so you can see my hands in the process of baking to get the full feel for how I do these methods.

My Cake Academy starts at the very beginning of the recipe, with organizing your ingredients, and takes you all the way through to the decorating. You can read through the whole chapter and get a fuller understanding of the baking techniques you'll see throughout the book, or you can refer back to this chapter as a refresher while you're making a particular recipe. I reference this section throughout the book in Cake Academy Review call-outs, so you can easily find your way back here. I want to be sure you have the information if and when you need or want it, but you can dive right in to the recipes and ignore this chapter all together if it feels like TMI.

Let's start at the beginning . . .

GATHER YOUR INGREDIENTS

Get in the habit of doing what the French call *mise en place* ("putting in its place"), or organizing a recipe (ingredients, equipment, music) before you do anything else. It is immensely helpful to read through a recipe, measure out everything, and confirm proper temperatures before you dive in to making the whole shebang, so you're prepared as you bake. This way, you also know what to expect during each step. You'll need to pull butter and eggs from the refrigerator long before you start so they're at the right consistency for baking. I weigh everything (more on that soon) and lay it out on a tray so it's ready to go in the mixer at the right moment. I am not naturally an A-type personality, and organization was a learned skill for me, but when I make several recipes in a day, having my mise en place ready to go is crucial to my speed and success. Now, organizing my recipes brings me great joy. Old dog, new tricks!

Weight versus Volume

If there is one piece of kitchen equipment you buy because of this book, I hope it's a digital kitchen scale. You can certainly bake everything included here without one, but using weights means consistent results every time you make a cake. If you use a scale, you know you're getting 120 grams (FYI—that's how much 1 cup of all-purpose flour should weigh for this book) every time, and your cakes will be more predictable. (See page 23 for a recommendation on what kind to get.)

How to Use a Digital Scale  Place the mixing bowl on the scale's platform, then hit the "tare" button. This will zero out the weight of the bowl, so you are only weighing what is inside and not the bowl itself. Next, place your first ingredient into the bowl until you've reached the desired amount. (You can weigh each ingredient in separate bowls or use the same bowl, as long as those ingredients are added to the recipe at the same time.) If you're weighing another ingredient into the same bowl, hit the "tare" button again, so it reads 0, and then add the next ingredient. Repeat. It's that easy.

How to Use the Spoon-and-Sweep Method If you do use measuring cups, do the spoon-and-sweep method. You spoon the flour into the measuring cup and then sweep the top clean with a knife. Spooning the flour into the cup aerates it, so it isn't so densely packed.

THE IMPORTANCE OF PREPPING

Preheating your oven and having the pans prepped and ready to go before you mix the cake batter are the small details that set you up for success. Cake batter likes to be baked as soon as it is mixed, so waiting on a slow preheat or tedious pan buttering (a well-buttered Bundt will take a few minutes) can cause the cake to deflate a bit in response.

Oven

I recall sending the little trays through my Easy-Bake Oven and being astonished that the heat of a light bulb could turn the batter into a cake. Your oven is more intricate than that, but they do essentially the same job. Your work of prepping and mixing ends and the magic of heat finishes the cake, so it is important to get the oven set up properly.

Preheat ▦ Oh, the moment you go to the oven and realize it's cold is bitter, so make sure to preheat straight off. (I may have learned this the hard way.) These recipes are written for specific temperatures. Some cakes need a jolt of high heat for a quick rise and a fast setting of the proteins to keep the cake lofty. Other cakes need to take it slow, so they will bake evenly and not be too dark and/or dry on the outside but undercooked inside. Preheating takes 10 to 15 minutes for most ovens, but that can be a lifetime to a perfectly mixed genoise or angel food cake, so do it first.

Wind or Flat Heat ▦ When I worked in professional kitchens, I had only "wind" or convection ovens, and we went to great lengths to mitigate the damage it caused to cakes. The wind in the oven was so strong that the cakes would come out uneven, looking like dunes on a beach. The other issue was the thick crust it created on top. I tried blocking the fan or covering the cake, with mixed results. My strong recommendation is to avoid convection heat when baking cakes. If you have no choice, then trimming off the cake tops (see page 47) is the only sanity-preserving solution.

Which Rack ▦ Unless otherwise noted in a recipe, always bake in the bottom third of the oven. Heat rises, so the top of the oven tends to be where the heat is the most intense. So if your cake is on an upper rack, the top will develop a crust before the center is set. The bottom is often where the heating elements are, so a cake right on the bottom can overbake. For the most even baking results, bake on only one rack at a time. If you have to bake several cakes at once, be sure to rotate them from top to bottom and front to back; this will create a more even bake. I only do this during the last 10 minutes of baking, when I am sure the cakes are set enough to be moved. DO NOT do the rotating switcheroo with "foam" cakes (see chapter 5), since they are delicate and will not respond kindly to having the door opened during baking.

Check the Temp ▦ Ovens, especially older ones, can be off the mark by quite a bit. I once had one that ran 80°F / 25°C cooler than the dial suggested. (It may have had something to do with the fact that I needed to prop a chair up against the door to keep it shut.) The results were devastating to anything I baked. By using an inexpensive oven thermometer, you can adjust your temperature and make sure your cakes bake well. If the oven is off by more than 20 degrees, you should have it calibrated by a professional.

Pans

The next thing I prep is the pan, doing this task beforehand can save the day with delicate recipes. Each kind of cake requires a different way of preparing the pan, so there really isn't a single rule of thumb, and every recipe indicates how the pan is to be prepared. Here are the things I have learned in my decades of baking cakes to prevent them from sticking to the pan, because there is nothing quite as disappointing as a perfectly baked cake that is stuck to the pan and has to be gouged out.

Grease ▦ Butter is my favorite for greasing a pan. You can use it softened for a really thick layer (as for Bundts) or melted for a thin layer (pretty much everything but Bundts). When I started writing this book, I was adamant (righteously so) about using only butter to grease a pan. I had very strong feelings about cooking spray, and none of them was good. As I baked hundreds of cakes and prepped as many pans, I softened my rhetoric about sprays. I still prefer butter because I *LOVE* butter and prefer to use an ingredient I'd actually want to eat. Having said that, cooking sprays, especially those with flour in the mix, really do work well. They may not be as tasty as butter, but they are super-quick.

Line and Flour ▦ Lining the pan with greased parchment paper after greasing will add a bit of insurance that the cake will release easily. Sometimes, I also call for flouring the pan to add even more releasing power. If it's a chocolate cake, I use cocoa powder instead of flour, so there isn't a light-colored, powdery film on the outside of the dark cake. When you dust with flour, be sure to tap any excess out of the pan, so you don't have a thick layer of flour on the cake. There should be just enough flour to create a buffer from the pan but still absorb into the cake as it bakes.

Brush for a Bundt ▦ When you're preparing a Bundt pan, you need to make sure that you get a thick layer of butter into all the nooks and crannies, so the batter doesn't stick to the pan as it bakes. A thick layer of soft butter (not melted, because that would be too thin), brushed on with a pastry brush, is the best move here. Adding a dusting of flour (or cocoa, if making a chocolate cake) is extra insurance that the cake will slip out. You can also use a cooking spray, but make sure you get the pan well covered. Baking spray made with flour is even better for ensuring the cake will release from the pan.

Go Naked ▦ For angel food, chiffon, or other cakes that require the cake to cling to the sides of the pan in order to help it rise, you don't grease the pan at all. These cakes often get hung upside down to cool (see Angel Food Cake, page 150) and the cake needs to cling to the sides so it doesn't fall out. For the same reason, you want to avoid nonstick pans for such cakes.

MIXING METHODS

There are really only a few mixing techniques you need to know in order to create beautiful cakes. Knowing how to cream ingredients, how to create foams, and when and how to fold will take you through this entire book successfully. They are sometimes done on their own; and other times, you'll be using all three in a single recipe. None of them is difficult; there are just some tricks to make the process super-easy and successful.

Creaming

Creaming involves whipping butter or other fats with sugar, then adding eggs, flour, and liquid. It is probably the most popular method of scratch-cake mixing in the home kitchen. It's also super-simple, but knowing just a little bit more about this process can take your cake from good to extraordinary.

Whipping air into fat is the key to the dreamy texture and rise of any cake that uses the creaming method. To achieve a smooth, tight texture and the highest rise possible (even if your recipe doesn't use any chemical leavener), you need to incorporate lots of air into the mix. This happens by having the right fat, temperature, mixing method, and ratio of liquids.

Fat and water don't naturally want to mix; but when we coax them into a glorious emulsion, magic happens. The goal is to whip air bubbles into the fat, which hold little droplets of liquid within them. When the batter is placed into the oven, the liquid in the fat bubbles turns to steam and expands, causing the batter to rise. Boom! That simple process is achieved by proper mixing. Here are a few things that will help you get the perfect mix.

Type and Ratio of Fats ▦ The fat is typically butter, because it tastes so good. The flavor can't be beat, but butter is particular about the temperature it likes in order to create an emulsion and bubbles. Some of my recipes also use a bit of shortening to help with this, since shortening is a champ at holding on to bubbles; but if you use too much, you'll have a lackluster flavor. Oil doesn't have enough structure on its own to hold the air bubbles, but when mixed with butter it makes for a super-luxurious cake.

Temperature of Ingredients ▦ All the ingredients need to be at room temperature (otherwise known as *softened*). If the ingredients are too cold, they won't emulsify or whip up with enough air to create a good rise. But if the fat is too warm, the batter won't have enough structure to trap the steam in the air bubbles, so it will be dense. The ideal temperature is about 70°F / 20°C. Having said this, I have NEVER taken the actual temperature. Here is the non-scientific way I know if the ingredients are the right temperature.

→ **Eggs** You don't want to add cold eggs to perfectly whipped butter or the butter will seize and you'll lose the fluffy air you created. If your eggs are not at room temperature (about 70°F / 20°C) when you are ready to mix your cake, warm them (in the shell) by placing in a bowl of hot tap water for about 5 minutes before adding to the recipe; change the water if it cools down too much.

→ **Fat** For the butter, you will know it's right if it is soft but still holds its shape when you pick it up. If the butter droops or your fingers melt right into it, it's too soft. If you can't easily press your fingers into the butter, it's too cold. You can warm the butter by microwaving it for a few seconds, then turn and repeat; but don't overdo this or you will have melted butter. You can also heat a glass bowl and put it over the butter like a dome. Cutting the butter into small pieces will help it to warm faster too. Some people swear by grating butter to warm it, but this strikes me as too much messy work.

→ **Liquid Dairy** Adding cold milk, sour cream, or heavy cream to a perfect bowl of whipped butter will ruin the emulsion. If the dairy is too cold, heat it for a few seconds in a microwave. Too hot, and you'll melt the butter; so just go for room temp.

Mixer Speed █ It's super-tempting to turn the machine on high and let it whip the butter and sugar into submission, but resist the urge. If you mix on medium-high instead, you'll get smaller air bubbles in the mixture; these will be stronger and create a far superior texture. If you've ever had a cake that has a coarse or tough crumb, it's likely because the air bubbles were too big. Letting the mixer rip on high speed will also cause a lot of friction that warms and weakens the structure of the butter. So, slow it down a bit. It may take an extra minute, but the cake will be worth it.

Adding Extracts █ Fat is the carrier of flavor, so add your extracts to the whipping butter and not at the end. This gives the extract time to work into the batter more thoroughly.

Scraping the Bowl █ There is just no way to make scraping the bowl seem sexy, but it's perhaps one of the keys to successful cake baking. I highly recommend you invest in a rubber-edged paddle attachment if you have a stand mixer. That rubber edge scrapes the bowl as it mixes; this greatly cuts down on the amount of times you need to stop the machine to make sure the bowl (especially the bottom) and paddle are cleaned off. If your ingredients stick to either, they are not being thoroughly incorporated into the batter. So, despite the tedium (I prefer to think of it as relaxing), scrape, scrape, scrape!

ADDING EXTRACTS

SCRAPING THE BOWL

ADDING LIQUIDS

ALTERNATING DRY AND WET INGREDIENTS

Adding Liquids ▮ Liquids are eggs, milk, yogurt, or anything not solid. You want to add them a little at a time and make sure you're maintaining the smooth emulsion the whole time. Just remember the temperature and speed rules and you'll be fine. Make sure the liquid is room temperature, add it in small slow increments, and mix on medium-low speed until smooth. Scrape the bowl often; just take a Zen approach to this necessary task. You don't want to add too much liquid at once or the fat won't be able to trap it and the batter will look curdled. This is why you alternate the liquid and dry ingredients in creamed cakes and always finish with the dry—to bring the mixture back into emulsion, even if it escaped perfection for a moment.

Alternating Dry and Wet Ingredients ▮ It may seem repetitive to go back and forth between the dry and wet ingredients, but there's a method to this madness. If you dump all the dry in first, the batter would be so tight you'd have to strong-arm it just to incorporate all of the flour, and that will create a cake that's too tough (more on that later). Equally as destructive is adding all the wet, which would deflate all the glorious air bubbles in the butter emulsion. So, alternating them is the kindest thing to do for your cake.

There are only two occasions when I sift flour. First, if the flour is lumpy. Cake flour, cocoa powder, and baking soda are the most frequent offenders of clumping after sitting in the bag. So after I measure, they often need to be sifted or the recipe can end up with unsightly lumps—and no one enjoys biting into that. The second reason for sifting is to lighten the dry ingredients when they are being folded into a delicate sponge batter (see page 42). By sifting the flour, you are adding air into it; this aeration will help you disperse the flour through your batter with less effort.

I do NOT sift dry ingredients together to distribute baking powder or baking soda. This just doesn't work as well as whisking, and it's not nearly as quick. I'm all for quick and easy when I can get away with it.

Flour Power ■ The flour helps to hold the cake together and gives it structure; but you want just a whisper of structure, not a brick house. Once you add the flour, especially all-purpose flour, you want to mix as little as possible so you don't get the gluten (see page 15) all excited. All of the dry ingredients should be thoroughly whisked together before they are added to the batter. This ensures that the leaveners and other dry ingredients are distributed evenly, even if there is minimal mixing once they are added to the wet mixture. Mix the dry into the batter only until it's combined and then stop. Some recipes call for adding the flour by hand to make sure the gluten doesn't go nuts and ruin the party. If so, heed that warning and mix by hand.

Light-as-Air Egg Foam

If you know my Instagram account, you are well aware of my love for meringue (which is just an egg foam) and all of its fluffy, fun, and delicious qualities. This method refers to the foam made by whipping air into eggs. The recipes may call for whole eggs, egg yolks, or just egg whites. No matter what kind of egg foam or meringue (there are three) you're making, it needs to be structurally strong, which seems like a contradiction since foam is so ethereal. A properly whipped egg foam can stand up to other ingredients being folded into it, albeit gently, and will hold its shape and create a hefty rise in the cake as it bakes. Typically, the foams are made by slowly whipping sugar into eggs. The sugar helps create a stretchier egg (resulting in more air bubbles to form a luxurious foam), and, as you will see, there are a few different ways to go about this, depending on the recipe you are making.

The egg proteins (mostly in the whites) will stretch and take on more air if they are warm when you are whipping them, so warm the eggs in the shell to about 100°F / 40°C before you begin. For foams, if your eggs are coming straight from the refrigerator, just let them soak in hot tap water for about 10 minutes. You may need to change the water a couple of times to get them warmed up quickly. Once the eggs feel warm to the touch, they are likely ready; there's no need to take their temperature, unless that's something that excites you.

Warm eggs   Sprinkle sugar   Ribbon stage

Whip It; Whip It Good! ▦ When whipping whole eggs or egg yolks, you need to whip the eggs and sugar until the foam is super-stable. On high speed, whip the eggs until foamy, about 30 seconds, then turn the speed to low and sprinkle the sugar slowly over the eggs until incorporated. Turn the machine to high speed and whip until the foam forms a ribbon when you lift the whisk out of the bowl—the ribbon will sit on top of the foam without sinking in for several seconds. The foam may look thick after a few minutes but the test is whether it is strong enough to suspend the weight of the ribbon for several seconds. To achieve real strength, it will take about 10 minutes, maybe longer if you are using a handheld mixer or doubling the recipe (such as in the Wedding Cake on page 199). Then turn the speed to medium and continue to whip the egg mixture for 1 minute. This crucial step will create smaller, more uniform air bubbles that are stronger and will hold up to the folding of other ingredients.

THE THREE MERINGUES

There are three types of meringues: French, Swiss, and Italian (I'm not sure how each country got assigned the different styles), and I love them all but use them for very different purposes. You won't be left guessing which one to use, since I will guide you through each recipe and which meringue to make.

→ **When Fat Is the Enemy** By now you know how much I love butter and fat in general. But, our beloved fat can wreak havoc when whipping meringues. If there is any fat in the bowl or on the whisk attachment, it will interfere with the egg white proteins and prevent them from forming the foam we so desire. Since egg yolks contain fat, they, too, are the enemy of whipping egg whites into meringues, so be very careful when separating the eggs (see page 10).

PEAKS

A **soft peak** is when the egg whites are firm enough that they don't drool off the whisk when lifted out of the bowl, but they just cling and even slouch a bit.

A **medium peak** is when the foam sits tall on the whisk but leans over and does a pronounced Dairy Queen–esque swirl at the top.

A **stiff peak** is when the meringue stands straight up with no apology. It should still be glossy and smooth but very firm and may have just a wisp of a curl at the very top.

→ **Peaks** When necessary, a recipe will indicate at what stage your egg whites should be before using in that recipe. The three most common stages are soft peak, medium peak, and stiff peak.

French Meringue

This meringue is simply raw egg whites whipped with sugar. It is the most common method used for cake batters, since the raw mixture will get added to the other ingredients and baked.

Whip the recipe's egg whites in a perfectly clean bowl on high speed until foamy, about 30 seconds. You want to establish that the eggs are free from fat and are going to create foam, giving them a head start. Oftentimes, a bit of acid, in the form of cream of tartar, is added to the egg whites in the beginning to increase the strength of the proteins. Turn the mixer speed to low, slowly sprinkle the sugar over the whites, so it doesn't crush the foam you've so diligently built up, and beat until incorporated.

Once all of the sugar has been added, turn the mixer speed to medium-high and whip to your desired peaks (see above). French meringue is the most likely to get overbeaten, so once it has reached the desired peak (as indicated in the recipe), stop the mixing and proceed with the recipe. If you go too far, the whites will look "broken" or "curdled," and there is very little (nothing really) you can do to go back from that.

"Broken" egg whites won't mix into your batter well, and that also means the egg whites have no more stretch, so they won't rise in the oven. You have to start again. It's a shame but not the end of the world.

Swiss Meringue

This method entails cooking egg whites and sugar together into a syrup, which makes for a stable meringue once whipped. This also cooks the meringue so it is safe to eat without baking; which is why this technique can be used as a cake topping (see page 217) and as the base for Swiss Meringue Buttercream (page 216).

Your saucepan should fit comfortably the mixing bowl of a stand mixer, with most of the bowl's surface within the pan. (If the pan is too small, you may get flames from a gas burner licking the bowl and cooking the eggs, so make sure both are a good fit.) The egg mixture will cook from the heat of the steam within the pan alone.

In the bowl of a stand mixer, combine the recipe's egg whites and sugar and use a whisk or rubber spatula to thoroughly mix together; the mixture will be very thick and grainy.

In a saucepan over medium-low heat, bring 1 inch / 2.5cm of water to a simmer. (There should be enough water to create steam but not so much that the bowl actually touches the water.)

Place the mixing bowl over the simmering water (this is a double boiler) and use a rubber spatula to stir the egg mixture until it is hot and all of the sugar has dissolved, about 5 minutes. Be sure to wipe down the sides of the bowl as the mixture cooks, so no grains of sugar cling and make your meringue grainy. Feel the egg mixture between your fingers to check for graininess. Once the mixture is completely smooth, put the bowl on the stand mixer fitted with the whisk attachment and beat on medium-high speed until the desired peaks form (see facing page).

If you are making buttercream, you will need to whip the meringue until it has cooled to room temperature (test by feeling the bowl), or it will melt the butter when you add it. Swiss meringue is very stable and will not "break" from over-mixing before it cools.

SWISS MERINGUE

Italian Meringue

This meringue has a reputation for being the most stable of the meringues and is made by pouring hot sugar syrup into whipping egg whites. I use this meringue for Italian Meringue Buttercream (page 215) when I want a super-light texture but need it to hold up well. It is a bit of a dance because you have to time the whipping eggs to be at medium peak (see page 38) just as the sugar reaches the correct temperature. You will need a candy thermometer (see page 25) to ensure a strong meringue that is also safe to eat without baking.

The first time you make this, turn the heat to medium so the sugar syrup won't reach the proper temperature before your eggs are done whipping. Once you've done it a couple of times, you'll have the timing of each just right. It may seem like diving into Double Dutch jump rope, but after a minute you'll get into the rhythm and it will feel like a natural move.

Pour the recipe's water into a saucepan and clip a candy thermometer to the side. Add the sugar and corn syrup to the center of the pan, trying to keep the sugar from hitting the sides. The corn syrup prevents the sugar from crystallizing (see page 19). Set the pan over high heat. Put the egg whites in the bowl of a stand mixer fitted with the whisk attachment.

ITALIAN MERINGUE

When the sugar reaches 230°F / 110°C, begin beating the egg whites on high speed. When the whites have formed medium peaks, turn the speed to low, until the sugar syrup is at the right temperature. The timing of the sugar will depend on the depth and width of your pan.

Remove the sugar syrup from the heat when it is 248°F / 120°C. (This number is exact, so it will cook the eggs and create the right consistency; if any lower, it won't be stable enough, and if any higher, it will set too firm.) Slowly add the syrup to the egg whites by dribbling it down the side of the bowl, avoiding the whisk attachment. If you hit the attachment, it will make spun sugar, which seems cool but not great for the purpose of this recipe. Once all the syrup has been added, turn the speed to high and whip until a glossy meringue is formed and it has cooled to room temperature, about 8 minutes. The exact timing will depend on your mixer.

Folding

There are many schools of thought about the best tool for folding flour into the batter. I like to use the whisk attachment from the mixer for light-as-air foams, and a rubber spatula when working with a thicker batter. The whisk attachment offers no resistance and allows you to move through the foam without breaking as many bubbles. The spatula is handy because you can clean the bottom and side of the bowl as you work. I run either one along the side of the bowl to the bottom and then up through the middle. As I gently push the batter upward and out of the bowl, I give the whip or spatula a little shimmy to disperse any lumps of flour that have collected. Always sift flour over the batter when adding more.

Folding Fat into a Foam ▨ If there is fat in a foam recipe, it will likely be melted and added at the very end, so as not to disrupt the whipped eggs. Put melted butter into a small bowl and mix a small amount of batter into it. You're trying to get the butter mixture to be similar in texture to the batter, so they blend together quickly with less mixing.

FOLDING

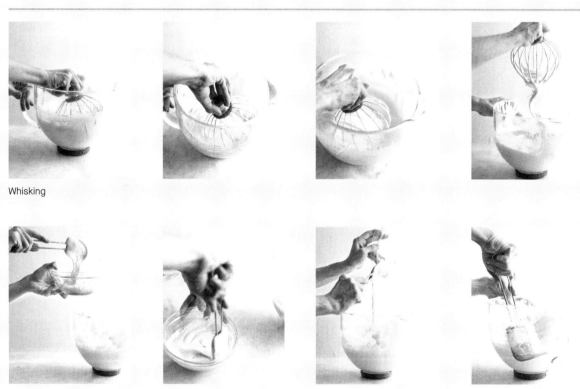

Whisking

Folding fat

FILLING THE PAN

Some cake batters are thin and flow to the edges of a pan and then lie flat. Other batters are quite thick and require scooping into the pan and then spreading so the cake will bake evenly. Such batters can be so thick that air bubbles can get trapped, so I thwack (between a tap and a bang) the pan on the counter several times to drive the large bubbles to the surface. I also push the batter up slightly to create a thick rim around the edge of the pan, so there is a slight dip in the center to help prevent a hump in the baked cake.

Thwack, Thwack, Thwack ▪ When to thwack the pan and when to be gentle? There is no guessing about this; I tell you in the recipe if it should be banged on the counter. However, the general rule of thumb for those family recipes you are baking is only bang if the cake is leavened with baking powder and/or soda. Cakes that are made with the egg-foam method (see page 36) should NOT be tapped, banged, or otherwise handled roughly, since we don't want to pop any of the beautiful air bubbles in the eggs. It's that air that makes these cakes rise. Just gently pour the batter into the pan, ever-so-gently spread it to the edges, and then get it into the oven ASAP!

IS IT DONE YET?

Each recipe will give you a visual cue for how to tell if the cake is done as well as a suggested baking time. In most cases, I go by color and feel.

How to Know? ▨ First, look through the window of your oven, assuming your oven has a window. It's best not to open the oven door until your cake is well set. The change in temperature from opening the door can cause the cake to collapse if it hasn't had ample time to set. Once the cake looks set (firm) and no longer wet, gently open the door, reach into the oven, and very carefully tap the top, right in the center, with the flat parts of your fingertips. The center of the cake is the last part to be fully baked—don't be fooled by a set edge; check the middle. If the cake wobbles under the delicate weight of your touch, it needs more time. If it feels spongy but solid, then it is done and needs to come out. To know for sure that it is baked through, poke the center with a cake tester or toothpick. If the tester comes out with a small amount of moist but not wet crumbs, then the cake is done. Some tight crumb cakes will come out completely clean. Another visual cue in some of the recipes is that the sides of the cake will just start to come away from the edges of the pan. This cue should be used only when I specify to look for it, because certain cakes may be baked in the center before you notice the pull from the edge and then they run the risk of overbaking.

COOLING AND STORING

Not to be forgotten is that the cooling process is a continuation of baking. And although the first step to success in fully releasing your cake from its pan was prepping the pan properly (see page 32), you also need to know how long to leave it in the pan before turning it out to cool completely. There is a sweet spot when the cake has cooled enough to have some structure but not so cooled that it glues itself to the pan. The most crucial example is the mighty Bundt that, because of all the fun details of the pan, has many more chances to stick. And freezing a fresh cake is a great way to bake ahead, so you're not scrambling on the day of your special occasion (which may just be coming home from school).

Cool It

Set the baked cake on a cooling rack, so that air can flow all the way around the pan and cool the cake faster. There are a couple of exceptions to this—Angel Food Cake (page 150) and Olive Oil–Chiffon Cake (page 153) like to hang upside down to cool so they keep their airy texture and don't collapse under their own weight. Some tube pans have "feet" on them that are meant to hold the inverted cake above the counter as it cools. If your pan, like mine, doesn't have this fancy feature, invert the cake over a water-filled wine bottle. (It needs some weight to it so it won't tip over with the top-heavy cake perched over it.) Leave the pan upside down until cooled completely.

Follow the cooling directions for each recipe, and your cakes will all come out of the pans with ease. If you've prepped your pan properly and have let the cake cool for 10 to 15 minutes, you're in the sweet spot—no sticking—just flip the cake out onto a serving plate. Let the cake cool completely before you begin decorating, since most of the frostings are butter-based and won't take kindly to being slathered over a warm cake.

Your Freezer Is Your Friend

You can make many cakes and frostings ahead of time; and freezing, as opposed to storing in the refrigerator, will prevent them from getting stale. Not all cakes and frostings like the freezer, so I mention the exceptions in the recipes.

How to Freeze ▧ The trick to successfully freezing cake layers is to cool the baked cake and immediately transfer to the freezer, locking in the moisture. Wrap the cakes very well in plastic wrap (there are now reusable, environmentally safe options) to avoid picking up any flavors or odors floating around your freezer (think fish sticks) and then freeze for up to two weeks. When you're ready to assemble the cake, defrost it, still wrapped, by leaving on the counter for about an hour (maybe longer for super-thick or dense cakes).

Unless otherwise noted in the recipe, you can freeze buttercream or other frostings for several weeks. Make the frosting and wrap really well in plastic (this is how it is done in professional kitchens) or transfer to an airtight container, before putting in the freezer. When ready to use, let the still-wrapped frosting defrost for a few hours at room temperature before remixing in a stand mixer fitted with the paddle attachment. The frosting may appear to have separated but should re-emulsify at room temperature. If the frosting hasn't thawed all the way through, pass it over a pan of simmering water for a few seconds and then mix again. Repeat as needed. I also use my blowtorch for this task because it's more fun and I can warm chilled frosting while it is mixing. Just wave the tip of the flame quickly over the metal bowl for a few seconds as the mixer is running. Repeat until the frosting is smooth.

IT'S TIME TO DECORATE

Decorating allows you to take a simple cake and make it fabulous. I will teach you how to ensure your cake layers are straight, any filling will stay put, and the frosting is free of crumbs and pristine. Then we can add elegant piping or whatever decor you choose. Knowing these tricks will make a homemade cake look professional.

Removing the Paper

Peel the parchment paper from the bottom cake layer. I know this seems obvious, but when I was working at a catering company, we sent out a cake (thankfully not my cake) that still had parchment between the layers, and it was a disaster. Lesson learned: Don't assemble a cake at 5:00 a.m., pre-coffee.

Using Cardboard Rounds

Set the cake on a cardboard round (see page 21)—this is a pro move. The cardboard should fit the size of the cake exactly, so trim the round accordingly, if needed. You could also set the cake directly on the plate from which you will be serving. If you intend to place the cake on a tall stand, it is easiest to decorate on a cardboard round and then transfer to the stand. A tall cake is too precarious to frost and decorate on a tall cake stand while also spinning on a cake turner (see page 21).

Adding Damp Paper

Place a damp (but not soaking wet) piece of paper towel under the cardboard round to prevent the cake from dancing around on the cake turner as you are trying to decorate. The paper towel should not poke out from beneath the round, or it will interfere with your ability to move the spatula as you frost the cake.

Trimming the Top

Some cakes, just by the nature of the recipe, rise up in the middle and produce a dome. I have never been alarmed or upset by this and, in fact, celebrate that cake hump, since it will get trimmed off and used as a "chef snack" as I decorate. If you leave the cake rounded, it may pose problems when stacking another layer on top. So, it needs to be trimmed. It is often easier to cleanly cut a cake if it has been refrigerated for about 30 minutes. Chilled cake will become denser and less likely to kick up as many crumbs. The goal is to slice off as little of the dome as possible; just enough to flatten the top. Perfection is not necessary, since we'll be covering it in icing anyway.

Setting the cake on a cake turner for this task is super-helpful. Use a long, serrated knife to gently saw the dome, while you slowly turn the cake. Turning the cake prevents having to push the knife too hard into the cake, since you're making small, gradual cuts into it as it turns. Keep the knife in one spot and slowly spin the cake turner as you saw. This is a very sweet and gentle motion—you're not hacking at the cake. As you turn and gently saw, the knife naturally slips deeper and deeper into the cake, until you are through to the other side. Use the same technique for slicing a cake into multiple layers.

FLIP IT!

If your cake isn't perfectly flat after trimming off the dome, just flip it over so the bottom of the cake is now the top. This will help ensure a level cake when you're all finished decorating.

Slicing and Filling the Layers

To slice a cake into thinner layers, measure the cake, find the midpoint in the layer, and gently mark that point with your knife all the way around to use as a guide. Then use the serrated knife to gently saw the cake, while you slowly turn the cake. Keep one hand on top of the cake; this will simultaneously hold it steady and help to achieve the most even layers.

If you are using a sponge cake, like Brown Butter Genoise (page 146), you'll want to brush it with a simple syrup (see page 226) to add flavor and needed moisture. Use a clean pastry brush to dab the syrup onto the cake; it shouldn't be drowning in syrup.

SLICING AND FILLING THE LAYERS

If you want to fill your cake with icing, whipped cream, a layer of fruit, or anything else you dream up, there are just a couple of tips that will make your life easier. If you are leaving the cake "naked," with no icing over the layers, then you can get away with your filling poking out a bit; see Victory (Victoria) Sponge on page 141. If you are covering the cake with icing, then you want to make sure the filling stays contained within the layers and doesn't interfere or poke out from the icing and is a hidden surprise when you cut into the cake. The fillings you use should be sturdy enough to hold up the cake layer above it; and in some cases, multiple layers. In other words, a super-soft whipped cream will want to smoosh out from between the layers with too much weight on top of it, so whip it to a nice stiff peak that will give it more body and don't use too much of it between layers. When filling a dense cake, like Ultimate Carrot Cake (page 136) or Chocolate Devil's Food Cake (page 125), I like to use a filling with enough body to support the weight, like Cream Cheese Frosting (page 209) or Ermine Frosting (page 206), and avoid using whipped cream.

Creating a Dam ▥ If you want to use a soft filling between layers, you'll need to create a dam around the outside edge of the cake layer to hold in the filling. Use a large round tip (Ateco #803) fitted into a pastry bag (see page 55) and pipe a ½-inch / 1.3cm rim of icing around the edge of the cake. You can then fill the inside with a soft filling, such as Thick Caramel Sauce (page 218), Lemon Curd (page 235), or Cherry Filling (page 234). This way, the filling will not breach the smooth sides of your finished cake.

Stacking and Trimming the Sides

After you fill the first layer of cake, be sure the next layer is on straight. It should be straight up and down. Bend down and take a look straight-on to make sure it isn't going all Cat-in-the-Hat lopsided on you, unless that is the look you are going for. It is easier to adjust the layers as you are stacking them than when it's all assembled, but that is possible as well.

If you've baked the cakes in multiple pans (brands vary slightly in dimensions), the sides may not line up exactly, so one layer may poke out a bit more than another. It's an easy issue to fix by trimming with your serrated knife from top to bottom. This is also how you'll remove any dark edges, which can either be dry or just visually distracting.

Crumb-Coating

You will want to lock in all the loose cake crumbs so they don't end up speckling the outside of your frosting. This is called a crumb coat. It is a particularly clever move when you have a dark chocolate cake, covered in white frosting. Simply take a small amount of whatever frosting you are using to cover the cake and spread it in a super-thin, even layer. It is okay and even expected that it will be chock-full of crumbs, hence the name. Be careful not to swipe your crumb-coated spatula back into the clean bowl of frosting. I usually swipe the blade clean along the edge of a small bowl.

Once the cake is completely covered, all the gaps in the layers are filled, and you've checked to make sure the sides are straight, refrigerate or freeze the cake until the crumb coat is no longer tacky, about 20 minutes. Now the crumbs are locked into this solid layer of frosting, and you can have a sense of serenity as you cover the cake in a final layer of frosting.

TO CRUMB OR NOT TO CRUMB?

The truth is, you don't HAVE to do the crumb coat, as long as you are confident you can cover the cake without kicking up all kinds of crumbs as you go. This will come with experience. I rarely bother with a crumb coat, but if you're just getting started in your cake-making journey, give yourself the peace of mind of a solid crumb coat.

Putting on the Final Layer of Frosting

Once your cake is trimmed, filled, stacked, and has a chilled crumb coat, you are ready to put on the final, pristine layer of frosting. Make sure your cake is perfectly centered on the cake turner, with a damp square of paper towel under the cardboard (see page 46). Put a large amount of frosting on the top of the cake and, using a metal decorating spatula, spread it over the surface; keep the frosting as flat and even as possible. Make the top of the frosting level. You'll push the frosting ever so slightly over the rim of the cake, just so it is teetering on the edge but not slouching down the side. This slight overhang of frosting will eventually end up creating the crisp right angle on the edge of your cake and takes it from pretty to sleek.

Spackle the sides of the cake with more frosting. If you've crumb-coated your cake, this will be easy, and you won't have to concern yourself with getting crumbs in the frosting as you go. Add a lot of frosting and don't worry about it being smooth at this point; just cover the cake. Once the whole thing is covered and rather rustic looking, it's time to clean up the excess frosting and create the smooth sides.

To smooth the frosting evenly, it is crucial to have the cake centered on the cake turner; otherwise, it will be wonky as it spins. Holding a metal icing spatula, a bench scraper, or a decorating comb straight up and down and at a 20-degree angle against the cake, steadily rotate the cake turner. Very gently press the spatula against the spinning cake. *Don't move the spatula.* Let the cake turner do all the work; by keeping the spatula in place and allowing the cake turner to do the spinning, you'll avoid scraping off too much of the frosting or getting swipe marks from the spatula. As frosting builds up on the spatula, wipe it clean. The more cakes you make, the more natural this will feel. Once the frosting is even and smooth, you'll want to make sure there are no gaps. If there are holes, fill them in and then smooth it out again. If there are pockmarks, you can heat the spatula with hot water to slightly melt the outer layer of frosting and make it as smooth as possible. Try not to overwork the frosting or you'll start to hit the cake beneath. If that happens, don't fret; just add more frosting and start again.

Once the sides are smooth, you should have a ridge of frosting that is jutting straight up around the edge of the cake, like a crown. Sometimes I leave this crown (see photograph on page 181); but for the sake of this lesson, I'm swiping it clean. Use the spatula to smooth the top edge by dragging it at a 20-degree angle from the outer edge of the "crown" to the center of the cake, then lift the spatula up; don't go beyond the center. Rotate the cake a quarter turn and repeat, wiping the spatula clean between each swipe. Continue until the top is flat and the sides are a crisp right angle. Don't be tempted to smooth the frosting up and over from the side to the top of the cake because this will result in a rounded edge. If your edges are not perfect, don't worry about it; that is why we invented decorative border edge piping (see page 56)—to hide any imperfection.

CARAMELIZATION MAGIC

Sugar cooked to the near-burning point, with a dark amber color and a perfectly bittersweet flavor, is the base for many recipes in the book. I use it to dip hazelnuts to create a tall elegant garnish for a torte (see page 180), as a sauce, mixed with heavy whipping cream to drizzle over Turtle Cake (page 179), and mixed with even more heavy cream that is then whipped into a rich, soft filling (see page 229). The trick to successful caramel is to avoid crystallization, when the caramel turns to rock candy instead of a beautiful amber liquid. If sugar crystals cling to the side of the pan and then fall into the boiling sugar water, it can cause a chain reaction and crystallization can happen. To avoid this, try to keep the side of the pan clean and add a bit of corn syrup, an invert sugar that doesn't crystallize, as extra insurance to keep your caramel smooth.

Place the recipe's sugar and corn syrup in the center of a saucepan. Be careful not to get the sugar on the sides of the pan.

Gently run the water down the sides of the pan, to wash any rogue sugar back into the center. Do not stir, but if the water doesn't saturate all the sugar, gently run your finger through the sugar, allowing the water to flow into dry spots.

Once the mixture is all wet, place the pan over high heat and bring the sugar to a boil. Do *not* stir!

Allow the mixture to boil until the sugar just starts to turn amber along the edge. You can now stir the caramel without fear of crystallizing.

Continue cooking until the caramel just starts to smoke; I like a darker caramel, but you will determine what is right for you. Just be careful not to let it go from a pleasant bitter note to incinerated. Remove from the heat to stop cooking.

CARAMELIZATION MAGIC

POURED GANACHE

ZOË'S GANACHE SOS

Depending on the chocolate you use, the temperature of the mixture, or if you are reheating the ganache, it may separate and look oily. Don't panic, it can be fixed in a number of ways. If the ganache is too cool to whisk easily, you'll want to heat it slightly over a double boiler or in a microwave for a few seconds. Once you can stir it, add in the following components a tiny bit at a time to fix your ganache. Read on for specifics about which additions are best for your situation. I have put them in order of easiest fix to most drastic.

Cream—If your ganache breaks (this is when the chocolate and fat start to separate), you can drizzle in more cream as you are whisking, a tablespoon at a time, until the ganache is emulsified and smooth.

Corn syrup—This is similar to adding more cream, but you'll end up with a thinner ganache that tends to be a touch shinier, so it is nice if you are using the ganache to pour over a cake.

Egg yolk—Egg yolks are great emulsifiers, meaning they will bring together the fat and chocolate. This is a very old French technique and requires you to whisk a raw yolk into the ganache, resulting in a very thick and luxurious mixture. Using raw eggs is no longer a common kitchen trick, so don't try this method if that makes you uneasy.

Blender—If your ganache won't come back together by whisking in one or all of the above, place the warm ganache in a blender or food processor and pulse until it all comes together. Remember that you are aerating the cream in the ganache as you blend it, so it will get thick if you go too far.

When I walk into a pastry shop, my eye is always caught by the glossy, perfectly smooth chocolate cakes covered with poured ganache. The finish is sophisticated and elegant, but it is one of the easiest ways to cover a cake once it is crumb coated. It can be a base for other decorations or left sleek and exquisitely understated.

To get a perfectly smooth finish on your cake with chocolate ganache you need to pour it in one go, otherwise you may have drips instead of sheen. After you have made your ganache, let it set so that it has thickened enough to cling to the cake. If it is still too warm, it will just run off and not create a thick enough layer to cover the cake. If it is too cool, it will be too dense and won't spread on its own. If it gets too firm, you can put it in the microwave or over a double boiler to warm for a few seconds.

If you are covering a layer cake, you'll want to do a ganache crumb coat to fill any gaps that will be accentuated by the glossy poured ganache. Separate about 1 cup / 240g of the ganache and allow it to set to room temperature. You can place the separated ganache in the refrigerator and stir every few minutes until it is firm enough to spread onto the cake, being careful not to let it get too firm. It will now be spreadable and you can use it to create your crumb coat (see page 49).

Line a baking sheet with parchment paper. Place the crumb-coated cake onto a wire rack and set over the prepared baking sheet—you will be pouring quite a bit of ganache over the cake, so this setup will catch the excess.

Starting in the center of the cake, pour the ganache in a steady stream and work your way out to the edge in a spiral, making sure there are no bare spots. Continue pouring over the edges, until the sides are completely covered. The ganache should be smoothing itself out as you pour. If there are any ripples, ever so gently lift and set down the whole baking sheet to settle the ganache; only do this right after you finish pouring or you may end up creating more ripples. Let the cake sit until set up enough that you can move it without disrupting the finish on the ganache, 15 to 20 minutes.

Run a metal icing spatula under the base of the cake to separate it from the wire rack before trying to lift it, or the ganache may tear.

POURED GANACHE

ROLLED FONDANT

Covering a cake in fondant or marzipan transforms a simple cake into something elegant and just a bit posh. The technique of creating a smooth finish on the fondant takes a minute to master; but with a little practice, you'll be covering cakes like a pro.

I suggest you buy a commercial fondant for your first try at covering a cake, since it is more forgiving. Once you have a feel for it, you will be more at ease with the home-made version on page 222. It is useful to place a thin sheet of vinyl or a Silpat on the work surface. This will give the fondant a smooth finish, and the fondant won't stick to it, so you'll need less cornstarch while working.

You want to have a smooth cake surface under the fondant or it will show any bumps and indents. The easiest way to achieve a smooth cake is to crumb-coat it (see page 49). Be sure to use a frosting that will not show through the rolled fondant.

Dust the work surface and rolling pin with a skim of cornstarch to prevent the fondant from sticking. Place the fondant on the prepared surface and roll it out to fit the diameter of the cake, plus the cake's height. Don't roll thinner than ⅛ inch / 3mm thick; otherwise, it may tear when molding it to the cake. If the fondant is a little short, you will be able to work it down as you are molding it to the cake.

Drape the rolled fondant over the cake. Using a special fondant-smoothing tool, which looks like a plastic iron, or putting a sheet of plastic wrap between your fingers and the cake (to keep the fondant from getting fingerprints), rub the fondant while simultaneously, very gently, stretching it downward. As you are rubbing it, the fondant will naturally start to mold to the cake, but it will also want to ruffle as you drape, so you need to very gently rub the sides smooth, while carefully stretching it. Continue this motion of rubbing and smoothing the fondant until it is snug on the cake. There will be an excess of fondant that gathers at the base of the cake.

Using a paring knife, carefully trim off the excess and then smooth the cut edges with your fingers or with the smoothing tool.

You can use fondant to make shapes. Cookie cutters are an easy way to get creative with fondant. The shapes will adhere to the cake with water.

ROLLED FONDANT

THE FINISHING TOUCH

Learning just a few easy piping techniques will allow you to put the finishing touch on any of the cakes you see in this book. You can use them all together to create a stylish pattern that looks more sophisticated than the effort might suggest. None of these techniques is difficult, but as with any new venture, it may take a few times to get comfortable holding and using a piping bag.

Setting Up and Filling the Piping Bag

Select a piping tip and slip it into a pastry bag, or use a tip coupler if you think you may switch tips along the way (see page 25). Cut the bottom of the bag to fit the tip or coupler. Start small, since you can always cut more, but if you cut the hole too big, there's no going back.

Make sure your frosting is nice and smooth by stirring it until all of the air bubbles are worked out. You can do this by hand or in a stand mixer fitted with the paddle attachment. Air bubbles in a piping bag mean an interruption in the flow of the frosting, so to get a clean line or flower, you want a smooth frosting. To fill the bag:

→   Fold over the top of the bag so you have about a 3-inch / 7.5cm collar. Use a spatula to fill the bag with frosting, trying to keep it as neat as possible. Any frosting that ends up on the outside of the bag will be all over your hands as you work. Every time you need to refill the bag, fold over the top again.

→   Unfold the top of the bag and use your fingertips to squeeze the frosting to the bottom of the bag. Twist the top of the bag until it creates tight pressure on the frosting inside and some comes out the bottom. It is now ready to use.

→   As you are piping, always maintain the tight twist and pressure on the bag, so you'll have to stop piping on occasion to twist the top. There should be so much pressure in the bag that you can easily squeeze out the frosting with one hand.

→   Your other hand should just be used as a guide to lead the tip. So don't wrap both hands around the bag to create pressure or your hands will warm the buttercream and melt it.

Practice Really Does Make Perfect   Make a batch of American Buttercream (page 213) and grab a glass of wine or a cup of tea and settle in for a bit of piping practice, or just dive right into your cake project—that's up to you. It may take a few goes at this to get the knack of it, but it's a tasty endeavor.

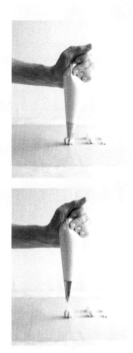

Star

Shell and Shell Border

Basic piping styles

Basic Piping Designs

These are some basic piping designs that are a great place to start your piping career. When added together, they can result in a gorgeous cake design; and with them, you can decorate all of the cakes in the book.

Star ▦ The star is the easiest shape and most of the others build on this. Fit your bag with a star tip; it doesn't matter what size, but you probably won't want to start with anything too enormous.

Hold the bag straight up and down, hovering over the practice surface (or cake) by about ¼ inch / 6mm. Squeeze the bag until a star forms, release the pressure from the bag, and lift up. Move to the next spot and repeat this action. The goal is to make a line of stars that are all the same size. This is meant to practice keeping control over your bag. Once you are decorating your cake, you can vary the pressure to get small or large stars. You can connect the stars to create a border around the edge of the cake or cover the entire cake in a series of giant stars, as for the Banana Cream Cake on page 132.

Rosette ▦ For a rosette, fit your bag with a star tip and hold it straight up and down. Start as if you are making a star but continue the pressure and draw a tight circle so there is no gap in the middle. End the motion by lifting up slightly over the point where you started, letting go of the pressure as you finish the circle.

Shell and Shell Border ▦ For shells, hold the bag at a 45-degree angle and squeeze the frosting until it hits the surface, ever so slightly rock the bag up and forward, so the frosting folds over the front, and then rock the bag back down and sweep it back, decreasing the pressure to create a tapering tail. Start the next shell over the tip of the tail so they are connecting in a border. Eventually, you can connect them without ever letting go of the pressure, by rocking up and down as you move around the cake.

PIPED ROSES

After you have mastered the basic piping design, you can move on to piped roses. If you know my work, you have seen my piped-rose cakes. They are my go-to for a particularly special occasion or if I am just feeling a bit romantic. The roses come together like magic out of a piping bag. These are not difficult to do but, like any craft, they take some practice and patience.

The Equipment You Will Need

→ Piping bags: 16-inch / 40cm pastry bags (if you are making multicolored roses, it is easier to use plastic disposable bags, so you can see where the painted stripe is in the bag as you are working)

→ Large rose tip: Ateco decorating tip #128 (the size of the rose is up to you)

→ Wooden skewer

→ Flower nail: Ateco flower nail, extra-large rose, 3-inch / 7.5cm diameter (this is what you will pipe the flower onto, so use one that fits the size of the rose you want to pipe)

→ Leaf tip: Wilton #366 leaf decorating tip

→ Kitchen shears

Preparing the Piping Bag

Decide on the color frosting you want for your roses. You can do them all the same color or have several different hues. Start your colors light, adding more coloring until it's just as you like.

Place the rose tip in the pastry bag. Line up the narrow end of the tip with the seam of the bag.

Along that seam, use a skewer to paint a thin line of food coloring, trying not to get it on the rest of the bag. This optional line of color will come out as the contrasting color on the tips of the petals.

Fill the bag one-third full with the frosting. Don't be tempted to overfill or the bag will be difficult to manage as you are piping. Push the frosting to the bottom of the bag. Twist the top of the bag to create pressure. Squeeze out the frosting, until the contrasting color is coming out clearly.

PREPARING THE PIPING BAG

Piping the Roses

Hold the rose nail between the fingers and thumb of your non-piping hand; you should be able to easily twirl the nail. Now pipe a nice wide blob of frosting onto the nail. This blob will act as the base of your rose, so make it large enough and wide enough to support the flower. The larger the rose (more petals), the larger the base. You'll snip the base from the nail to transfer to the cake.

Pipe the bud (or center) of the rose by holding your rose tip straight up and down, with the narrow end of the tip up. The wide end of the tip will be touching the frosting blob, about halfway down from the center.

Squeeze out a ribbon of frosting while turning the nail with your thumb and forefinger; once you've created a circle with the frosting, draw the tip down to the nail, anchoring the bud to the base.

To create the first row of petals, hold the tip so the wide end is touching the base of the bud, right where the bud finished off. Tilt the narrow end of the tip slightly away from the center, at a 20-degree angle.

Squeeze out the frosting, turning the nail, and move the tip up very slightly (increasing the pressure) and then down (decreasing the pressure) in an arch that spans half the bud. Repeat this motion to complete the first two petals on either side of the bud.

PIPING THE ROSES

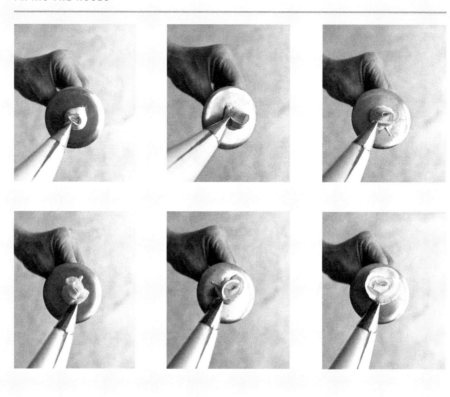

TRANSFERRING THE ROSES TO THE CAKE

Form the next row of three petals in the same way, starting each one where the last petal finished. Overlap the petals to hide any openings between them. For each row, increase the number of petals. Tilt the tip out even more if you want it to appear that the flower is opening up.

You can stop at any point. You may want just a few petals for a young rose, or you can continue on for a more mature flower. The roses should be a variety of sizes to make them look more realistic.

Transferring the Roses to the Cake

Once you have piped as many petals as you like, you will need to lift the rose off the nail and onto the cake. I do this by using a pair of kitchen shears. You will want to cut only partway through, so you can lift the rose on the blades.

Carefully place the rose onto the cake and slide the shears out from under it. You will need to make sure it is well anchored, so it will not move around.

Finish by using the leaf tip to pipe a few leaves around the base of the rose. This is a wonderful way to hide any imperfections in your flowers. Repeat with as many roses as you like.

BAKING AT HIGH ALTITUDES

I live in the Midwest, which is perhaps the flattest place in the country, so I am by no means the reigning expert on high-altitude baking, but I have baked a few cakes in the mountains of Colorado, and this is what I learned. There can be a big difference in how cakes behave if you live above 5,280 feet / 1.6km. With less air pressure, the rising batter balloons up too quickly and then collapses abruptly, giving you a dense, if not sunken, result. The following adjustments can help you avoid disappointment.

→ Decrease the baking soda or baking powder by half.

→ Increase baking temperature by 15 to 25 degrees, which will set the proteins faster and stop the bubbles from expanding too much.

→ Decrease the baking time, due to the higher temperature.

→ Decrease the amount of sugar by just a tablespoon per cup. Sugar is a tenderizer, so it can weaken the structure of the cake. This means it can't trap the gas as well and too much may cause the cake to collapse.

→ Increase the amount of flour by a tablespoon per cup. This will lend more structure to the cake.

For more detailed information, visit the Colorado State University website (colostate.edu) and search for high-altitude food preparation.

1   pound cakes, quick breads, and bundts

The comfort foods of the cake world, pound cakes, quick breads, and Bundts deliver without pretension or fuss, just flavor. There is nothing more satisfying than a perfect vanilla-bean pound cake. Despite how easy it is to make and its humble appearance, it deserves all the respect in the world. In fact, my professor at the Culinary Institute of America (CIA) told us that we were not to talk down about Sara Lee and that ubiquitous pound cake until we were making something as beloved by all of America. I still prefer the homemade version, but my professor had a point. Rounding out this chapter are quick breads, which are really just cakes you are allowed to eat for breakfast. And to fancy up the simplest of cakes, bake them in a Bundt pan and you've taken the recipe to a sensational finish. These are classic cakes, and ones I make regularly—especially banana breads—but they're also simple and a great introduction for new bakers.

The measurements are all in the name, so there is no forgetting this recipe. Mix together a pound of butter, a pound of sugar, a pound of eggs, and a pound of flour and you have a simply perfect blank canvas for all kinds of flavor-adds. For my version, I like vanilla, as it is the darling of all pound cakes, but you can give this cake a kick with citrus zest, such as lemon, grapefruit, orange, or lime, or spices. Make it your own. This recipe is also remarkable in that it has no chemical leavener, on which so many cakes rely. It is all about whipping air into the butter until the batter is light and fluffy to create the rise once it hits the oven. The outcome is a dense, buttery crumb that is Midwestern in its straightforward nature, and pure comfort. No wonder pound cakes are one of the most popular cakes in history. It's wonderful to have on hand, and it serves as a nice excuse to invite a friend for coffee.

You can bake this cake in two loaf pans—so you can send one home with your friend—or in a Bundt to fancy it up a bit. The texture and simplicity of the cake make it a perfect match for a simple-syrup soak or a sugar glaze, which are other ways to add moisture and flavor.

vanilla-bean pound cake

Makes two 8-inch / 20cm loaves

cake academy review

CREAMING → page 33

1 lb / 454g unsalted butter, at room temperature

1 lb / 454g confectioners' sugar

2 Tbsp vanilla extract (see page 12)

Scraped seeds from 1 vanilla bean

2 tsp citrus zest (optional)

1 lb / 454g eggs (about 9 large), at room temperature

1 lb / 454g all-purpose flour

1 tsp kosher salt

½ cup / 120ml Confectioners' Sugar Icing (page 204) or Simple Syrup (page 226)

1 Preheat the oven to 325°F / 165°C. Generously grease two 8 by 4-inch / 20 by 10cm loaf pans and then line them with greased parchment paper.

2 In a stand mixer fitted with the paddle attachment, cream the butter on medium-high speed until creamy and smooth, about 1 minute.

3 Turn the mixer speed to low, add the confectioners' sugar to the butter, and mix until incorporated. Turn the speed to medium-high and beat until very light and fluffy, about 5 minutes. Scrape the bowl often for even incorporation.

4 Add the vanilla extract, vanilla seeds, and citrus zest (if using) and mix until incorporated.

5 Turn the speed to medium-low and add the eggs, one at a time, beating just until combined. Scrape the bowl after every couple of eggs.

6 In a separate bowl, whisk together the flour and salt. Add one-third of the flour mixture to the butter mixture, mixing on low speed just until combined. Repeat with another one-third flour and then the final one-third, scraping the bowl and paddle after each addition.

7 Scrape the batter into the prepared pans. Smooth the tops and tap the pans on the counter a few times to release excess air bubbles. Set the pans on a baking sheet.

8 Bake until the cakes are golden and a tester comes out clean, about 1 hour 10 minutes. Let the cakes cool in the pans for 10 minutes, then invert onto serving plates and let cool completely. Pour the icing over the cakes and let set before serving.

CONTINUED

POUND CAKES, QUICK BREADS, AND BUNDTS

VARIATION: VANILLA-RASPBERRY BUNDT

Beautiful raspberries, studded like hidden gems, offer a sweet surprise to those expecting plain ol' pound cake. Generously butter and flour a 12-cup / 2.8L Bundt pan. Gently fold 2 cups / 240g fresh (or frozen) raspberries into the batter and then pour into the prepared pan. Bake until a tester comes out clean, about 50 minutes. (If you use frozen fruit, the baking time can be longer, up to 1 hour 15 minutes.) Let cool as directed. Glaze with raspberry Confectioners' Sugar Icing (see variation, page 204) before serving.

marble pound cake

While there are similarities to the original pound-for-pound version (Vanilla-Bean Pound Cake, page 63), this variety tastes a bit more twenty-first century. The balance of butter and sugar still allows for the simplicity of the vanilla to shine through, but the addition of buttermilk and cake flour adds a bit more lightness to the interior crumb. Then there is the cocoa marbling to shift this into high gear. It's an excellent everyday cake—an easy way to send a bit of love in school lunches or reward yourself after a long, hard Wednesday out in the world.

Makes one 8-inch / 20cm loaf

cake academy review

CREAMING → page 33

1 cup / 120g all-purpose flour

4 Tbsp / 40g cake flour, sifted

½ tsp kosher salt

1 cup / 220g unsalted butter, at room temperature

1½ cups / 300g granulated sugar

1 Tbsp vanilla extract (see page 12)

Scraped seeds from ½ vanilla bean

3 eggs, at room temperature

¼ cup / 60ml buttermilk, at room temperature

3 Tbsp Dutch-processed cocoa powder (sifted if lumpy)

1   Preheat the oven to 325°F / 165°C. Generously grease an 8 by 4-inch / 20 by 10cm loaf pan, then line it with greased parchment paper.

2   In a medium bowl, whisk together both flours and the salt, then set aside.

3   In a stand mixer fitted with the paddle attachment, cream the butter on medium-high speed until creamy and smooth, about 1 minute.

4   Turn the mixer speed to low, add the sugar to the butter, and mix until incorporated. Turn the speed to medium-high and beat until very light and fluffy, about 5 minutes. Scrape the bowl often for even incorporation.

5   Add the vanilla extract and vanilla seeds, turn the speed to medium, and mix until incorporated.

6   Turn the speed to medium-low and add the eggs, one at a time, beating just until combined. Scrape the bowl after each addition.

7   Add one-third of the flour mixture to the butter mixture, mixing on low speed, just until combined. Add half the buttermilk and mix on low speed just until combined. Repeat with another one-third flour, the remaining buttermilk, and the final one-third flour, scraping the bowl and paddle after each addition.

8   Divide the batter in half. Stir the cocoa powder into half of the batter.

CONTINUED

9   Using an ice-cream scoop or a spoon, alternate scoops of the vanilla and chocolate batters into the prepared pan. Drag a knife or skewer through the batter to create a marbled effect. Smooth the top and tap the pan on the counter a few times to release excess air bubbles. Set the pan on a baking sheet.

10 Bake until a tester comes out clean, about 1 hour 10 minutes. Let the cake cool in the pan for 10 minutes, then remove from the pan and place onto a serving plate and let cool completely before serving.

lemon-curd pound cake

Every bite of this bright and dreamy cake has all the enthusiasm of a spring morning. There are layers of tartness from the luxurious lemon curd, lemon zest, and pieces of baked lemon that nestle perfectly into the buttery rich batter. A light and easy drizzle of lemon syrup, made from baked lemon slices, makes a simple bite feel like the warm, sunny promise of a new day.

Makes one 9-inch / 23cm loaf

cake academy review

CREAMING → page 33

2 lemons, sliced ⅛ inch / 3mm thick, plus zest of 2 lemons

Scraped seeds from 1 vanilla bean

1 cup / 240ml Simple Syrup (page 226)

¾ cup / 165g unsalted butter, at room temperature

1½ cups / 300g granulated sugar

2 tsp vanilla extract (see page 12)

1 tsp lemon extract

2 eggs, at room temperature

4 egg yolks, at room temperature

2 cups plus 2 Tbsp / 240g cake flour

1 tsp baking powder

¼ tsp baking soda

½ tsp kosher salt

¾ cup / 180g sour cream, at room temperature

½ cup / 140g Lemon Curd (page 235)

1 Preheat the oven to 325°F / 165°C. Generously grease a 9 by 4-inch / 23 by 10cm Pullman pan (or a 10 by 5-inch / 25 by 13cm loaf pan), then line it with greased parchment paper. Set aside.

2 Put the lemon slices and vanilla seeds in the bottom of a 9-inch / 23cm baking dish, pour the simple syrup over the top, and cover tightly with aluminum foil.

3 Bake until the lemons are very soft, 40 to 45 minutes. Set aside.

4 In a stand mixer fitted with the paddle attachment, cream the butter on medium-high speed until creamy and smooth, about 1 minute.

5 Turn the mixer speed to low; add the sugar, vanilla extract, lemon extract, and lemon zest to the butter; and mix until incorporated. Turn the speed to medium-high and beat until light and fluffy, about 5 minutes. Scrape the bowl often for even incorporation.

6 Turn the speed to medium-low and add the eggs and egg yolks, one at a time, beating just until combined. Scrape the bowl after each addition.

7 In a separate bowl, whisk together the flour, baking powder, baking soda, and salt. Sift to remove any lumps.

8 Add one-third of the flour mixture to the butter mixture and mix on low speed, just until combined. Add half of the sour cream, mixing until incorporated. Repeat with another one-third flour, then the remaining sour cream, and finish with the final one-third flour, scraping the bowl and paddle after each addition.

9 Fold the lemon curd into the batter. It's okay if there are a few streaks of curd left throughout the batter.

10 Scrape the batter into the prepared pan. Smooth the top and tap the pan on the counter several times to release excess air bubbles. Lay five baked lemon slices over the top of the batter. Set the pan on a baking sheet.

11 Bake just until the top sets, about 45 minutes; the sliced lemons will have slipped beneath the surface. Lay another four lemon slices over the top and continue to bake until a tester comes out clean, 25 to 30 minutes more. As soon as you take the cake out of the oven, drizzle with 2 Tbsp of the lemon syrup from the baked lemons.

12 Let the cake cool in the pan for 20 minutes, then remove from the pan and set on a wire rack to cool completely before serving.

POUND CAKES, QUICK BREADS, AND BUNDTS

When I was growing up, coming home from school meant digging into snacks such as carob and dehydrated banana chips. It wasn't until I tasted actual chocolate that I realized there was a giant world out there (and everyone else was probably eating better snacks than I was). Thus began a long and storied quest to find the good sweet stuff that eventually led me to Nutella. Swirling hazelnut-y chocolate into the center of this banana bread is so satisfying and delicious. It's the after-school snack we all deserve. If you are a banana-bread purest, you can leave the Nutella out of the bread and top it with Cream Cheese Frosting (page 209) instead.

I like my bananas mashed by hand, so there are some small chunks in the bread. If you like a more even crumb, then you are more of a pureed-banana person—and that will work too.

banana bread with swirls of nutella

Makes two 8-inch / 20cm loaves

2 cups / 480g mashed very ripe bananas (about 4 large)

1 cup / 200g lightly packed brown sugar

½ cup / 110g unsalted butter, melted

½ cup / 120ml whole milk

2 eggs, at room temperature

2 tsp vanilla extract (see page 12)

3⅓ cups / 400g all-purpose flour

2 tsp baking powder

1½ tsp baking soda

1½ tsp kosher salt

½ cup / 140g Nutella

1   Preheat the oven to 350°F / 175°C. Generously grease two 8 by 4-inch / 20 by 10cm loaf pans, then line them with greased parchment paper.

2   In a large bowl, combine the bananas, brown sugar, butter, milk, eggs, and vanilla and mix well with a wooden spoon.

3   In a separate bowl, whisk together the flour, baking powder, baking soda, and salt. Add the dry ingredients to the banana mixture and stir just until smooth.

4   Heat the Nutella in the microwave for about 20 seconds to soften.

5   Divide half of the banana batter between the prepared pans. Drizzle half of the Nutella over the two pans and run a knife through the batter in a zigzag pattern to distribute.

6   Add the remaining batter to the pans, top with the remaining Nutella, and swirl into the batter with the knife again.

7   Bake until a tester comes out clean, about 50 minutes. Let the cakes cool in the pans for 10 minutes, then remove from the pans and set on a wire rack to cool completely before serving.

Poor zucchini and its permanent record of overabundant productivity. What other vegetable gets thrust into neighbors' hands with the same desperate need to share as these guys? There's always one day in August where an optimistic gardener (my dad) becomes wild-eyed, slightly demented, and determined to divvy up the borderline unmanageable bounty. He delivers his harvest with such glee, and in return I deliver zucchini cakes, like this pure and simple option or the richest Best-Ever Chocolate-Zucchini Bundt Cake on page 74.

Any neighbor will be happy to see you returning to share this gently spiced cake with its creamy just-sweet-enough frosting.

zucchini cake

Makes one 9 by 13-inch / 24 by 36cm sheet cake or two 8-inch / 20cm loaves

cake academy review

BASIC PIPING DESIGNS: ROSETTES → page 56

1¾ cups / 350g granulated sugar

¾ cup / 255g honey

½ cup / 120ml mild-flavored oil (such as vegetable oil)

3 eggs, at room temperature

1 tsp vanilla extract (see page 12)

3 cups / 470g packed grated unpeeled zucchini (see Baker's Note)

2¾ cups / 330g all-purpose flour

2 tsp baking powder

1 tsp baking soda

4 tsp ground cinnamon

½ tsp ground nutmeg

½ tsp ground ginger

¼ tsp kosher salt

1 cup / 120g chopped walnuts, plus whole toasted walnuts for topping

1 recipe Cream Cheese Frosting (page 209)

1 Preheat the oven to 325°F / 165°C. Generously grease a 9 by13-inch / 24 by 36cm cake pan (or two 8 by 4-inch / 20 by 10cm loaf pans), then line it with greased parchment paper.

2 In a large bowl, whisk together the sugar, honey, oil, eggs, and vanilla. Then add the zucchini and mix until incorporated.

3 In a separate bowl, whisk together the flour, baking powder, baking soda, cinnamon, nutmeg, ginger, and salt.

4 Stir the dry ingredients into the honey mixture, just until combined, then fold in the chopped walnuts.

5 Scrape the batter into the prepared pan. Smooth the top and tap the pan on the counter a few times to release excess air bubbles. Set the pan on a baking sheet.

6 Bake until the cake is set and a tester comes out clean, about 55 minutes (or about 1 hour if you are using loaf pans). Let the cake cool in the pan for 10 minutes, then invert onto a serving platter to cool completely.

7 Use the frosting to pipe rosettes onto the cake and then top each rosette with a toasted walnut before serving.

BAKER'S NOTE

To easily grate zucchini, cut off both ends and then cut into quarters. If the zucchini are large and at all tough, remove the seeds. Then use a box grater or the grater attachment on a food processor to shred the zucchini.

Bless whomever first thought to combine zucchini and chocolate. These two unlikely partners make fantastic cake together. The moisture in the vegetables translates to a super-rich cake—and all rich cakes are made even better with chocolate. I love the bittersweet edge of a darker chocolate, but semisweet works beautifully here as well.

I've been baking versions of this cake since 1986, when I was an art student at the University of Vermont in Burlington. While working as a photography assistant where we were shooting a woman with her zucchini bounty, I became transfixed by the deep, dark chocolate cake we were photographing. Not until I had convinced the baker to send the cake and recipe home with me did she reveal that the secret ingredient was, indeed, zucchini. Although I have since lost her original recipe, this matches my memory perfectly.

best-ever chocolate-zucchini bundt cake

Makes one Bundt cake

cake academy review

CREAMING → page 33

Dutch-processed cocoa powder for dusting, plus ⅔ cup / 50g

2¼ cups / 270g all-purpose flour

1 tsp baking soda

1 tsp kosher salt

½ cup / 110g unsalted butter, at room temperature

1 cup / 200g lightly packed brown sugar

¾ cup / 150g granulated sugar

½ cup / 120ml mild-flavored oil (such as vegetable oil)

1 tsp vanilla extract (see page 12)

2 eggs, at room temperature

½ cup / 120g plain full-fat yogurt or sour cream

2 cups / 315g packed grated unpeeled zucchini (see Baker's Note, page 73)

4 oz / 115g bittersweet or semisweet chocolate, melted and cooled to room temperature

1 Preheat the oven to 325°F / 165°C. Generously grease a 12-cup / 2.8L Bundt pan and dust with cocoa powder.

2 In a medium bowl, sift together the flour, baking soda, salt, and ⅔ cup / 50g cocoa powder. Sift to remove any lumps.

3 In a stand mixer fitted with the paddle attachment, cream the butter on medium-high speed until creamy and smooth, about 1 minute.

4 Turn the mixer speed to low, add both sugars to the butter, and mix until incorporated. Drizzle in the oil and vanilla, turn the speed to medium-high, and beat until very light and fluffy, about 5 minutes. Scrape the bowl often for even incorporation.

5 Turn the speed to medium-low and add the eggs, one at a time, beating just until combined. Scrape the bowl after each addition.

6 Add one-third of the flour mixture to the butter mixture, mixing on low speed, just until combined. Add half of the yogurt, mixing until incorporated. Repeat with another one-third flour, then the remaining yogurt, and finish with the final one-third flour, scraping the bowl and paddle after each addition.

7 Remove the bowl from the mixer and stir in the zucchini until it is evenly distributed. Then add the chocolate and stir until combined.

8 Pour the batter into the prepared pan. Gently tap the pan on the counter several times to make sure the batter has fully settled into the nooks of the Bundt.

9 Bake until a tester comes out with moist crumbs, about 1 hour. DO NOT OVERBAKE. Let the cake cool in the pan for 10 minutes, then flip it out onto a serving plate and dust the top with cocoa before serving.

chocolate ganache bundt cake

This is an irresistible development in the evolution of the humble pound cake. It is peak indulgence with the addition of rich ganache, a dark and creamy chocolate that gives an incredible depth of flavor. Use a really great bittersweet chocolate if you want this cake to sing.

Dusting the Bundt pan with cocoa maintains that fudgy dark look on the outside, while making it easy to pop out of the pan.

Makes one Bundt cake or two 8-inch / 20cm loaves

cake academy review

CREAMING → page 33

POURED GANACHE → page 52

Dutch-processed cocoa for dusting, plus ½ cup / 40g

½ cup / 120ml heavy whipping cream

½ cup / 100g chopped bittersweet chocolate

¼ cup / 60ml buttermilk

1½ cups / 180g all-purpose flour

½ tsp baking soda

½ tsp kosher salt

¾ cup / 165g unsalted butter, at room temperature

1½ cups / 300g granulated sugar

1 Tbsp vanilla extract (see page 12)

2 eggs, at room temperature

3 egg yolks, at room temperature

1 cup / 240g Dark Chocolate Ganache (page 221)

1 Preheat the oven to 325°F / 165°C. Generously grease a 12-cup / 2.8L Bundt pan (or two 8 by 4-inch / 20 by 10cm loaf pans) and dust with cocoa powder.

2 In a small saucepan over medium-low heat, bring the heavy cream to a gentle simmer. Turn off the heat, add the chocolate, and swirl the pan, so the chocolate is submerged in the cream. Let the chocolate and cream sit for 3 minutes, then whisk until smooth. Pour the chocolate mixture into a bowl and whisk in the buttermilk. Set aside to cool.

3 In a medium bowl, whisk together the flour, ½ cup / 40g cocoa powder, baking soda, and salt. Sift to remove any lumps.

4 In a stand mixer fitted with the paddle attachment, cream the butter on medium-high speed until creamy and smooth, about 1 minute.

5 Turn the mixer speed to low, add the sugar and vanilla to the butter, and mix until incorporated. Turn the speed to medium-high and beat until light and fluffy, about 5 minutes. Scrape the bowl often for even incorporation.

6 Turn the speed to medium-low and add the eggs and egg yolks, one at a time, beating just until combined. Scrape the bowl after each addition.

7 Add one-third of the flour mixture to the butter mixture and mix on low speed, just until combined. Add half of the cooled chocolate-buttermilk mixture and mix until just incorporated. Repeat with another one-third flour, the remaining chocolate-buttermilk mixture, and then the final one-third flour, scraping the bowl and paddle after each addition.

8 Scrape the batter into the prepared pan. Smooth the top and gently tap the pan on the counter a few times to make sure the batter has fully settled. Set the pan on a baking sheet.

9 Bake until a tester comes out clean, about 50 minutes. Let the cake cool in the pan for 15 minutes, then invert onto a serving plate and let cool completely.

10 Pour the ganache over the top of the cake before serving.

pumpkin–mocha swirl bundt cake

PSL* lovers, this one's for you. The instant that first cool breeze blows in after Labor Day, it's time to start gushing about sweater weather and decorative gourds. This cake takes all the warm spices that herald the change of season and combines them with creamy, rich pumpkin into a cake that pretty much blows all others out of the water. Then, just to gild the lily, I added a stripe of chocolate and espresso, because they marry so well with pumpkin and make the cake look like your favorite striped sweater.   *pumpkin spice latte

---

Makes one Bundt cake

Dutch-processed cocoa powder for dusting, plus 2 Tbsp

1 cup / 240ml mild-flavored oil (such as vegetable oil)

1 cup / 200g granulated sugar

1 cup / 200g lightly packed brown sugar

3 eggs, at room temperature

One 15-oz / 425g can pumpkin puree

½ cup / 120ml evaporated milk

1 Tbsp vanilla extract (see page 12)

2¼ cups / 270g all-purpose flour

1½ tsp baking soda

1 tsp kosher salt

1 Tbsp pumpkin pie spice, divided (see Baker's Note)

1 tsp instant espresso

¼ cup / 25g confectioners' sugar

1 Preheat the oven to 325°F / 165°C. Generously grease a 12-cup / 2.8L Bundt pan and dust with cocoa powder.

2 In a large bowl, combine the oil, both sugars, and eggs and stir until well incorporated. Then stir in the pumpkin puree, evaporated milk, and vanilla.

3 In a separate bowl, whisk together the flour, baking soda, salt, and 2 tsp of the pumpkin pie spice. Add the dry ingredients to the pumpkin mixture and mix until it all comes together in a smooth batter.

4 Divide the batter into two bowls and stir the espresso and 2 Tbsp cocoa powder into one of them.

5 Pour one-fourth of the pumpkin batter into the prepared pan. Pour one-fourth of the cocoa batter evenly over the pumpkin. Repeat these layers, alternating the pumpkin and cocoa batters in the pan until they are both used up. Gently tap the pan on the counter several times to make sure the batter has fully settled into the nooks of the Bundt.

6 Bake until a tester comes out clean, about 1 hour 15 minutes. Let the cake cool in the pan for 15 minutes, then turn out onto a serving dish.

7 Meanwhile, in a small bowl, combine the confectioners' sugar and remaining 1 tsp pumpkin pie spice and stir to mix. Sprinkle over the top of the cake before serving.

BAKER'S NOTE

To make your own pumpkin pie spice, blend together 1¼ tsp ground cinnamon, 1 tsp ground ginger, ¼ tsp ground cloves, and ½ tsp ground nutmeg.

2 fruit-studded cakes— upside down or otherwise

I'm an enormous fan of fruit-filled cakes that are on the pretty but less polished side of the cake world. Rustic Grape and Almond Paste Cake (page 86, and pictured opposite) is a perfect example. They are like the comfy chair at Grandma's house, all warm and soothing. Some of them are super-simple and require just a spoon or a Danish dough whisk, which is the coolest and simplest tool in the kitchen (see page 24). Others require a tiny bit more fuss, but nothing complicated, and they are 100 percent worth the small extra effort. I also think these treats should be breakfast cakes (I mentioned eating cake in the morning in the previous chapter, which shows you my dietary habits) because they tend not to be overly sweet, so the fruit shines through. They are excellent served with a cup of coffee or tea. Start with Blueberry Muffin Cake (page 83), and you'll understand what I mean.

There's no better way to celebrate the little indigo berries of summer than with a fluffy muffin. And isn't a muffin really just a tiny cake yearning to grow into greatness? This cake adds a little almond flour, whole-wheat flour, and walnuts to amp up the heartiness that sets off the tart explosions of blueberry flavor. As the name might suggest, this cake is perfect for breakfast with a dollop of yogurt and a few fresh berries or as a school-lunch treat.

blueberry muffin cake

Blueberries make the most famous muffin fruit, but don't feel constrained; try this cake with any fruit you want. Fresh or frozen fruit works equally well, but check out the Baker's Note for best results.

Makes one 8-inch / 20cm cake

10 Tbsp / 140g unsalted butter, at room temperature

1 cup / 200g granulated sugar

1 cup / 120g all-purpose flour

¼ cup / 35g whole-wheat flour

½ cup / 60g almond flour

1 tsp baking powder

¼ tsp kosher salt

2 eggs, at room temperature

½ cup / 120ml whole milk, at room temperature

1 tsp vanilla extract (see page 12)

2 cups / 310g fresh or frozen blueberries (see Baker's Note)

TOPPING

½ cup / 60g chopped walnuts

3 Tbsp granulated sugar

½ tsp ground cinnamon

1 pinch kosher salt

2 Tbsp unsalted butter, cut into 8 pieces

Perfect Whipped Cream (page 227), plain yogurt, or ice cream for serving

1 Preheat the oven to 375°F / 190°C. Generously grease an 8-inch / 20cm springform pan, then line the bottom and sides with greased parchment paper.

2 In a food processor, combine the butter, sugar, all three flours, baking powder, salt, eggs, milk, and vanilla and process until smooth.

3 Pour the batter into the prepared pan. Add the blueberries to the top of the batter. Run a knife around the batter to distribute the berries and release any large air bubbles. (If you use frozen berries, they will sink as the cake bakes; fresh ones will stay closer to the top.)

4 Bake until the cake is starting to set in the middle and is golden brown, about 45 minutes.

5 To make the topping: Meanwhile, in a small bowl, toss together the walnuts, sugar, cinnamon, and salt.

6 Sprinkle the topping over the cake, distribute the butter evenly over the topping, and continue to bake until a tester comes out clean, about 25 minutes more. (The cake may take 5 minutes longer to bake if you are using frozen berries.) Let the cake

cool in the pan, to just about room temperature, and then run a knife around the edge. Remove the sides of the springform and transfer to a serving plate.

7 Serve the cake warm with a dollop of whipped cream or yogurt or a scoop of ice cream.

VARIATION: APPLE, PEACH, OR RHUBARB MUFFIN CAKE

This cake is the perfect canvas for just about any type of fruit, depending on the season. Just substitute apples, peaches, all sorts of other berries, or rhubarb for the blueberries and proceed as directed.

BAKER'S NOTE

Keeping the blueberries frozen until ready to mix in ensures that their juices will not streak the batter with their natural color and add a bunch of liquid to the overall recipe. Tossing them with 1 Tbsp flour before adding to the batter will help prevent them from sinking to the bottom of the cake during baking.

I grew up in New England, and the apples from my childhood were McIntosh. They are deliciously tart and have a soft flesh that practically turns to applesauce on a hot day. It wasn't until I moved to Minneapolis that my apple horizons were broadened, and now I am spoiled by the riches of so many local. As a result, I always use a couple different kinds in a recipe; I'll pick sweet (Honeygold), tart (Haralson), saucy (McIntosh still makes the cut), and firm (Prairie Spy). You'll have your own local favorites. Infusing apples with a golden honey-bourbon caramel is like matchmaking two friends. Honey as the basis for caramel is a bold and absolutely spectacular flavor.

Shredding the apples into the cake retains the moisture and packs in the flavor but also adds a measured consistency of apple throughout that I just love. I'll leave it to you to decide if you want to peel the apples; I do not. It's easier, and the apple pieces are so small that having the skin on doesn't bother me in the least. My mom wanted walnuts in her cake when she tested it for me, so there they are!

apple cake with honey-bourbon glaze

Apple season falls right around Rosh Hashanah, which is the time to celebrate the Jewish new year with family and friends. This cake will quickly become an old family tradition for the holiday.

Makes one Bundt cake

1¼ cups / 300ml mild-flavored oil (such as vegetable oil)

1½ cups / 300g granulated sugar

⅔ cup / 130g lightly packed brown sugar

3 Tbsp bourbon

2 tsp vanilla extract (see page 12)

3 eggs, at room temperature

2 cups / 300g packed grated apples, plus 2 cups / 300g apple chunks (about 4 medium apples), ¼-inch / 6mm pieces

2 cups / 240g all-purpose flour, plus 1 Tbsp

1 cup / 130g whole-wheat flour

1 Tbsp ground cinnamon

1 tsp baking soda

¾ tsp kosher salt

1 cup / 100g chopped walnuts (optional)

HONEY-BOURBON GLAZE

¼ cup / 60ml heavy whipping cream

¼ cup / 50g granulated sugar

3 Tbsp honey

2 Tbsp bourbon

1 Tbsp unsalted butter

1 pinch kosher salt

---

1   Preheat the oven to 325°F / 165°C. Generously grease and flour a 12-cup / 2.8L Bundt pan.

2   In a large bowl, combine the oil, both sugars, bourbon, vanilla, and eggs and stir with a spoon to mix. Then stir in the grated apples.

3   In a separate bowl, whisk together the 2 cups / 240g all-purpose flour, whole-wheat flour, cinnamon, baking soda, and salt. Add the dry ingredients to the apple mixture and mix only until it all comes together in a smooth batter.

4   Toss the apple chunks and chopped walnuts (if using) with the 1 Tbsp all-purpose flour and then fold into the batter.

5   Pour the batter into the prepared pan. Gently tap the pan on the counter several times to make sure the batter has fully settled into the nooks of the Bundt.

6   Bake until a tester comes out clean, about 1 hour 15 minutes. Let the cake cool in the pan for 15 minutes, then turn out onto a serving plate.

7   To make the glaze: In a medium saucepan over medium-low heat, combine the cream, granulated sugar, honey, bourbon, butter, and salt; stir to mix; and simmer for 2 minutes.

8   Drizzle half of the glaze over the still-warm cake. Save the remaining glaze to drizzle over the fully cooled cake when ready to serve.

It's curious why grapes are rarely used in baking, unless dried into raisins. They are juicy and have such a wide range of sweetness and flavor, depending on the variety. They're also a perfect match for almond paste, an ingredient with which I'm more than just a bit smitten; there are so many ways to play with the slightly creamy, earthy flavor. Together with the earthiness of olive oil, the combination makes a gorgeous cake that's just as suited for a holiday table as it is for a Tuesday-night dessert.

rustic grape and almond paste cake

To get the dreamy texture of this cake, the batter is made in a food processor so the almond paste is blended smoothly. It yields a crumb that is dense and tender at the same time. Try the variation with kirschwasser-soaked dried cherries in place of the grapes.

Makes one 10-inch / 25cm cake

1 cup plus 1 Tbsp / 120g cake flour

½ tsp baking powder

⅛ tsp kosher salt

7 oz / 200g almond paste, cut into small pieces, plus 4 oz / 115g, cut into ¼-inch / 6mm cubes (see Baker's Note)

1 cup / 200g granulated sugar

¾ cup / 175ml olive oil, or ½ cup / 120ml olive oil plus ¼ cup / 60ml mild-flavored oil (such as vegetable oil)

1 tsp vanilla extract (see page 12)

1 tsp almond extract

1 tsp orange zest

5 eggs, at room temperature

1½ cups / 240g halved grapes (any seedless variety will do)

TOPPING

½ cup / 60g almond slivers, lightly crushed in mortar and pestle

¼ cup / 50g granulated sugar

1 tsp orange zest

4 drops orange blossom water

1   Preheat the oven to 325°F / 175°C. Generously grease and flour a 10-inch / 25cm tube pan.

2   In a medium bowl, whisk together the flour, baking powder, and salt.

3   In a food processor, combine the pieces of almond paste, sugar, olive oil, vanilla, almond extract, and orange zest and process until smooth. Add the eggs, one at a time, pulsing to combine after each addition.

4   Add one-third of the flour mixture to the oil mixture and pulse just until combined. Repeat with another one-third flour and then the final one-third. Using a spoon or rubber spatula, fold the cubes of almond paste and half of the grapes into the batter.

5   Scrape the batter into the prepared pan and top with the remaining grapes.

6   To make the topping: In a small bowl, combine the almonds, sugar, orange zest, and orange blossom water and rub together with your fingertips.

7   Sprinkle the topping over the batter and smooth with a spatula. Set the pan on a baking sheet.

8   Bake until the cake is deep golden and a tester comes out clean, about 1 hour 15 minutes. Let the cake cool in the pan for 10 minutes, then remove from the pan and set onto a wire rack to cool completely before serving.

VARIATION: DRIED CHERRY AND KIRSCHWASSER CAKE

The intensity of dried cherries is a perfect pairing with the almond-paste batter of this cake, and I've added a bit of kirschwasser (cherry liqueur) to make it a party. Place 1¼ cups / 175g dried cherries and ¼ cup / 60ml kirschwasser in a microwave-safe bowl and microwave for about 1 minute, then let cool to room temperature. Substitute the cherry-kirschwasser mixture for the grapes and proceed as directed.

BAKER'S NOTE

The almond paste needs to be soft, or it won't incorporate smoothly. If it is old and dried out, it will just stay in clumps.

plum cake

This may be my favorite cake in the whole book. That's a big statement, since I created them all and put my heart into each one. This one is perfectly balanced with sweet, buttery, tender, yet hearty cake and the freshness of tart plums. The spiral of plums sinks into the cake and turns a stunning fuchsia in the oven. I can't ever wait to transfer it from the baking pan to a plate before cutting a warm slice and devouring it. Add some softly whipped cream, and this cake is my idea of pure joy.

Makes one 9-inch / 23cm cake

10 Tbsp / 140g unsalted butter, at room temperature

1 cup / 200g granulated sugar

2 eggs, at room temperature

½ cup / 120ml whole milk, at room temperature

1 tsp vanilla extract (see page 12)

1 cup / 120g all-purpose flour

½ cup / 60g almond flour

¼ cup / 35g whole-wheat flour

1 tsp baking powder

¼ tsp kosher salt

4 plums, quartered

TOPPING

2 Tbsp granulated sugar

¼ tsp ground cinnamon

2 Tbsp unsalted butter, cold, cut into ¼-inch / 6mm cubes

1 Preheat the oven to 375°F / 190°C. Generously grease a 9-inch / 23cm springform pan, then line the bottom and sides with greased parchment paper.

2 In a food processor, combine the butter, sugar, eggs, milk, and vanilla and process until smooth. Add all three flours, the baking powder, and salt and mix together by pulsing several times, just until smooth.

3 Scrape the batter into the prepared pan and smooth the top with a spatula. Gently tap the pan on the counter several times to release excess air bubbles. Add the plums in a spiral on top of the batter. Set the pan on a baking sheet.

4 Bake for about 45 minutes.

5 To make the topping: Meanwhile, in a small bowl, mix together the sugar and cinnamon.

6 Carefully sprinkle the topping over the baked cake and then dot with the butter.

7 Continue baking until the cake is golden and a tester comes out clean, about 20 minutes. Let the cake cool in the pan for 20 minutes and then run a knife around the edge. Remove the sides of the springform and transfer to a wire rack to cool completely before serving.

Scandinavian baking, especially around the holidays, always makes me think of cardamom. It's indispensable in so many classic desserts but is especially tied to Nordic baked goods. The perfumed sweetness of the pears in this cake meets the warmth of candied ginger and cardamom to create a sophisticated combination that tastes as comforting as Grandma's house feels.

pear-cardamom cake

To get the perfect ratio of cake to fruit, you'll want to choose thin, tall pears. I like Bosc, Concorde, Starkrimson, and Bartlett for their shapes and flavors in this cake.

Makes one 10-inch / 25cm cake

cake academy review

CREAMING → page 33

¾ cup / 165g unsalted butter, at room temperature

1 cup / 200g granulated sugar

2 Tbsp molasses

1½ tsp vanilla extract (see page 12)

1 Tbsp finely chopped candied ginger

2 eggs, at room temperature

1¾ cups / 210g all-purpose flour

1½ tsp baking powder

½ tsp kosher salt

¾ tsp ground cardamom

½ cup / 120ml buttermilk, at room temperature

6 small ripe pears, peeled and cored (leave stems on for drama)

1 recipe cardamom Confectioners' Sugar Icing (see variation, page 204)

1   Preheat the oven to 350°F / 175°C. Generously grease and flour a 10-inch / 25cm tube pan.

2   In a stand mixer fitted with the paddle attachment, cream the butter on medium-high speed until creamy and smooth, about 1 minute.

3   Turn the mixer speed to low; add the sugar, molasses, and vanilla to the butter; and mix until incorporated. Then turn the speed to medium-high and mix until light and fluffy, about 3 minutes. Add the ginger and mix until incorporated.

4   Turn the speed to medium-low and add the eggs, one at a time, beating just until combined. Scrape the bowl after each addition.

5   In a separate bowl, whisk together the flour, baking powder, and salt.

6   Add one-third of the flour mixture to the butter mixture, mixing on low speed, just until combined. Add half of the buttermilk and mix to incorporate. Repeat with another one-third flour, the remaining liquid, and then finish with the final one-third flour, scraping the bowl and paddle after each addition.

7   Scrape the batter into the prepared pan and smooth the top with a spatula. Gently tap the pan on the counter several times to release excess air bubbles. Press the pears, upright, halfway into the batter, spacing them evenly around the pan. Set the pan on a baking sheet.

8   Bake until the cake is golden and a tester comes out clean, about 1 hour 15 minutes. Check the cake at about 20 minutes to make sure the pears aren't slumping over. If they are, use the stem to right them in the batter and continue baking. Transfer the cake to a wire rack and let cool completely in the pan.

9   Run a knife around the edge of the cake, the center tube, and the bottom of the pan and then carefully transfer, using a large spatula to lift it off the base, to a serving plate.

10 Drizzle with the icing before serving.

pineapple upside-down cake

Pineapple Upside-Down Cake reminds me of thumbing through old recipe books from the 1960s. (Yes, I have a collection of them.) Back then, the dishes were usually shown as an illustration in color-saturated pictures. Versions of this recipe included fake-red cherries as a bull's-eye in pineapple rings. Since that was also the era of Jell-O salad served as a vegetable, it's safe to say some things could stand for some updating. I set out to use fresh pineapple but quickly realized the cake came out too dry. The canned pineapple is juicier and makes for a better cake. I think of it as a nod to the cake's '60s past.

The lightly spiced cornmeal cake batter is the perfect match for the caramelized pineapple. It is both velvety and bold.

Makes one 8-inch / 20cm cake

cake academy review

CREAMING → page 33

PINEAPPLE TOPPING

¾ cup / 150g lightly packed brown sugar

6 Tbsp / 85g unsalted butter

3 Tbsp rum

⅛ tsp kosher salt

3 whole star anise (optional)

One 20-oz / 567g can pineapple rings or chunks in 100% juice (see Baker's Note; reserve the juice)

½ cup / 60g chopped pecans (optional)

1 cup plus 1 Tbsp / 120g cake flour

⅓ cup / 60g cornmeal

¾ tsp baking powder

¾ tsp ground cinnamon

¼ tsp ground nutmeg

¼ tsp kosher salt

8 Tbsp / 115g unsalted butter, at room temperature

1¾ cups / 230g confectioners' sugar

2 tsp vanilla extract (see page 12)

2 eggs, at room temperature

¼ cup / 60ml heavy whipping cream, at room temperature

¼ cup / 60ml canned pineapple juice

2 Tbsp rum

1 Preheat oven to 375°F / 190°C. Generously grease an 8-inch / 20cm cake pan. (If using a springform pan, line it with a 9-inch / 23cm piece of greased parchment paper to prevent leaking.)

2 To make the topping: In a medium bowl, combine the brown sugar, butter, rum, and salt and stir until smooth. Spread the mixture into the prepared pan and top with the star anise (if using).

3 Arrange the pineapple over the mixture, then sprinkle with the pecans (if using). Set aside.

4 In a medium bowl, whisk together the flour, cornmeal, baking powder, cinnamon, nutmeg, and salt. Set aside.

5 In a stand mixer fitted with the paddle attachment, cream the butter on medium-high speed until creamy and smooth, about 1 minute.

6 Turn the mixer speed to low, add the confectioners' sugar and vanilla to the butter, and mix until incorporated. Then turn the speed to medium-high and beat until light and fluffy, about 5 minutes. Scrape the bowl often for even incorporation.

7 Turn the speed to medium-low and add the eggs, one at a time, beating just until combined. Scrape the bowl after each addition.

CONTINUED

FRUIT-STUDDED CAKES—UPSIDE DOWN OR OTHERWISE

8   In a measuring cup, stir together the cream, pineapple juice, and rum.

9   Add one-third of the flour mixture to the butter mixture, mixing on low speed, just until combined. Add half of the pineapple juice mixture and mix to incorporate. Repeat with another one-third flour, the remaining liquid, and then finish with the final one-third flour, scraping the bowl and paddle after each addition.

10   Scrape the batter into the prepared pan, covering the pineapple. Smooth the top with a spatula and tap the pan on the counter several times to release excess air bubbles. Set the pan on a baking sheet.

11   Bake until the cake is golden and a tester comes out clean, about 40 minutes. Immediately run a knife around the edge of the pan and invert the cake onto a serving plate. Let cool for about 20 minutes. Serve the cake warm or at room temperature.

BAKER'S NOTES

If you are using pineapple rings, overlap them around the edge of the batter and then place one in the center. This way, you use up all of the rings and have pineapple in every bite.

My friend Sara shared this tip. If you have a baking stone, preheat it with the oven and then bake the cake on the hot stone. This creates a "hot bottom" and helps the pineapple topping cook evenly.

rhubarb upside-down cake

Where I'm from, everyone has a personal rhubarb source. Either it's a backyard plant that came with your house or there's one tucked away in your parents' yard. At my home, it's customary to snap off a stalk in late spring and drag the ends through a plate of sugar to eat crunchy and raw. It's a pucker-y bite for those brave souls willing to try it. Even if you do that, save a few stalks to luxuriate in the sweet embrace of this cake. The crème de cassis (black currant liqueur) gives it a pleasant kick that plays beautifully with the rhubarb. Making this cake provides a perfect excuse to share a slice over the backyard fence, maybe with someone who's short on their own rhubarb hookup.

Makes one 9-inch /
23cm cake

cake academy review

CREAMING → page 33

1 cup / 220g unsalted butter, at room temperature, divided

1½ cups / 300g granulated sugar, divided

4 Tbsp crème de cassis, divided

Kosher salt

4 cups / 480g coarsely chopped fresh or frozen rhubarb, 1-inch / 2.5cm pieces (see Baker's Note)

1½ tsp vanilla extract (see page 12)

2 eggs, at room temperature

1¾ cups / 210g all-purpose flour

1½ tsp baking powder

½ cup / 120ml buttermilk, at room temperature

1 Preheat the oven to 350°F / 175°C. Generously grease a 9-inch / 23cm springform pan, then line the bottom and sides with greased parchment paper.

2 In a small saucepan over low heat, combine ¼ cup / 55g of the butter, ½ cup / 100g of the sugar, 2 Tbsp of the crème de cassis, and a pinch of salt and cook, stirring with a wooden spoon, just until melted.

3 Pour the mixture into the prepared pan, then arrange the rhubarb over the top and set aside.

4 In a stand mixer fitted with the paddle attachment, cream the remaining ¾ cup / 165g butter on medium-high speed until creamy and smooth, about 1 minute.

5 Turn the mixer speed to low, add the remaining 1 cup / 200g sugar and the vanilla to the butter, and mix until incorporated. Then turn the speed to medium-high and mix until light and fluffy, about 5 minutes. Scrape the bowl often for even incorporation.

6 Turn the speed to medium-low and add the eggs, one at a time, beating just until combined. Scrape the bowl after each addition.

7 In a medium bowl, whisk together the flour, baking powder, and ½ tsp salt.

8 In a liquid measuring cup, stir together the buttermilk and remaining 2 Tbsp crème de cassis.

9 Add one-third of the flour mixture to the butter mixture, mixing on low speed, just until combined. Add one-half of the buttermilk mixture and mix to incorporate. Repeat with another one-third flour, the remaining liquid, and then finish with the final one-third flour, scraping the bowl and paddle after each addition.

10 Scrape the batter into the pan, covering the rhubarb, and smooth the top with a spatula. Gently tap the pan on the counter several times to release excess air bubbles. Set the pan on a baking sheet.

CONTINUED

FRUIT-STUDDED CAKES—UPSIDE DOWN OR OTHERWISE

11 Bake until the cake is golden and a tester comes out clean, about 1 hour. Let the cake cool in the pan for 5 minutes, then run a knife around the edge and undo the side of the springform. Invert onto a serving plate, allowing the base to drop with the cake, and gently peel off the base and parchment. Serve the cake slightly warm.

VARIATION: CRANBERRY–GRAND MARNIER UPSIDE-DOWN CAKE

Around the Thanksgiving and Christmas holidays, try this cranberry version, which is equally tart and wonderful but has an even more spectacular color. Replace the rhubarb with 4 cups / 400g fresh or frozen cranberries, swap the crème de cassis for Grand Marnier, and proceed as directed.

BAKER'S NOTE

If using rhubarb late in the season, it can have a tough outer layer that will need to be removed with a vegetable peeler.

3 soaked cakes

There is a brilliant tradition of adding sweet syrups and milks to cakes, so the cakes are both infused with flavor and can be kept for days without going dreadfully dry. I'm certain this technique was born in the kitchens of wise bakers who had a stale cake they were determined not to waste. By soaking cake in either sweet-flavored milk or sugar syrup, it was made new again. The soaking gives an almost pudding quality to the cakes, placing these among my favorites in this book. On my forty-five-mile cake walk across Manhattan, the top of the list was Greek Orange-Phyllo Cake (page 114, and pictured opposite), soaked with orange syrup and topped with baked oranges, but I also love, love, love Grandma Ellen's Trinidad Rum Cake (page 103), and everyone will want seconds of boozy, rich Tiramisu (page 113). Actually, I love them all!

semolina-walnut cake with orange blossom soak

This is technically a cake, but once you pour the orange blossom soak over it, you've got something closer to a pudding. The ground nuts and semolina create a rich, super-tender base that soaks up the fragrant floral syrup. This cake is at its very best served warm in a bowl with a dollop of rich Greek full-fat yogurt and topped with a sprinkle of candied walnuts. The orange flavor intensifies as the cake sits, so save a slice as a fragrant breakfast treat for the next morning.

Makes one 8-inch / 20cm cake

cake academy review

CREAMING → page 33

¾ cup / 90g finely ground toasted walnuts

½ cup / 80g semolina

½ cup / 60g almond flour

1 tsp baking powder

¼ tsp ground cardamom

¼ tsp ground cinnamon

¼ tsp ground nutmeg

¼ tsp kosher salt

½ cup / 110g unsalted butter, at room temperature

¾ cup / 150g granulated sugar

1 tsp vanilla extract

3 eggs, at room temperature

ORANGE BLOSSOM SOAK

½ cup / 100g granulated sugar

½ cup / 120ml freshly squeezed orange juice

2 Tbsp freshly squeezed lemon juice

1 Tbsp orange blossom water

½ tsp orange zest

2 Tbsp honey

1 pinch kosher salt

CANDIED WALNUTS

1 cup / 200g granulated sugar

1 cup / 240ml water

2 tsp orange zest

1 tsp orange blossom water

2 cups / 200g toasted walnut halves

Plain Greek yogurt for serving

1 Preheat the oven to 350°F / 175°C. Generously grease an 8-inch / 20cm square baking dish.

2 In a medium bowl, whisk together the ground walnuts, semolina, almond flour, baking powder, cardamom, cinnamon, nutmeg, and salt.

3 In a stand mixer fitted with the paddle attachment, cream the butter on medium-high speed until creamy and smooth, about 1 minute.

4 Turn the mixer speed to medium, add the sugar and vanilla to the butter, and beat for about 5 minutes, until the mixture is light in color and about double in volume.

5 Turn the speed to medium-low and add the eggs, one at a time, beating just until combined. Scrape the bowl after each addition.

6 Add the dry ingredients to the butter mixture and mix until just combined.

7 Scrape the batter into the prepared dish.

8 Bake until the cake is golden and a tester comes out clean, about 30 minutes.

CONTINUED

SOAKED CAKES

9 To make the soak: Meanwhile, in a small saucepan over medium heat, combine the sugar, orange juice, lemon juice, orange blossom water, orange zest, honey, and salt and cook, stirring, until the sugar dissolves. Pour into a liquid measuring cup and allow to cool slightly until the cake is finished baking.

10 When the cake comes out of the oven, using a skewer, poke holes every ½ inch / 1.3cm, through to the bottom, then pour the soak over the cake. Allow to sit for 1 hour.

11 To make the candied walnuts: In a medium saucepan over medium-high heat, bring the sugar and water to a boil and cook, stirring, until all the sugar is dissolved. Stir in the orange zest, orange blossom water, and walnuts; turn the heat to medium-low; and simmer until the liquid thickens to the consistency of maple syrup, it will be reduced by about half. Strain the walnuts with a fine-mesh sieve, reserving the syrup.

12 Serve the cake with a big dollop of yogurt, sprinkled with the candied walnuts and drizzled with the reserved walnut syrup.

When I got married, I had two wedding cakes: a traditional tiered cake, made by Barbara McKeon, my mom's BFF (more on that cake on page 199), and a Trinidadian rum cake (also known as black cake), made by my husband's grandmother, Ellen François. Grandma Ellen made this cake every year at Christmastime and for special occasions, like weddings. It is a fruitcake, but nothing like the infamous Christmas variety you might dread. This one is made with dried fruit (raisins, apricots, dates, prunes, cherries, cranberries, currants, and/or any other favorite dried fruit) that has soaked in rum for days and is then baked in a spiced batter. Trinidad, where my husband's family is from, is an island known for its exceptional rum, so it makes sense that Grandma Ellen's cake has all the rum in it. That's the magic spell, and you'll feel it! Grandma Ellen didn't write down the recipe, as far as I can tell, so this one is based on years of experimenting. The bit of marmalade added to the mix is something that I borrowed from pastry chef Helen Goh's fruitcake recipe, because a touch of citrus was needed, and I love marmalade more than just about anything.

grandma ellen's trinidad rum cake

Makes one 8-inch / 20cm cake

cake academy review

CREAMING → page 33

ROLLED FONDANT → page 53

4 cups / 560g coarsely chopped dried fruit (see headnote)

2¾ cups / 650ml rum, divided (see Baker's Note)

1¾ cups / 210g all-purpose flour

¼ cup / 30g almond flour

1½ tsp baking soda

¾ tsp ground nutmeg

½ tsp ground cinnamon

½ tsp ground ginger

½ tsp ground cardamom

½ tsp ground cloves

½ tsp kosher salt

¾ cup / 165g unsalted butter, at room temperature

½ cup / 100g lightly packed brown sugar

2 tsp vanilla extract (see page 12)

¼ cup / 80g blackstrap molasses (see Baker's Note)

Rounded 2 Tbsp orange marmalade

3 eggs, at room temperature

16 oz / 450g marzipan (optional; see Baker's Note)

1   In a large bowl, combine the dried fruit and 1½ cups / 360ml of the rum and let soak at room temperature for at least 24 hours or up to 3 days. The longer it soaks, the more rum the fruit will absorb and the stronger it will taste.

2   Preheat the oven to 350°F / 175°C. Generously grease an 8-inch / 20 cm cake pan, then line it with greased parchment paper.

3   In a separate bowl, whisk together both flours, the baking soda, nutmeg, cinnamon, ginger, cardamom, cloves, and salt. Set aside.

4   In a stand mixer fitted with the paddle attachment, cream the butter on medium-high speed until creamy and smooth, about 1 minute.

5   Turn the mixer speed to medium, add the brown sugar and vanilla to the butter, and beat for about 5 minutes, until the mixture is light in color and about double in volume. Add the molasses and marmalade and mix until incorporated.

6   Turn the speed to medium-low and add the eggs, one at a time, beating just until combined. Scrape the bowl after each addition. Add ¼ cup / 60ml rum and mix until evenly incorporated.

7   Add the dry ingredients to the butter mixture and mix until just combined. Fold in the soaked fruit and any remaining soaking liquid. Scrape the batter into the prepared pan; it will be VERY full.

CONTINUED

8 Bake until a tester comes out clean, about 1 hour 15 minutes. While the cake is still hot, brush the top with about 2 Tbsp rum. Let the cake cool completely, then invert from the pan onto a plate. Brush the sides and top of the cake with about ¼ cup / 60ml rum. Wrap the bottom and sides of the cake in wax paper and set it into a clean cake pan. Brush the top of the cake with another 2 Tbsp rum every few hours until the rum is used up.

9 If desired, roll out the marzipan into a ⅛-inch / 3mm-thick disk. Drape the rolled marzipan over the cake. Rub the marzipan and simultaneously, very gently, stretch it downward. As you are rubbing it, the marzipan will naturally start to mold to the cake, but it will also want to drape, so you need to very gently rub the drapes smooth, while carefully stretching it. Use a paring knife to carefully trim off the excess, then smooth the cut edges with your fingers or a smoothing tool.

10 Serve the cake immediately or store in the refrigerator for up to 1 week.

BAKER'S NOTES

This cake is boozy, which is what my family loves about it. But if you'd like to turn that down, decrease the amount of rum you use to soak to ½ cup / 120ml.

You can use your favorite dark or even spiced rum for the cake.

Blackstrap molasses has a more intense flavor than regular molasses and really gives this cake its signature color and flavor.

For Christmas, I use a cookie cutter to create marzipan holly leaves, then add the veins with the back of a knife and roll tiny balls of marzipan to create the berries. I like the white-on-white look, but you can color the marzipan if you want more drama.

When my friend Steven Brown asked me to design a dessert program for his now-famous Tilia restaurant, he had two requests: There had to be a butterscotch pudding and a sticky toffee–date cake. His instincts for what people want to eat is impeccable, and both of these desserts became house favorites. The cake is made with the honey-sweetness of dates, which are cooked and pureed; so even if you think you don't like dates, you'll absolutely love this cake. The fresh ginger gives it a warmth that goes beautifully with the toffee sauce that soaks through the cake while it's fresh from the oven. I bake them in individual servings so they can be tipped out and topped with a scoop of ice cream (I use rum raisin), like a crown.

sticky toffee–date cake

Makes 12 individual cakes

cake academy review

CREAMING → page 33

12 oz / 340g dates

1 cup plus 2 Tbsp / 270ml water

1 tsp baking soda

1 tsp grated fresh ginger

6 Tbsp / 85g unsalted butter, at room temperature

1 cup / 200g lightly packed brown sugar

2 tsp vanilla extract (see page 12)

2 eggs, at room temperature

2 Tbsp rum

2 cups / 240g all-purpose flour

1 Tbsp baking powder

½ tsp kosher salt

TOFFEE SAUCE

½ cup / 120ml heavy whipping cream

1 cup / 200g lightly packed brown sugar

2 Tbsp rum

2 Tbsp unsalted butter

½ tsp kosher salt

Ice cream for serving

1   Preheat the oven to 325°F / 165°C. Generously grease twelve 6-oz / 170g ramekins or a muffin tin and set on a baking sheet.

2   In a medium saucepan over medium heat, combine the dates and water, cover, and simmer for about 5 minutes to soften. Turn off the heat and let sit for another 5 minutes until tender; it may take up to 10 minutes if your dates are dried out.

3   In a blender, puree the dates with their soaking water until smooth. Return the puree to the saucepan and bring to a gentle boil over medium heat. Remove from the heat and stir in the baking soda and ginger; the mixture will foam and darken. (The baking soda neutralizes the acid in the dates and creates a rich dark color.) Let cool slightly.

4   In a stand mixer fitted with the paddle attachment, cream the butter on medium-high speed until creamy and smooth, about 1 minute.

5   Turn the mixer speed to medium, add the brown sugar and vanilla to the butter, and beat for about 5 minutes, until the mixture is light in color and about double in volume.

6   Turn the speed to medium-low and add the eggs, one at a time, beating just until combined. Scrape the bowl after each addition. Add the rum and mix until evenly incorporated.

7   In a separate bowl, whisk together the flour, baking powder, and salt.

8   Add one-third of the flour mixture to the butter mixture, mixing on low speed, just until combined. Add half of the dates and mix to incorporate. Repeat with another one-third flour, the remaining dates, and then finish with the final one-third flour, scraping the bowl and paddle after each addition. Mix only enough to combine.

CONTINUED

9   Evenly scrape the batter into the prepared ramekins.

10 Bake until the cakes are golden and a tester comes out with moist crumbs, about 30 minutes. Don't overbake; you want them to be slightly pudding-like, but the tester shouldn't be wet.

11 To make the sauce: While the cakes are baking, in a small saucepan over medium-high heat, combine the cream, brown sugar, rum, butter, and salt and bring to a boil, stirring constantly. Then turn the heat to medium-low and simmer until thicker, about 5 minutes. Remove from the heat.

12 When the cakes come out of the oven, using a skewer, poke holes every ½ inch / 1.3cm, through to the bottoms, and spoon two-thirds of the sauce over the tops. If the sauce doesn't get completely absorbed into the cake, poke a few more holes.

13 Let the cakes cool for about 10 minutes, then invert onto individual plates and spoon the remaining sauce over the tops. Serve immediately with ice cream.

BAKER'S NOTE

If you don't need all the cakes at once, keep them in their ramekins, tightly covered, and refrigerate for up to 24 hours. Microwave for several seconds before serving with the sauce.

This cake is a bit of an overachiever when it comes to how many milks it jams into a relatively small space. The cake mix itself is made with whole milk (1), then it is soaked with the traditional trio of evaporated milk (2), condensed milk (3), and heavy whipping cream (4) to give it the rich taste and soft texture we all love. But I've added a layer of whipped sour cream (5) to the top that makes a great contrast to the sweetness of the cake. That's five milks, because sometimes more is better! I learned the trick of reducing the sweetened condensed milk even more before making the milk soak from the good folks at America's Test Kitchen. It adds a caramelized note to the mix that I find worth the extra minutes of prep.

cinco leches— tres leches all grown up

Makes one 9 by 13-inch / 23 by 33cm sheet cake

cake academy review

LIGHT-AS-AIR
EGG FOAM → page 36
BASIC PIPING:
STARS → page 56
(OPTIONAL)

MILK SOAK

One 14-oz / 396g can sweetened condensed milk

One 12-oz / 354ml can evaporated milk

1 cup / 240ml heavy whipping cream

1 tsp vanilla extract (see page 12)

2 Tbsp rum

CAKE

1¾ cups / 210g all-purpose flour

1½ tsp baking powder

1 tsp ground cinnamon

½ tsp kosher salt

1 cup / 240ml whole milk, at room temperature

½ cup / 110g unsalted butter, at room temperature

2 tsp vanilla extract (see page 12)

4 eggs, at room temperature

1¾ cups / 350g granulated sugar

TOPPING

1½ cups / 360ml heavy whipping cream

¼ cup / 60g sour cream or crème fraîche

3 Tbsp confectioners' sugar

2 tsp vanilla extract (see page 12)

Ground cinnamon for dusting

1 To make the soak: Put the condensed milk into a large microwave-safe bowl, cover, and microwave on low power for about 10 minutes, stirring every few minutes, until it is thick and slightly darker. Stir in the evaporated milk, whipping cream, vanilla, and rum. Set aside.

2 To make the cake: Preheat the oven to 325°F / 165°C. Generously grease a 9 by 13-inch / 23 by 33cm baking dish.

3 In a medium bowl, whisk together the flour, baking powder, cinnamon, and salt.

4 In a separate microwave-safe bowl, combine the whole milk and butter, cover, and heat on low power until the butter is melted, about 1 minute. Let cool completely. Stir in the vanilla.

5 In a stand mixer fitted with the whisk attachment, whip the eggs on medium-high speed until foamy, turn the speed down to low and slowly add the granulated sugar. Return the speed to medium-high and whip until thick and glossy, about 7 minutes.

6 Turn the speed to low and slowly add the cooled milk mixture. Then add the flour mixture in three additions, mixing just until the flour is incorporated after each addition.

CONTINUED

7   Transfer the batter to the prepared baking dish.

8   Bake until a tester comes out clean, about 35 minutes. Let the cake cool for 10 minutes and then, using a skewer, poke holes every ½ inch / 1.3cm, through to the bottom. Evenly pour the milk soak over the cake. Let sit until the cake cools to room temperature, then refrigerate, uncovered, for at least 3 hours, but overnight is best. When ready to serve, remove the cake from the refrigerator and let sit at room temperature for 30 minutes.

9   To make the topping: In a stand mixer fitted with the whisk attachment, combine the heavy cream, sour cream, confectioners' sugar, and vanilla and whip on medium speed until medium peaks form, about 2 minutes.

10 Spread the topping over the cake or pipe on the top using a large star tip. (I use Wilton tip #1M.) Dust with cinnamon before serving.

This is a dessert I first tasted in Little Italy in New York City, when I was a kid in the 1970s. At the time, I felt as if I was getting away with something a little scandalous because of the coffee-and-booze-soaked cake; it all seemed so grown-up and sophisticated. The cake still leaves me feeling as though something special is taking place. The trick is to balance the delicately soaked cake with rich mascarpone and custard and then lighten the whole thing with soft whipped cream. I put the layers together in a soufflé dish, but an 8-inch / 20cm glass trifle bowl would work nicely, too, so you can see the layers.

tiramisu

Makes about 10 servings

cake academy review

BASIC PIPING → page 56

COFFEE SOAKING SYRUP

⅓ cup / 80ml hot coffee

3 Tbsp granulated sugar

⅓ cup / 80ml cognac, brandy, or Amaretto

2 cups / 480ml heavy whipping cream

2 Tbsp confectioners' sugar

1 cup / 240g mascarpone cheese

½ recipe Pastry Cream (page 231)

1 Espresso Sponge Cake (page 144)

1 Tbsp cocoa powder, divided, plus more for dusting

Milk chocolate for shaving (see page 8)

1   To make the syrup: In a liquid measuring cup, stir together the coffee and sugar until the sugar dissolves, then stir in the cognac. Set aside.

2   In a stand mixer fitted with the whisk attachment, combine the heavy cream, confectioners' sugar, and mascarpone and beat on medium speed until medium-soft peaks form, about 1 minute. In a large bowl, combine ½ cup / 60ml of the soaking syrup with the pastry cream and whisk until smooth. Stir one-third of the whipped mascarpone into the pastry cream, then gently fold in another one-third mascarpone. Set aside the last one-third mascarpone for decorating.

3   Cut the cake into two equal layers. Place one of the layers in the bottom of an 8-inch / 20cm soufflé dish, brush with half of the remaining soaking syrup. Dust the soaked cake with 1½ tsp of the cocoa powder and use a fine-rasp grater to top with 1 oz / 30g of chocolate shavings. Layer with half the mascarpone cream. Repeat with a second layer of cake, soak, cocoa powder, chocolate shavings, and mascarpone cream.

4   Decorate the top as desired by piping with the remaining one-third mascarpone. (I use Wilton tip #125.) Transfer to the refrigerator and let the dish set for several hours or up to overnight.

5   Dust the tiramisu with cocoa powder just before serving.

greek orange-phyllo cake

This cake (pictured on page 98) has no business being in this book. It's not a typical cake in any way; instead, it is layers of phyllo tossed together with a sweet, creamy mixture of Greek yogurt, olive oil, and tangy orange juice. On my cake-walking odyssey across Manhattan, I fell head over heels in love with this dessert, which I had at Pi Bakery, a little Greek spot in Tribeca. It looked like cake, so naturally I'm putting it in my book. It took me a while and several baking fails to figure out what exactly was going on with it, but then after watching a lovely elderly Greek man make something similar on YouTube, I figured out the secret. The only problem was, I don't speak a word of Greek (well, one word: Zoë means "life" in Greek), and this man spoke only Greek, so I interpreted as best I could and came out victorious. Baking the layers of phyllo first allows the "cake" to absorb more liquid, and that is what creates the fantastic texture. I added baked oranges to the top, because they're so dreamy and something you should experience in this life.

Makes 12 servings

BAKED ORANGES

Twelve ⅛-inch / 3mm-thick orange slices (easiest done on a mandoline), plus zest of 1 orange

1 cup / 240ml freshly squeezed orange juice

¼ cup / 60ml orange liqueur (such as Grand Marnier)

1 cup / 240ml water

1 cup / 200g granulated sugar

2 cinnamon sticks

PHYLLO CAKE

8 oz / 225g phyllo, thawed

Semolina for dusting, plus 1 Tbsp

2 eggs, at room temperature

¾ cup / 150g granulated sugar

⅔ cup / 160ml freshly squeezed orange juice

½ cup / 120ml mild olive oil

½ cup / 120g plain Greek yogurt

2 tsp baking powder

1 tsp vanilla extract (see page 12)

Plain Greek yogurt for serving

1   To prepare the oranges: Preheat the oven to 325°F / 165°C.

2   Put the orange slices in the bottom of a 9 by 13-inch / 23 by 33cm baking dish, pour the orange juice and orange liqueur over top, and cover tightly with aluminum foil.

3   Bake until the oranges are very soft, 40 to 45 minutes.

4   In a large saucepan over medium-high heat, combine the water, sugar, orange zest, and cinnamon sticks and bring to a boil. Cook for 5 minutes, then remove from the heat.

5   Pour the syrup over the orange slices and let cool completely. (At this point, you can transfer them to an airtight container and store in the refrigerator for up to 2 days.)

6   To make the cake: Using your hands, separate the sheets of phyllo, scrunch up the individual sheets into a shaggy ball, and place on a baking sheet. (This step is tedious but so worth the effort.)

7   Bake the phyllo until the sheets are dry, about 15 minutes. If they do not seem to be baking evenly, flip them. Once they are dry, break them up into small pieces.

8   Generously grease a 9-inch / 23cm square baking dish and dust with semolina. Set aside.

9   In a stand mixer fitted with the whisk attachment, combine the eggs and sugar and beat on high speed until pale and thick, about 5 minutes.

10 In a separate bowl, mix together the orange juice, olive oil, yogurt, baking powder, vanilla, and 1 Tbsp semolina.

11 Turn the mixer speed to low, add the orange juice mixture to the eggs, and mix until just combined. Remove the bowl from the mixer and fold in the phyllo.

12 Spread the mixture into the prepared dish. Turn the oven temperature to 350°F / 175°C.

13 Bake until lightly browned, 35 to 40 minutes. Remove from the oven and, while the cake is still hot, pour all the syrup from the oranges evenly over the top, then let cool.

14 Cut the cake into twelve squares and top each square with a baked orange slice. Serve with a dollop of Greek yogurt.

4 cake layers, loaves, and sheets

These are the foundational layers for the special-occasion cakes in chapter 6, but they can also be baked as sheet cakes or in a loaf pan for something a wee bit more humble during the week—when perhaps the day calls for cake but less fuss. All of them can move from simple to sensational and back; it's up to you and your mood.

I have been baking cakes for decades, and yet it was really in the writing of this book that I nailed down my favorite versions of these options. Chocolate Devil's Food Cake (page 125) has been a longtime staple in my house and, along with Ultimate Carrot Cake (page 136), a popular request at birthdays. I struggled to find white cake that excited me, and now my own White Cake (page 119) is way up there on the delicious scale. Whether you want something classic and universally loved, like yellow or chocolate cakes, or a Southern traditional cake such as Red Velvet Cake (page 128) or Hummingbird Cake (page 135), these all deliver and will make your friends and family happy, happy!

This is the grande dame of cakes, the elegant wedding invitee who classes up the room just by her mere presence. In fact, it's probably the most popular wedding cake flavor. No matter the reason, a classic white cake creates an occasion. It also goes with any topping. Because it's such an icon, nailing just the right crowd-pleasing texture and flavor is crucial. After years of tinkering, I am pleased to present my perfect white cake for every occasion. I discovered the magic of whipping heavy cream and folding it into the batter from Shirley O. Corriher, a food scientist and recipe developer. It not only adds the richness of the cream but also the lightness of the air it contains. A stroke of brilliance.

white cake

Makes one 8-inch /
20cm triple-layer cake

cake academy review

CREAMING → page 33

PEAKS → page 38

CRUMB-COATING →
page 49 (OPTIONAL)

PUTTING ON THE
FINAL LAYER OF
FROSTING → page 49

8 Tbsp / 112g unsalted butter, at room temperature

7 Tbsp / 80g vegetable shortening

2 cups / 400g granulated sugar

1 Tbsp vanilla extract (see page 12)

¾ tsp almond extract

1 cup / 240ml egg whites (from about 6 eggs), at room temperature

3 cups / 330g cake flour

2 tsp baking powder

¾ tsp kosher salt

½ cup / 120ml buttermilk, at room temperature

¾ cup / 175ml heavy whipping cream

1 recipe American Buttercream (page 213) or Chocolate Frosting (page 205)

1 Preheat the oven to 350°F / 175°C. Generously grease three 8-inch / 20cm cake pans, then line them with greased parchment paper.

2 In a stand mixer fitted with the paddle attachment, cream the butter and shortening on medium-high speed until creamy and smooth, about 1 minute.

3 Turn the mixer speed to medium; add the sugar, vanilla, and almond extract to the butter; and beat for about 5 minutes, until the mixture is light in color and about double in volume.

4 Turn the speed to medium-low, add the egg whites, a little at a time, about six equal additions, mixing each until completely incorporated before adding the next. Scrape the bowl after each addition. This takes some patience with this many eggs; don't be tempted to add them too fast.

5 In a separate bowl, whisk together the flour, baking powder, and salt until well combined. Sift to remove any lumps.

6 Add one-third of the flour mixture to the egg white mixture and mix until combined. Scrape the bowl and add half of the buttermilk, mixing until combined. Repeat with another one-third flour, the remaining buttermilk, and then the final one-third flour. Scrape down after each addition.

7 In another bowl, using a whisk, whip the heavy cream to medium peaks. Then, using a rubber spatula, fold the whipped cream into the batter until no streaks remain.

8 Pour the batter into the prepared pans and spread evenly using an offset spatula. Gently tap the pans on the counter several times to release excess air bubbles.

9 Bake until a tester comes out clean, 25 to 30 minutes. Allow to cool for 15 minutes in the pans, then remove from pans and transfer to a wire rack to cool completely. (This cake will shrink slightly in the pan as it cools, so don't be alarmed.)

CONTINUED

10   Remove the parchment paper and place one cake layer on a serving plate.

11   Using an offset spatula, spread a ¼-inch / 6mm-thick layer of the buttercream over the cake, making sure it goes all the way to the edge. Place the next cake over that and top with another layer of buttercream. Repeat with the last cake. If desired, at this point, you could crumb-coat the cake.

12   Decorate the cake with a smooth layer of the remaining buttercream.

13   Serve the cake immediately or store in the refrigerator, covered, for up to 24 hours.

VARIATION: FUNFETTI CAKE

The pristine color of the cake makes it the natural match for adding sprinkles to create the perfect party cake. Just before pouring the batter into the prepared pan, fold in ½ cup / 100g candy sprinkles. (I use Wilton Brand sprinkles, since they don't bleed color into the batter.) Proceed as directed.

To decorate with sprinkles, press them onto the soft buttercream just after putting on the final layer.

BAKER'S NOTE

To make as 24 cupcakes, evenly divide the batter among the wells of a cupcake pan and bake for 20 minutes, or until a tester comes out clean.

This is probably the most-consumed birthday cake in all the land. Its mellow, satisfying flavor suits any palate. Probably derived from an egg-and-butter pound cake in Europe, the yellow cake really caught on in the United States as a celebration cake. With all respect to Duncan and Betty, we mere mortals really can create a cake from scratch that rivals the box. The action of mixing remains the same, but the ability to use real ingredients means a fresh depth of flavor. Just slicing into raspberry buttercream and being greeted by this sunny color mean happy days are here.

yellow cake

Makes one 8-inch /
20cm triple-layer cake
or one 9 by 13-inch /
24 by 36cm sheet cake

cake academy review

CREAMING → page 33

CRUMB-COATING →
page 49

PUTTING ON THE
FINAL LAYER OF
FROSTING → page 49

8 Tbsp / 112g unsalted butter, at room temperature

½ cup / 120ml mild-flavored oil (such as vegetable oil)

2¼ cups / 450g granulated sugar

1 Tbsp vanilla extract (see page 12)

4 eggs, at room temperature

5 egg yolks, at room temperature

2⅔ cups / 320g all-purpose flour

2½ tsp baking powder

¾ tsp kosher salt

½ cup / 120ml whole milk, at room temperature

½ cup / 120g sour cream, at room temperature

1 recipe American Buttercream (page 213) or Whipped Milk Chocolate Mascarpone Frosting (page 237)

1 Preheat the oven to 350°F / 175°C. Generously grease three 8-inch / 20cm cake pans (or a 9 by 13-inch / 24 by 36cm cake pan), then line them with greased parchment paper.

2 In a stand mixer fitted with the paddle attachment, cream the butter on medium-high speed until creamy and smooth, about 1 minute.

3 Turn the mixer speed to medium; add the oil, sugar, and vanilla to the butter; and beat for about 5 minutes, until the mixture is light in color and about double in volume.

4 Turn the speed to medium-low and add the eggs and egg yolks, one at a time, mixing each until incorporated before adding the next. Scrape the bowl after each addition.

5 In a medium bowl, whisk together the flour, baking powder, and salt until well combined. In a liquid measuring cup, whisk together the milk and sour cream.

6 Add one-third of the flour mixture to the butter mixture and mix until combined. Scrape the bowl and add half of the milk mixture, mixing until combined. Repeat with another one-third flour, the remaining milk mixture, and then finish with the final one-third flour, scraping the bowl and paddle after each addition.

7 Pour the batter into the prepared pans and spread evenly using an offset spatula. Gently tap the pans on the counter several times to release excess air bubbles.

8 Bake until a tester comes out clean, 25 to 30 minutes (45 minutes for a sheet cake). Let the cakes cool completely before removing from the pans by inverting onto wire racks.

9 Remove the parchment paper and place one cake layer on a serving plate.

10 Using an offset spatula, spread a ¼-inch / 6mm-thick layer of the buttercream over the cake, making sure it goes all the way to the edge. Place the next cake over that and top with another layer of buttercream. Repeat with the last cake. If desired, at this point, you could crumb-coat the cake.

11 Decorate the cake with a smooth layer of the remaining buttercream.

12 Serve the cake immediately or store at room temperature, covered, for up to 48 hours.

chocolate devil's food cake

This is a cake that I have been baking and tweaking since my very first job in a professional kitchen in 1995. D'Amico was a large-scale catering company in Minneapolis, and this was the base of the most popular cakes we created for bar/bat mitzvahs, birthdays, weddings, and holiday soirees. It has a super-intense chocolate flavor and dense crumb that make it the perfect match for all kinds of fillings and toppings. The coffee and rum are not pronounced as individual flavors but just balance out the sweetness of the high ratio of sugar. It's the BEST chocolate cake I've ever made, and I've tried them all. Well, pretty close to all.

Makes one 9-inch / 23cm Pullman loaf or one 8-inch / 20cm double-layer cake

2⅓ cups / 280g all-purpose flour

2 cups / 400g granulated sugar

⅔ cup / 50g Dutch-processed cocoa powder (sifted if lumpy)

1 tsp baking soda

1 tsp kosher salt

1¼ cups / 300ml hot strong coffee

2 Tbsp rum or brandy

2 eggs

1 cup / 240ml buttermilk

½ cup / 120ml mild-flavored oil (such as vegetable oil)

1 tsp vanilla extract (see page 12)

1 recipe Chocolate Frosting (page 205) or Cream Cheese Frosting (page 209)

Chocolate shavings (see page 8) for topping

1 Preheat the oven to 350°F / 175°C. Generously grease a 9 by 4-inch / 23 by 10cm Pullman pan (or two 8-inch / 20cm round cake pans), then line it with greased parchment paper. Set aside.

2 In a large bowl, whisk together the flour, sugar, cocoa powder, baking soda, and salt until well combined. In a small bowl, stir together the coffee and rum.

3 In a separate bowl, whisk together the eggs, buttermilk, oil, and vanilla until well combined. Add the egg mixture and half the coffee-rum to the dry ingredients and mix with a spoon until smooth. Slowly add the remaining coffee-rum and whisk until totally blended and smooth. The batter will be quite thin.

4 Pour the batter into the prepared pan. Gently tap the pan on the counter several times to release excess air bubbles.

5 Bake until a tester comes out clean, about 1 hour 10 minutes (30 minutes for 8-inch rounds). Let the cake cool completely before removing from the pan and inverting onto a serving plate.

6 Using a metal decorating spatula, cover the cake with an even layer of the frosting and top with chocolate shavings. Serve at room temperature.

BAKER'S NOTES

If you aren't a fan of coffee and rum, substitute with a flat cola or stout beer.

To make as 24 cupcakes, fill the well of a cupcake pan two-thirds full of batter and bake for about 20 minutes, or until a tester comes out clean.

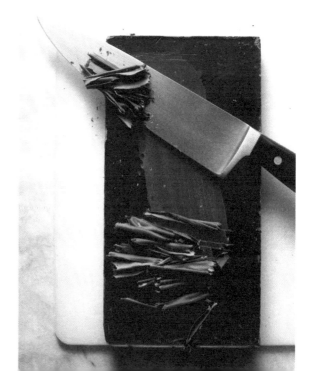

hot chocolate cake

This cake is a little bit more easygoing in flavor than its intense cousin, Chocolate Devil's Food Cake (page 125), making it an ideal children's birthday cake. Slather it in creamy chocolate frosting with a tower of toasted homemade Marshmallows (page 240; or store-bought if you're in a hurry). It's impossible not to break into an unabashed grin when you see this cake making its way to the table. This is also a base option for Black Forest Cake (page 172), when layered with whipped cream and cherries.

Makes one 8-inch / 20cm triple-layer cake

cake academy review

CREAMING → page 33

CRUMB-COATING → page 49

PUTTING ON THE FINAL LAYER OF FROSTING → page 49

8 Tbsp / 112g unsalted butter, at room temperature

½ cup / 120ml mild-flavored oil (such as vegetable oil)

2 cups / 400g granulated sugar

4 eggs, at room temperature

5 egg yolks, at room temperature

2 cups / 240g all-purpose flour

¾ cup / 60g Dutch-processed cocoa powder (sifted if lumpy)

1½ tsp baking powder

¼ tsp baking soda

¾ tsp kosher salt

½ cup / 120ml whole milk, at room temperature

½ cup / 120g sour cream, at room temperature

1 recipe Chocolate Frosting (page 205)

Toasted marshmallows for topping

1   Preheat the oven to 350°F / 175°C. Generously grease three 8-inch / 20cm cake pans, then line them with greased parchment paper.

2   In a stand mixer fitted with the paddle attachment, cream the butter on medium-high speed until creamy and smooth, about 1 minute.

3   Turn the mixer speed to medium, add the oil and sugar to the butter, and beat for about 5 minutes, until the mixture is light in color and about double in volume.

4   Turn the speed to medium-low and add the eggs and egg yolks, one at a time, mixing each until incorporated before adding the next. Scrape the bow after each addition.

5   In a medium bowl, whisk together the flour, cocoa powder, baking powder, baking soda, and salt until well combined.

6   In a liquid measuring cup, whisk together the milk and sour cream.

7   Add one-third of the flour mixture to the butter mixture and mix until combined. Scrape the bowl and add half of the milk mixture, mixing until combined. Repeat with another one-third flour, the remaining milk mixture, and then finish with the final one-third flour. Scrape the bowl after each addition.

8   Divide the batter into the prepared pans and spread evenly using an offset spatula. Gently tap the pans on the counter several times to release excess air bubbles.

9   Bake until a tester comes out clean, about 30 minutes. Allow the cakes to cool in the pans for 15 minutes, then transfer to a wire rack to cool completely.

10   Remove the parchment paper and place one cake layer on a serving plate.

11   Using a metal decorating spatula, spread a ¼-inch / 6mm-thick layer of the frosting over the cake, making sure it goes all the way to the edge. Place the next cake over the frosting and top with another layer of frosting. Repeat with the last cake. If desired, at this point, you could crumb-coat the cake.

12   Decorate the cake with a smooth layer of the remaining frosting. Top with marshmallows.

13   Serve the cake immediately or store at room temperature, covered, for up to 48 hours.

My stepmother, Patricia, is from Alabama, and she introduced me to the Southern red velvet cake. Her mother used to make it on Patricia's birthday, layered with soft Ermine Frosting, and now I have taken up the honor; but I like the tangy contrast of Cream Cheese Frosting. The cake's origins are a little murky, but the bright-red version we see today was invented in the 1920s by an extract company and then suddenly became one of the most beloved cakes in every city, not just in the South.

What a remarkable evolution to see how some recipes, created by companies to sell products, like red food coloring, found their way onto clipped recipe cards, passed around by grandmas, and eventually tucked into the back of an old recipe box that holds the entire history of a family's way of eating.

I tried my best to use a natural food dye, derived from ruby-red beets, to tint the cake, but all my efforts resulted in a bright-purple cake. I consulted food scientists, but the solution required adding so much more acid (the consensus favored cream of tartar), that it would have changed the flavor of the cake. I went with the artificial color on this one, but you decide if you want a true red or if the natural purple velvet is your deal.

red velvet cake

Makes one 8-inch /
20cm triple-layer cake

cake academy review

CREAMING → page 33

CRUMB-COATING →
page 49

PUTTING ON THE
FINAL LAYER OF
FROSTING → page 49

8 Tbsp / 112g unsalted
butter, at room temperature

½ cup / 120g mild-flavored
oil (such as vegetable oil)

2¼ cups / 450g
granulated sugar

1 Tbsp vanilla extract
(see page 12)

1 Tbsp red food coloring,
plus more as needed

4 eggs, at room temperature

5 egg yolks,
at room temperature

2⅓ cups / 280g
all-purpose flour

3 Tbsp Dutch-processed
cocoa powder (sifted
if lumpy)

2½ tsp baking powder

½ tsp kosher salt

1 cup / 240ml buttermilk,
at room temperature

1 recipe Cream Cheese
Frosting (page 209) or
Ermine Frosting (page 206)

1 Preheat the oven to 350°F / 175°C. Generously grease three 8-inch / 20cm cake pans, then line them with greased parchment paper.

2 In a stand mixer fitted with the paddle attachment, cream the butter on medium-high speed until creamy and smooth, about 1 minute.

3 Turn the mixer speed to medium; add the oil, sugar, and vanilla; and beat for about 5 minutes, until the mixture is light in color and about double in volume. Add the food coloring and continue beating, until the batter is a uniform color.

4 Turn the speed to medium-low and add the eggs and egg yolks, one at a time, mixing each until incorporated before adding the next. Scrape the bowl after each addition.

5 In a separate bowl, whisk together the flour, cocoa powder, baking powder, and salt until well combined.

6 Add one-third of the flour mixture to the butter mixture, mixing on low speed until combined. Add half of the buttermilk, mixing until incorporated. Repeat with another one-third flour, the remaining buttermilk, and then finish with the final one-third flour, scraping the bowl and paddle after each addition.

7   Pour the batter into the prepared pans and spread evenly using a small offset spatula. Gently tap the pans on the counter several times to release excess air bubbles.

8   Bake until a tester comes out clean, 25 to 30 minutes. Let the cakes cool in the pans for 15 minutes and then transfer to a wire rack to cool completely.

9   Remove the parchment paper and place one cake layer on a serving plate.

10 Using an offset spatula, spread a ¼-inch / 6mm-thick layer of the frosting over the cake, making sure it goes all the way to the edge. Place the next cake over the frosting and top with another layer of frosting. Repeat with the last cake. If desired, at this point, you could crumb-coat the cake.

11 Decorate the cake with a smooth layer of the remaining frosting.

12 Serve the cake immediately or store in the refrigerator, covered, for up to 24 hours. If refrigerated, bring the cake to room temperature before serving.

coconut– candy bar cake

This will become a family favorite, with just the right level of coconut intensity balanced with the plush interior and chewy shreds of coconut. Here, we cover the layers with Sticky Coconut Filling and enrobe with Dark Chocolate Ganache to create a coconut–candy bar of a cake.

Makes one 8-inch / 20cm triple-layer cake

cake academy review

CREAMING → page 33

CRUMB-COATING → page 49

POURED GANACHE → page 52

BASIC PIPING DESIGNS: STARS → page 56

COCONUT CAKE

2 cups / 200g loosely packed sweetened shredded coconut

8 Tbsp / 112g unsalted butter, at room temperature

2¼ cups / 450g granulated sugar

⅓ cup / 80ml mild-flavored oil (such as vegetable oil)

1 Tbsp vanilla extract (see page 12)

1½ tsp coconut extract

4 eggs, at room temperature

5 egg yolks, at room temperature

2⅓ cups / 280g all-purpose flour

2¼ tsp baking powder

¾ tsp kosher salt

1 cup / 240ml unsweetened coconut milk, at room temperature

1 recipe Sticky Coconut Filling (page 233)

1 recipe Dark Chocolate Ganache (page 221), divided

1   To make the cake: Preheat the oven to 350°F / 175°C. Generously grease three 8-inch / 20cm cake pans, then line them with greased parchment paper.

2   In a food processor, break up the long strands of shredded coconut by pulsing for about 30 seconds.

3   In a stand mixer fitted with the paddle attachment, cream the butter on medium-high speed until creamy and smooth, about 1 minute.

4   Turn the mixer speed to medium; add the sugar, oil, vanilla, and coconut extract; and beat for about 5 minutes, until the mixture is light in color and about double in volume.

5   Turn the speed to medium-low and add the eggs and egg yolks, one at a time, mixing each until incorporated before adding the next. Scrape the bowl after each addition.

6   In a separate bowl, whisk together the flour, baking powder, and salt until well combined.

7   Add one-third of the flour mixture to the butter mixture and mix just until combined. Add half of the coconut milk, mixing until incorporated. Repeat with another one-third flour, the remaining coconut milk, and then finish with the final one-third flour, scraping the bowl and paddle after each addition. Fold in the shredded coconut.

8   Pour the batter into the prepared pans and spread evenly using a small offset spatula. Gently tap the pans on the counter several times to release excess air bubbles.

9   Bake until a tester comes out clean, about 35 minutes. Let the cakes cool completely before removing from the pans. Remove the parchment paper and place one cake layer on a serving plate.

10 Using an offset spatula, spread a ½-inch / 1.3cm-thick layer of the coconut filling over the cake, making sure it goes all the way to the edge but not beyond. Place the next cake over the filling and top with another layer of filling. Top with the last cake.

11 Using 1 cup / 260g of the ganache, crumb-coat the cake. Fill a pastry bag fitted with a small star tip (Ateco #821) with room-temperature ganache. Warm the remaining ganache to a pourable consistency.

12 Line a baking sheet with parchment paper. Set the assembled cake on a wire rack, place on the baking sheet, and pour the liquid ganache over the cake. Once the cake is set, transfer to a serving plate. Using the prepared pastry bag, pipe a border of shells to decorate the cake.

13 Serve the cake immediately or store in the refrigerator, covered, for up to 48 hours. (It slices better when chilled.)

banana cream cake

This cake is a touch lighter than its banana bread cousin (see page 70), yet it still has all the banana flavor; it's just a bit more refined. I like to bake this in a sheet pan and top it with pastry cream, fresh bananas, and perfectly whipped cream. It's like a cake version of the famous banana cream pie. This cake is also lovely all dressed up with honey buttercream in Beehive Cake (page 194) or simply baked and topped with Cream Cheese Frosting (page 209) for a lunch-box snack. I like the cake with nuts, but then half of my family won't touch it, so only on occasion do I risk mutiny and add them.

Makes one 9 by 13-inch / 24 by 36cm sheet cake or one 8-inch / 20cm triple-layer cake

cake academy review

PEAKS → page 38

BASIC PIPING DESIGNS → page 56

BANANA CAKE

3 cups / 360g all-purpose flour

2¼ cups / 450g granulated sugar

2¼ tsp baking powder

¼ tsp baking soda

¾ tsp kosher salt

2 cups / 480g mashed very ripe bananas (about 4 large)

¾ cup / 175ml mild-flavored oil (such as vegetable oil)

1 Tbsp vanilla extract (see page 12)

3 eggs, at room temperature

1 cup / 240ml heavy whipping cream

1 cup / 100g chopped walnuts (optional)

1 recipe Pastry Cream (page 231), chilled

1 recipe Perfect Whipped Cream (page 227), divided

3 ripe bananas, sliced, at room temperature

1. To make the cake: Preheat the oven to 350°F / 175°C. Generously grease a 9 by 13-inch / 24 by 36cm cake pan (or three 8-inch / 20cm cake pans), then line it with greased parchment paper.

2. In a large bowl, whisk together the flour, sugar, baking powder, baking soda, and salt until well combined.

3. In a separate bowl, whisk together the mashed bananas, oil, vanilla, and eggs.

4. Add the wet ingredients to the flour mixture and stir together until just combined.

5. In another bowl, using a whisk, whip the heavy cream to medium peaks. Using a rubber spatula, fold the whipped cream into the batter, then fold in the walnuts (if using).

6. Pour the batter into the prepared pan and spread evenly using a small offset spatula. Gently tap the pan on the counter several times to release excess air bubbles.

7. Bake until a tester comes out clean, 40 to 45 minutes (about 30 minutes for 8-inch rounds). Let the cake cool completely before removing from the pan, then invert it onto a serving platter.

8. Stir the pastry cream until smooth, then fold in 1 cup / 240ml of the Perfect Whipped Cream with a rubber spatula. Spread the pastry cream over the cake, then cover with the sliced bananas. Pile or pipe (I use Ateco star tip #869) the remaining whipped cream over the bananas. Be sure to cover the bananas well so they don't turn brown before serving.

9. Store in the refrigerator, covered, for up to 24 hours.

hummingbird cake

During my epic forty-five-mile cake walk across Manhattan, Jen, my BFF, joined me for a stretch that included a stop at Magnolia Bakery. There, she declared the hummingbird cake her favorite cake, so naturally it was going to have a prominent spot in this book. I always thought of the South as the birthplace of this tasty cake, but it has Caribbean roots. The hummingbird is the national bird of Jamaica, which is where this cake originated and how it got its sweet, fluttery name. The fruity combination of tropical flavors includes honey-sweet pineapple, bananas, and a toasty note of cinnamon. Ermine Frosting is the classic topping for this cake, but I like the tang of Cream Cheese Frosting too. Either way, press toasted pecans onto the sides to add crunch. Scooping up a forkful of this cake, it's almost possible to feel the swing of a hammock and a soft, warm breeze on your cheek.

Makes one 8-inch / 20cm triple-layer cake

cake academy review

CRUMB-COATING → page 49

PUTTING ON THE FINAL LAYER OF FROSTING → page 49

3 cups / 360g all-purpose flour

2 cups / 400g granulated sugar

2 tsp ground cinnamon

1 tsp baking soda

½ tsp kosher salt

3 eggs, at room temperature

1 cup / 240g crushed pineapple, with juice

1 cup / 240g mashed very ripe bananas (about 2 large), at room temperature

1 cup / 240ml mild-flavored oil (such as vegetable oil)

2 tsp vanilla extract (see page 12)

2½ cups / 300g finely chopped pecans, lightly toasted, divided

1 recipe Ermine Frosting (page 206) or Cream Cheese Frosting (page 209)

1. Preheat the oven to 350°F / 175°C. Generously grease three 8-inch / 20cm cake pans, then line them with greased parchment paper.

2. In a large bowl, whisk together the flour, sugar, cinnamon, baking soda, and salt until well combined.

3. In a separate bowl, mix together the eggs, pineapple with juice, bananas, oil, and vanilla.

4. Add the wet ingredients to the flour mixture, stir together until well combined, and then stir in 1 cup / 120g of the pecans.

5. Pour the batter into the prepared pans and spread evenly using a small offset spatula. Gently tap the pans on the counter several times to release excess air bubbles.

6. Bake until a tester comes out clean, about 25 minutes. Let the cakes cool completely before removing from the pans.

7. Remove the parchment paper and place one cake layer on a serving plate.

8. Using a metal decorating spatula, spread a ¼-inch / 6mm-thick layer of the frosting over the cake, making sure it goes all the way to the edge. Place the next cake over the frosting and top with another layer of the frosting. Repeat with the last cake. If desired, at this point, you could crumb-coat the cake.

9. Decorate the cake with a smooth layer of the remaining frosting. Use the tip of the offset spatula to gently zigzag along the top of the cake. Press the remaining 1½ cups / 180g pecans into the sides of the cake.

10. Serve the cake immediately or store in the refrigerator, covered, for up to 48 hours. If refrigerated, bring the cake to room temperature before serving.

Carrot cake reminds me of growing up on a commune in Vermont. Just the mention of this iconic 1970s cake, and I hear Joni Mitchell playing in my mind! The cake I grew up with would have been ultra-earnest, sweetened with honey from my dad's bees and made with 100 percent whole-wheat flour, with a dash of wheat bran added just for good measure. My version is less sturdy and way more delicious. This cake is one of my most requested, because it's chock-full of carrots, shredded coconut, dried fruit, and spices. It is barely held together with a bit of flour, but, man, is it moist and delicious. I served this cake to both of my boys on their first birthdays. To take this from its hippie roots to something a bit more elegant, candy the carrot peels (see page 248) and use them to decorate the sides.

ultimate carrot cake

If you would like to level this up into a triple-layer cake, simply bake the batter in three 8 by 2-inch / 20 by 5cm pans. Slathered in Cream Cheese Frosting, this cake is perfect for any party or even for breakfast.

Makes one 8-inch / 20cm double-layer cake

cake academy review

CRUMB-COATING →
page 49

PUTTING ON THE
FINAL LAYER OF
FROSTING → page 49

4 cups / 450g loosely packed finely grated carrots

2⅓ cups / 280g all-purpose flour

1½ tsp baking powder

1 tsp baking soda

½ tsp kosher salt

1 tsp ground cinnamon

¼ tsp ground ginger

¼ tsp ground cloves

¼ tsp ground nutmeg

1¼ cups / 250g granulated sugar

1 cup / 200g lightly packed brown sugar

1¼ cups / 300ml mild-flavored oil (such as vegetable oil)

4 eggs, at room temperature

2 tsp vanilla extract (see page 12)

Finely grated zest of ½ large orange

3½ cups / 300g loosely packed sweetened shredded coconut, divided

1 cup / 160g chopped dried fruit (such as apricots, raisins, cherries)

1 recipe Cream Cheese Frosting (page 209)

1 Preheat the oven to 350°F / 175°C. Generously grease two 8 by 3-inch / 20 by 8cm round cake pans, then line them with greased parchment paper.

2 In a food processor, chop the grated carrots finely.

3 In a large bowl, whisk together the flour, baking powder, baking soda, salt, cinnamon, ginger, cloves, and nutmeg until well combined.

4 In a separate bowl, whisk together both sugars, the oil, eggs, vanilla, orange zest, 1¾ cups / 150g of the coconut, dried fruit, and carrots. Then add the dry ingredients and mix just until uniformly combined.

5 Divide the batter into the prepared pans and spread evenly using a small offset spatula. Gently tap the pans on the counter several times to release excess air bubbles.

6 Bake until a tester comes out clean, 50 to 55 minutes. Let the cakes cool completely before removing from the pans. Remove the parchment paper and place one cake layer on a serving plate.

7 Using a metal decorating spatula, spread a ½-inch / 1.3cm-thick layer of the frosting over the cake, making sure it goes all the way to the edge. Place the next cake over the frosting and top with another layer of frosting. If desired, at this point, you could crumb-coat the cake.

8 Decorate the cake with a smooth layer of the remaining frosting. Press the remaining 1¾ cups / 150g coconut to the sides of the cake.

9 Serve the cake immediately or store in the refrigerator, covered, for up to 48 hours. If refrigerated, bring the cake to room temperature before serving.

5 light-as-air cakes

After I made a pavlova and posted it on Instagram, things went nutty. By the end of the week, hundreds of people had made my recipe for this ethereal tutu of a cake. What I learned from that experience was that the world loved this light, airy, sweet cloud of a dessert as much as I did. I find meringue to be the most glorious element of a cake, and I love the process of making it almost as much as the eating of it. Check out page 37 to learn more about meringues, especially if you have ever had difficulty with them. I promise to change all that.

All of the cakes in this chapter are based on whipped eggs. Some use whole eggs, some include just the whites, and others whip them up separately and then fold them back together for the lightest, most exquisite texture imaginable. In most of these recipes, such as Angel Food Cake (page 150, and pictured opposite), whipped eggs alone are responsible for the lofty rise. The magic that an egg can perform is endlessly fascinating—and delicious.

hot milk sponge cake

Hot milk sponge sounds like something I need in the dead of a Minnesota winter. But it's actually a tempting and gorgeous cake that you can dress up as you see fit, either layered with pastry cream and chocolate ganache as a classic Boston Cream Pie (page 168) or served with nothing more than berries in the heat of summer. Its delightfully fluffy texture is made by whipping up whole eggs with a couple of additional yolks for good measure. The batter clings to the sides of the pan as it creeps ever higher while baking.

Makes two 9-inch / 23cm cake layers

cake academy review

LIGHT-AS-AIR
EGG FOAM → page 36

2 cups plus 1 Tbsp / 230g cake flour

2 tsp baking powder

½ tsp kosher salt

3 eggs, at room temperature

2 egg yolks, at room temperature

1½ cups / 300g granulated sugar, divided

¾ cup / 175ml whole milk

2 Tbsp mild-flavored oil (such as vegetable oil)

1 Tbsp vanilla extract (see page 12)

1 recipe Lemon Curd (page 235)

1. Preheat the oven to 350°F / 175°C. Line the bottoms of two 9-inch / 23cm cake pans with greased parchment, but leave the sides of the pans untouched. The cakes need to cling to the ungreased pans to rise properly.

2. In a large bowl, whisk together the flour, baking powder, and salt and then sift back into the bowl. Set aside.

3. In a stand mixer fitted with the whisk attachment, whip the eggs and egg yolks on high speed. Once the eggs are well combined and starting to foam, about 1 minute, turn the speed to medium-low and sprinkle ¾ cup / 150g of the sugar slowly over top. Turn the speed to high and let it whip for about 5 minutes.

4. While the eggs are whipping, in a small saucepan over medium heat, bring the milk, oil, and remaining ¾ cup / 150g sugar to a boil. Turn off the heat and stir in the vanilla.

5. Once the eggs are light in color and thick, they should be able to form a ribbon of batter that sits on top of the egg foam for a few seconds when you lift the whisk out of the foam. Turn the mixer speed to low, slowly add the boiling milk mixture, and then add the flour mixture, a few tablespoons at a time, scraping down the bowl several times.

6. Immediately pour the batter into the prepared pans and gently run a spatula through the batter to pop any large air bubbles.

7. Bake until a tester comes out clean, 15 to 20 minutes. Let the cake cool completely in the pans. Run a knife around the edge before turning out onto serving plates. The cakes can be served simply sliced with dollops of lemon curd.

I have to admit I hadn't ever made a Victoria sponge cake until British food writer Mary Berry came into my life through *The Great British Baking Show*. You'll notice that the ratio of ingredients here is very similar to a traditional pound cake (see page 63).

I finally had a proper Victoria sponge while on a trip to Dublin, and it was so light and really nothing like its distant pound-cake relative. When I got back home I had a difficult time replicating that texture, because US flour is different and produces a denser cake. Once I employed "self-raising" flour, a common British ingredient, which contains baking powder and salt in the mix, I had a total victory! The traditional filling is whipped cream and jam with a simple dusting of confectioners' sugar. I added a bit of fresh fruit for flavor and texture, and it's just straight up pretty. Try it, you'll be chuffed!

victory (victoria) sponge cake

Makes one 8-inch / 20cm double-layer cake

cake academy review

CREAMING → page 33

LIGHT-AS-AIR
EGG FOAM → page 36

FRENCH MERINGUE →
page 38

PEAKS → page 38

1 cup / 220g unsalted butter, at room temperature

1 cup plus 2 Tbsp / 220g superfine sugar

1 Tbsp vanilla extract (see page 12)

4 eggs, at room temperature

1¾ cups / 220g self-raising flour

12 oz / 340g strawberries, stemmed and quartered, plus whole and halved strawberries with stems left on for decorating

1 Tbsp granulated sugar

1 tsp lime zest

1 pinch ground pink peppercorn (optional)

1¾ cups / 225g strawberry Quick Jam (see page 236) or store-bought preserves

1 recipe Perfect Whipped Cream (page 227), whipped to stiff peaks

Confectioners' sugar for dusting

1 Preheat the oven to 350°F / 175°C. Generously grease two 8 by 3-inch / 20 by 8cm round cake pans, then line them with greased parchment paper.

2 In a stand mixer fitted with the paddle attachment, cream the butter on high speed until creamy and smooth, about 1 minute.

3 Turn the mixer speed to medium-low, add the super-fine sugar and vanilla to the butter, and mix until incorporated. Then turn the speed to medium-high and beat until very light and fluffy, about 5 minutes. Scrape the bowl often.

4 Turn the speed to low and add the eggs, one at a time, beating just until combined. Scrape the bowl after each addition.

5 Add one-third of the flour to the butter mixture and mix on low speed, just until incorporated. Repeat with another one-third flour until just incorporated. Add the final one-third flour. It will be a thick batter.

6 Divide the batter among the prepared pans and smooth the tops using a small offset spatula. Gently tap the pans on the counter several times to release excess air bubbles.

7 Bake until the cakes are golden and a tester comes out clean, 20 to 25 minutes. Let the cakes cool in the pans for 20 minutes, then remove from the pans and let cool completely on a wire rack.

CONTINUED

LIGHT-AS-AIR CAKES

8 In a medium bowl, toss together the quartered strawberries, granulated sugar, lime zest, and pink pepper (if using). Allow to macerate until the sugar dissolves, about 15 minutes.

9 Remove the parchment paper and place one cake layer on a serving plate.

10 Spread the jam over the top of the cake, then cover the jam with a 1-inch / 2.5cm layer of the whipped cream. Distribute half the macerated strawberries over the whipped cream.

11 Place the second cake on the whipped cream and dust the top generously with confectioners' sugar and decorate with whole and halved strawberries.

12 This cake is best served right away, with the remaining macerated strawberries and whipped cream, but any leftovers can be stored, covered, in the refrigerator for up to 1 day.

espresso sponge cake

Here is a light and airy sponge that's kicked up with a dose of espresso. Whipping the egg whites and egg yolks separately and then marrying them back together once they're at their heavenly best creates the ultimate foam. Since egg whites can reach their full potential without the fat of the yolks, they get even loftier than a foam created from a whole egg (see Brown Butter Genoise, page 146). This cake is perfect for any occasion. Serve it with some boozy coffee soak, pastry cream, and a dusting of cocoa in a tiramisu (see page 113) or layer it with ganache and a sprinkle of confectioners' sugar. The only deciding factor is whether you want something light and bright or dark and intense, like the chocolate variation.

Makes one 8-inch / 20cm cake

cake academy review

LIGHT-AS-AIR
EGG FOAM → page 36

FRENCH MERINGUE →
page 38

PEAKS → page 38

FOLDING → page 42

½ cup / 55g cake flour

1½ tsp espresso powder

4 eggs, separated,
at room temperature

⅓ cup / 65g
superfine sugar

1 pinch kosher salt

2 tsp vanilla extract
(see page 12)

Cocoa powder for dusting

1   Preheat the oven to 375°F / 190°C. Line the bottom of an 8 by 3-inch / 20 by 8cm round cake pan with lightly greased parchment, but leave the sides of the pan untouched. The cake needs to cling to the ungreased pan to rise properly.

2   In a large bowl, whisk together the flour and espresso powder and then sift back into the bowl. Set aside.

3   In a stand mixer fitted with the whisk attachment, whip the egg yolks on high speed. Once the eggs are well combined, turn the speed to medium-low and slowly sprinkle in half the sugar. Turn the speed to high and let it whip for about 5 minutes; it should be light in color and texture and about doubled in volume. When you lift the whisk out of the mixture, the batter should form a ribbon that sits on top of the egg foam for several seconds.

4   In a clean mixer bowl with a clean whisk attachment, combine the egg whites and salt and beat on low-medium speed until foamy. Slowly sprinkle in the remaining sugar to create a French meringue and, once it is all added, turn the speed to high and beat until stiff, glossy peaks form, 1 to 2 minutes more.

5   Fold the meringue into the egg yolk foam and then gently stir in the vanilla.

6   Sift one-third of the flour mixture over the egg foam and gently fold it in. Repeat with the next one-third flour and then the final one-third flour.

7   Immediately pour the batter into the prepared pan and gently smooth the top with a small offset spatula.

8   Bake until a tester comes out clean, about 20 minutes. Let the cake cool completely in the pan. Run a knife around the edge before turning out onto a serving plate. The cake can be served simply sliced with a dusting of cocoa powder.

VARIATION: CHOCOLATE SPONGE JELLY-ROLL CAKE

Just like the Brown Butter Genoise, this cake can be baked as a sheet and formed into a jelly-roll. Generously grease a 16 by 11-inch / 41 by 28cm jelly-roll pan, then line it with greased parchment paper. Increase the amount of cake flour to ¾ cup plus 1 Tbsp / 90g and replace the espresso powder with 4 tsp Dutch-processed cocoa powder. Sift together the flour and cocoa, then proceed as directed. Bake at 400°F / 200°C until a tester comes out clean, 12 to 15 minutes.

joconde (almond sponge cake)

This cake is nutty and rich but still light as a sponge cake should be. It provides the perfect base for Blackberry Diva Cake (page 196), not only because the flavors are ideally suited to one another but also because it is named after the ultimate diva of a painting, the Mona Lisa. Da Vinci's Italian model was named Lisa Goconde, which translates in French to Joconde. How could a diva cake be made with anything else? It is also a great choice for a traditional Bûche de Noël (page 191) or simply rolled with cream and berries.

Makes one 11 by 16-inch / 41 by 28cm sheet cake

cake academy review

LIGHT-AS-AIR EGG FOAM → page 36

FRENCH MERINGUE → page 38

PEAKS → page 38

3 Tbsp all-purpose flour

1 cup / 120g almond flour

3 eggs, at room temperature

½ cup / 100g superfine sugar, plus 2 Tbsp

3 egg whites, at room temperature

1 pinch kosher salt

Confectioners' sugar for dusting

1 recipe Perfect Whipped Cream (page 227)

4 cups / 480g fresh berries

1 Preheat the oven to 350°F / 175°C. Generously grease an 11 by 16-inch / 41 by 28cm jelly-roll pan, then line the bottom with greased parchment paper.

2 In a large bowl, sift together the all-purpose flour and almond flour. Set aside.

3 In a stand mixer fitted with the whisk attachment, whip the eggs and ½ cup / 100g sugar on high speed for about 8 minutes. The batter should be very light in color and texture. When you lift the whisk out of the mixture, the batter should form a ribbon that sits on the surface of the egg foam for several seconds. Turn the speed to medium and continue to whip for 1 minute more. Remove the bowl from the mixer and, using the whisk attachment or a rubber spatula, gently fold the almond mixture into the egg foam in three additions.

4 In a clean mixer bowl with a clean whisk attachment, whip the egg whites and salt on medium speed just until they start to foam. Slowly sprinkle in the remaining 2 Tbsp sugar to create a French meringue, then whip on high speed until glossy, stiff peaks form, 1 to 2 minutes. Remove the bowl from the mixer and, using the whisk attachment or a rubber spatula, gently fold the meringue into the almond batter.

5 Pour the batter into the prepared pan and spread evenly with an offset spatula.

6 Bake until the cake is set and just golden on top, 12 to 15 minutes. Let the cake cool completely in the pan.

7 Dust a clean kitchen towel with confectioners' sugar. Invert the joconde onto the prepared towel and carefully peel off the parchment paper.

8 Cover the joconde with half of the whipped cream, then top with half of the berries.

9 Using the towel to get started, roll the joconde, starting at the short end, into as tight a log as you can manage. Transfer the log to a serving platter. Cover with plastic wrap and refrigerate for 1 hour.

10 Remove the log from the refrigerator, then top with the remaining whipped cream and berries. Dust with confectioners' sugar before serving.

brown butter genoise

Taking creamy, lush butter down to dark and nutty brown butter adds a bit of backbone to a light and fluffy cake such as this—a total secret-weapon flavor that gives each slice of cake a hint of sophistication. A genoise is all about getting the eggs whipped up into a thick, luxurious web that looks super-delicate but is strong enough to carry the flour and butter as it rises in the oven. This cake is a classic choice for wedding cakes. It's a blank canvas that requires a good soak to be at its peak flavor and texture, and that's where your creativity comes in. Or you may choose to add one of my Simple Syrup variations (see page 226).

Makes one 9-inch / 23cm sheet cake

cake academy review

LIGHT-AS-AIR
EGG FOAM → page 36
FOLDING → page 42

4 whole eggs (in shell), at room temperature

1 egg yolk, at room temperature

½ cup / 55g cake flour

⅓ cup / 45g cornstarch

1 pinch kosher salt

½ cup / 100g superfine sugar

2 Tbsp Brown Butter (facing page)

1 tsp vanilla extract (see page 12)

Confectioners' sugar and fresh fruit for serving

1   Preheat the oven to 375°F / 190°C. Line the bottom of a 9-inch / 23cm cake pan with lightly greased parchment, but leave the sides of the pan untouched. The cake needs to cling to the ungreased pan to rise properly.

2   Put the whole eggs in a large bowl, cover with hot water, and let sit for about 10 minutes. (You may have to change the water if it gets cold. You are trying to get them to about 100°F / 38°C; they should feel warmer than room temperature).

3   In a large bowl, whisk together the flour, cornstarch, and salt and then sift back into the bowl. Set aside.

4   In a stand mixer fitted with the whisk attachment, crack in the warm eggs, add the egg yolk, and whip on high speed until well combined.

5   Turn the mixer speed to medium-low and slowly sprinkle the sugar over the eggs. When all the sugar is added, turn the speed to high and whip for about 8 minutes. The batter should be very light in color and texture and about tripled in volume. When you lift the whisk out of the mixture, the batter should form a ribbon that sits on top of the egg foam for several seconds.

6   Sift one-third of the flour mixture over the egg foam and gently fold it in using the whisk attachment or a rubber spatula. Repeat with the next one-third flour and then the final one-third flour.

7   Place ½ cup / 120ml of the batter in a small bowl and stir in the brown butter and vanilla. Very gently fold the butter mixture into the bowl of batter.

8   Immediately pour the batter into the prepared pan and gently smooth the top with a small offset spatula. Set the pan on a baking sheet.

9   Bake until the cake is golden and a tester comes out clean, about 20 minutes. Let the cake cool completely in the pan. Run a knife around the edge before turning out onto a serving plate. The cake can be served simply sliced with a dusting of confectioners' sugar and some fresh fruit.

VARIATION: GENOISE JELLY-ROLL CAKE

This genoise can also be baked in a sheet pan and used to make a Yule log (see pages 191 and 192) or Raspberry Charlotte Royale (page 187), or rolled up with whipped cream and fresh fruit and then dusted with confectioners' sugar. Generously grease a 16 by 11-inch / 41 by 28cm jelly-roll pan, then line it with greased parchment. Proceed as directed and bake in a 400°F / 200°C oven until a tester comes out clean, 10 to 12 minutes.

brown butter

16 oz / 450g
unsalted butter

1 In a small saucepan over medium-low heat, melt the butter. Turn the heat to medium-high and boil until the butter is frothy. Turn the heat to low and cook gently, until the milk solids have settled to the bottom of the pan, are golden brown, and smell slightly toasted. (Once the milk solids start to caramelize, it goes quickly, so don't walk away.) Remove from the heat once the butter is a deep amber color. Strain through a fine-mesh sieve, if desired.

2 Allow the butter to cool completely, then cover and refrigerate for up to 2 weeks.

anna's hazelnut–brown butter cake

This is a cake I've been chasing for thirty years. It's the one my husband's mom used to make for him when he was growing up, and the cake by which he judges all others. "This is delicious," he often said, "but I wish you could make the hazelnut cake my mom used to bake." Anna François, my mother-in-law, is a potter and one of the most talented people I know, but writing down recipes is not her style. She tried to talk me through how to make it, but I just wasn't able to replicate hers, and it drove me to near madness. Since this book wouldn't have been complete without this recipe, I persevered and finally got the enthusiastic approval of my husband. It was September when I finally nailed it, so I used fresh figs that were in season, but the cake is also brilliant served with peaches, cherries, berries, or just a simple dusting of confectioners' sugar.

Makes one 8-inch / 20cm cake

cake academy review

LIGHT-AS-AIR EGG FOAM → page 36

FRENCH MERINGUE → page 38

PEAKS → page 38

1¼ cups / 250g superfine sugar, divided

½ cup / 60g all-purpose flour

½ cup / 60g hazelnut flour

6 Tbsp / 85g Brown Butter (page 147), melted

2 Tbsp honey

1 tsp vanilla extract (see page 12)

1 pinch kosher salt

4 eggs, separated, at room temperature

½ recipe Perfect Whipped Cream (page 227)

Figs, peaches, berries, cherries, or any other fruit you desire for topping

1 Preheat the oven to 375°F / 190°C. Line an 8-inch / 20cm cake pan with a large piece of ungreased parchment paper, so it comes all the way up the sides. Set aside.

2 In a medium bowl, mix together ¼ cup / 50g of the sugar, both flours, the brown butter, honey, vanilla, salt, and egg yolks. Set aside.

3 In a stand mixer fitted with the whisk attachment, beat the egg whites on high speed until foamy. Turn the speed to medium-low and slowly sprinkle in the remaining 1 cup / 200g sugar to create a French meringue. Turn the speed to high and beat until medium-stiff, glossy peaks form, 1 to 2 minutes more.

4 Stir about 1 cup / 240ml of the meringue into the egg yolk–flour mixture to lighten. Gently fold in another one-third of the meringue. Repeat with two more additions, until the yolk mixture is light and smooth with no streaks of whites left in the batter.

5 Pour the batter into the prepared pan and smooth the top with a small offset spatula.

6 Bake until the cake is light brown and has risen, about 20 minutes. Turn the oven temperature to 350°F / 175°C and bake until a tester comes out clean, about 20 minutes more. Let the cake cool completely in the pan, then turn out onto a serving plate. Remove the parchment paper.

7 Serve the cake dolloped with the whipped cream and topped with fresh fruit.

An enduring bit of classic elegance, angel food cake is a canvas waiting for a little seasonal paint. Dress it up with fresh raspberries in summer, or drizzle it with a wickedly dark ganache in the dead of January. Once upon a time, I would have served a simple dollop of cream on top. That was before I saw my friend, and fellow baker, Jessie Sheehan grace an angel food cake with a fruit-studded sheath of whipped cream in her book *The Vintage Baker*. She boldly slathered the colorful topping over the whole cake (pictured on page 138). She forever ruined naked angel food cake for me, and I'm so grateful.

angel food cake

Makes one 10-inch / 25cm cake

cake academy review

LIGHT-AS-AIR
EGG FOAM → page 36
PEAKS → page 38

1¼ cups / 250g superfine sugar, divided

1 cup plus 1 Tbsp / 120g cake flour

1 Tbsp cornstarch

1 pinch kosher salt

6 oz / 170g fresh raspberries, plus more for garnish

1¾ cups / 415ml egg whites (from about 12 eggs), at room temperature

1 Tbsp freshly squeezed lemon juice

1 tsp cream of tartar

1 tsp vanilla extract (see page 12)

1 Tbsp lemon zest

Confectioners' sugar for dusting or 1 recipe Raspberry Whipped Cream (see variation, page 227)

1 Preheat the oven to 350°F / 175°C. Prepare a 10-inch / 25cm tube or angel food pan by doing NOTHING. The batter needs to grab the sides to rise in the oven and to successfully hang upside down to cool.

2 In a large bowl, whisk together half of the sugar, the flour, cornstarch, and salt. Sift the mixture three times to aerate, then set aside. Toss the 6 oz / 170g raspberries with 1 Tbsp of the flour mixture, then set aside.

3 In a stand mixer fitted with the whisk attachment, whip the egg whites, lemon juice, and cream of tartar on high speed until the whites are foamy. Turn the speed to medium-low and slowly add the remaining sugar. Turn the speed to medium-high and continue to whip the mixture until medium-stiff peaks form, about 3½ minutes. Add the vanilla, turn the speed to medium, and whip until incorporated.

4 Sift one-fourth of the sugar-flour mixture over the egg foam and, using a rubber spatula, gently fold them together. Repeat with another one-fourth sugar-flour mixture and gently fold together. Continue in this way until all the sugar-flour is incorporated. Fold in the lemon zest.

5 Spoon half of the batter into the ungreased pan, distribute 3 oz / 85g of the floured raspberries over the batter. Add the remaining batter and top with remaining 3 oz / 85g floured raspberries. Run a knife or metal spatula through the batter to release any large air bubbles.

6 Bake until the top is golden and a tester comes out clean, about 40 minutes. Immediately invert the pan onto a wine bottle and let rest to prevent the cake from compressing. Leave suspended upside down until completely cool, about 45 minutes.

7 Using a paring knife, very carefully loosen the cake away from the edge of the pan and the center. Invert the cake (using a cardboard round with a hole cut in the middle makes this task easier) onto a serving plate.

8 Dust the cake with confectioners' sugar or cover with the whipped cream. Garnish with fresh raspberries. Using a serrated bread knife or angel food comb, cut into individual slices to serve.

olive oil–chiffon cake

This cake melds the sleek fruity elegance of great olive oil and the brightness of oranges, two classic Italian flavors that give this fluffy treat some authority. Use freshly squeezed juice if you can. I was lucky enough to be gifted a case of oranges from my mother-in-law, who got them from a grower near her house. Oh, the joy of opening that box of fruit with their vibrant color and sweet perfume in the dead of a Minnesota winter. Even if you aren't lucky enough to have an orange source, grabbing a few from the store and squishing out that juicy sunshine is worth it. Serve this cake with nothing more than a cup of coffee, or go a bit more festive and pair with a fruit sauce. I like the filling on page 234, but made with blueberries.

Makes one 10-inch / 25cm cake

cake academy review

LIGHT-AS-AIR
EGG FOAM → page 36

PEAKS → page 38

FRENCH MERINGUE → page 38

BASIC PIPING DESIGNS:
ROSETTES → page 56

1¾ cups / 210g all-purpose flour

1½ cups / 300g granulated sugar, divided

2 tsp baking powder

1 tsp kosher salt

6 eggs, separated, at room temperature

½ cup / 120ml freshly squeezed orange juice

¼ cup / 60ml fruity olive oil

¼ cup / 60ml mild-flavored oil (such as vegetable oil) or olive oil (if you want a stronger flavor)

1 tsp vanilla extract (see page 12)

3 egg whites, at room temperature

½ tsp cream of tartar

1 recipe Perfect Whipped Cream (page 227; if covering the whole cake in rosettes, increase the amount of heavy whipping cream in the recipe to 3 cups / 720ml)

1. Preheat the oven to 350°F / 175°C. Prepare a 10-inch / 25cm tube pan by doing NOTHING. The batter needs to grab the sides to rise in the oven and to successfully hang upside down to cool.

2. In a large bowl, whisk together the flour, 1 cup / 200g of the sugar, baking powder, and salt. Set aside.

3. In a separate bowl, stir together the egg yolks, orange juice, orange zest, fruity olive oil, mild-flavored oil, and vanilla.

4. Add the dry ingredients to the yolk mixture and whisk together until smooth. Set aside.

5. In a stand mixer fitted with the whisk attachment, combine the egg whites and cream of tartar and beat on high speed until medium peaks form, about 2 minutes. Turn the speed to medium-low and slowly sprinkle in the remaining ½ cup / 100g sugar to create a French meringue. Turn the speed to high and beat until stiff, glossy peaks form, 1 to 2 minutes more.

6. Stir one-third of the meringue into the egg yolk–flour mixture to loosen it up. Using the whisk attachment or a rubber spatula, fold the remaining meringue into the yolk mixture.

7. Pour the batter into the ungreased pan. Run a knife or metal spatula through the batter to release any large air bubbles.

8. Bake until the cake bounces back to the touch and a tester comes out clean, 50 to 55 minutes. Immediately invert the pan onto a wine bottle and let rest to prevent the cake from compressing. Leave suspended upside down until completely cool, about 45 minutes.

9. Using a paring knife, very carefully loosen the cake away from the edge of the pan and the center. Invert the cake (using a cardboard round with a hole cut in the middle makes this task easier) onto a serving plate.

10. Spread or pipe the whipped cream over the cake. I use a large star tip (1M by Wilton) to pipe the rosettes. Using a serrated bread knife, cut into individual slices to serve.

As I mentioned in the introduction, the story of my life with sweets started with an auspicious meeting with Twinkies (see page 1). I would never presume to create anything as iconic as the original, but this version is freakin' delicious. My son, when tasting them for the first time, declared, "These taste way too good—you didn't get it quite right!" Love that kid. The chiffon cake is baked in a Twinkie-shaped pan (it's actually a hot dog–bun pan) to give it the essential look. It is super-tender and has the squish that is so beloved in the original cake snack. I offer a few choices of frosting to inject into the cylinder cake, since the original hyper-white Twinkie stuffing is a bit of a mystery and because each of my testers liked different fillings.

the og snack cake

I sometimes use a small star tip to pipe a bit of frosting on the tops of the cakes before dusting with confectioners' sugar and decorating with edible flowers, just to jazz them up for a special occasion.

Makes about 16 individual cakes

cake academy review

PEAKS → page 38

FRENCH MERINGUE → page 38

BASIC PIPING DESIGNS → page 56

¾ cup plus 2 Tbsp / 110g all-purpose flour

¾ cup / 150g granulated sugar, divided

1 tsp baking powder

½ tsp kosher salt

3 eggs separated, at room temperature

¼ cup / 60ml mild-flavored oil (such as vegetable oil) or olive oil (if you want a stronger flavor)

¼ cup / 60ml freshly squeezed orange juice

1 tsp orange zest

1 tsp vanilla extract (see page 12)

2 egg whites, at room temperature

½ tsp cream of tartar

¼ recipe Ermine Frosting (page 206), Italian Meringue Buttercream (page 215), or American Buttercream (page 213)

1   Preheat the oven to 350°F / 175°C. Lightly grease a nonstick hot dog–bun pan.

2   In a large bowl, whisk together the flour, ½ cup / 100g of the sugar, baking powder, and salt until combined. Set aside.

3   In a separate bowl, stir together the egg yolks, oil, orange juice, orange zest, and vanilla.

4   Add the dry ingredients to the egg yolk mixture and whisk together until smooth. Set aside.

5   In a stand mixer fitted with the whisk attachment, combine the egg whites and cream of tartar and beat on high speed until medium peaks form, about 2 minutes. Turn the speed to medium-low and slowly sprinkle in the remaining ¼ cup / 50g sugar to create a French meringue. Turn the speed to high and beat until stiff, glossy peaks form, 1 to 2 minutes more.

6   Stir one-third of the meringue mixture into the egg yolk mixture to loosen it up. Then, using the whisk attachment or a rubber spatula, fold the remaining meringue into the yolk mixture.

7   Fit a 16-inch / 40cm pastry bag with a large round tip (Ateco #9807), pour the batter into the bag, and then pipe into the prepared pan, filling each mold only two-thirds full.

8   Bake until golden and a tester comes out clean, 15 to 20 minutes. Invert the pan and tap gently to remove the cakes onto a sheet of parchment paper. Let cool completely.

CONTINUED

9 Fit a 12-inch / 30cm pastry bag with a Bismark piping tip (Ateco #230) and fill with the frosting. Inject the frosting from the bottom of each cake by poking the tip into it about three-fourths of the way through; fill until the cake begins to bulge. Repeat injecting the frosting every ½ inch / 1.3cm.

10 Serve the cake immediately or store in the refrigerator, covered, for up to 24 hours. If refrigerated, bring the cake to room temperature before serving.

VARIATION: DOUBLE-LAYER TWINKIE CAKE

This batter also bakes up as a super-soft, wonderful 8-inch / 20cm double-layer cake, for such occasions that call for a giant Twinkie-like confection. Line the bottoms of two UNGREASED 8-inch / 20cm cake pans with parchment paper. (The cake needs to cling to and climb up the sides.) Mix the batter as directed and then divide among the prepared pans. Bake until a tester comes out clean, 20 to 25 minutes. Let the cakes cool completely in the pans. If the cakes seem to be sinking, flip the pans upside down on a wire rack. Once cool, run a paring knife around the edges of the pans and invert onto plates. Remove the parchment and fill and decorate with the frosting as desired.

dacquoise with cream and berries

A dacquoise (da-KWOZ) is a very French dessert, made of a crisp, nutty meringue baked in disks and assembled into a cake. The word *dacquoise* refers to both the layers and the cake itself. This redundancy makes perfect sense, because everything about it is delicious—you just want to say the word over and over. I use salted almonds in this recipe to balance the sweetness of the meringue, but you can replace them with hazelnuts, pistachios, or any other nuts. The lightness of the crisp dacquoise pairs with so many flavors. In the summer months, I serve it with chilled whipped cream and fresh berries (blueberries, raspberries, and blackberries), making it a super-simple and easy dessert that's still a knockout. In the winter months, I puree roasted chestnuts and add them to buttercream (see page 216); this is a stunner when topped with boozy cherries and whipped cream and makes a rather rustic, yet festive dessert for the holidays. There are countless options for fillings, so go nuts (or berries)!

Makes about 10 servings

cake academy review

LIGHT-AS-AIR
EGG FOAM → page 36

FRENCH MERINGUE → page 38

PEAKS → page 38

FOLDING → page 42

½ cup / 60g almond flour

½ cup / 60g confectioners' sugar

1 cup / 140g whole roasted and salted almonds

1 cup / 240ml egg whites (from about 6 eggs), at room temperature

¼ tsp cream of tartar

1 cup / 200g superfine sugar

1 recipe Perfect Whipped Cream (page 227)

1 cup / 300g lime curd (see variation, page 235)

2 pints / 240g fresh berries (see headnote)

1 Preheat the oven to 225°F / 107°C. Trace two 8-inch / 20cm circles on each of two sheets of parchment paper and set them, upside down, on two 16 by 11-inch / 41 by 28cm jelly-roll pans. Set aside.

2 In a large bowl, sift together the almond flour and confectioners' sugar. Set aside.

3 In a food processor, pulse the almonds to crush them. You want the pieces to be just big enough to add texture.

4 In a stand mixer fitted with the whisk attachment, combine the egg whites and cream of tartar and beat on medium-high speed, until they start to foam, about 45 seconds. Turn the speed to medium-low and slowly sprinkle in the sugar to create a French meringue. Turn the speed to high and beat until stiff, glossy peaks form, 1 to 2 minutes more.

5 Using the whisk attachment, fold in the almond flour mixture, then fold in the crushed almonds.

6 Divide the batter evenly among the circles on the prepared parchment paper. Using an offset cake spatula, spread the batter, making sure all the circles are even so they bake at the same rate.

7 Bake until the dacquoise are dry, about 90 minutes. Turn off the oven (don't open the door), turn on the oven light (if your oven doesn't have a light, continue baking for 15 minutes more), and let the dacquoise sit in the cooling oven for at least 2 hours; it can be stored like this overnight or even up to 24 hours. Leaving the light on ensures it will stay dry.

8 Place one dacquoise disk on a serving plate, cover with one-fourth of the whipped cream, swirl one-fourth of the lime curd into the cream, and top with one-fourth of the berries. Repeat with the remaining disks, whipped cream, curd, and berries.

9 Refrigerate the dacquoise for 1 hour before serving to make cutting easier.

CONTINUED

VARIATION: CHESTNUT-CHERRY DACQUOISE

Adding chestnut buttercream is a very traditional way to serve a dacquoise and makes for a slightly more decadent version. A perfect addition to your holiday table. Bake and cool the dacquoise as directed. When assembling, replace the lime curd and fresh berries with ½ recipe of chestnut Swiss Meringue Buttercream (see page 216) and 1 recipe of Cherry Filling (page 234). Put 2 Tbsp of buttercream on the serving plate and top with the first disk of dacquoise; the buttercream will adhere the cake to the plate. Spread one-fourth of the buttercream over the disk, building up the edges slightly to create a dam for the cherries. Place one-fourth of the cherries in the center of the buttercream. Top with one-fourth of the whipped cream and sprinkle with one-fourth of the remaining crushed nuts. Repeat with the remaining dacquoise, buttercream, cherries, whipped cream, and nuts.

The pavlova is the ballerina of the baking world. Literally. It was named for a Russian dancer who was visiting Australia. (Or was it New Zealand? Both countries claim the dessert's origin.) I have played with the shape to give it a more elegant look, reminiscent of the tutus that Pavlova, the dancer, would have worn.

A pavlova is a study in perfect imperfection. It bakes into a delicate, smooth shell that collapses in the middle, begging for any manner of filling. Scoop in fresh berries, fill the center with a citrusy curd and passion fruit, or use all of them—the options are limitless. Plus, because there's zero flour in the shell, pavlovas are naturally a gluten-free dessert if you need something spectacular that fits that bill. Besides, who doesn't want to dig into a crackling, sweet cloud?

There are a few parts of this method that will set you up for success. If possible, use really fresh egg whites. They'll make a stronger egg foam that will be less likely to crack while it bakes. The water in the mix helps to thin out the egg white protein, creating a more ethereal pavlova that will melt in your mouth. If you make your own superfine sugar (see page 18), sift it first to make sure it is truly fine so it will dissolve into the eggs more easily, giving the pavlova a smoother surface. The low oven temperature is key to keeping the meringue from cracking or browning too much. An oven thermometer is a great tool to determine your oven's temperature for sure.

pavlova

Makes about 8 servings

cake academy review

LIGHT-AS-AIR
EGG FOAM → page 36
PEAKS → page 38

5 egg whites, at room temperature

1 pinch kosher salt

⅛ tsp cream of tartar (optional, but adds some strength if using older eggs)

3 Tbsp cold water

1¼ cups / 250g superfine sugar

1 Tbsp plus 1 tsp cornstarch

1 tsp vanilla extract (see page 12)

1 tsp vinegar (white wine, cider, or distilled)

1 recipe Perfect Whipped Cream (page 227)

½ recipe Lemon Curd (page 235), divided

Fresh berries and/or passion fruit for filling and topping

Confectioners' sugar for dusting

1 Preheat the oven to 275°F / 135°C and place a rack in the bottom third of the oven. Trace a 6-inch / 15cm circle on a piece of parchment paper and set it, upside down, on a baking sheet.

2 In a stand mixer fitted with the whisk attachment, combine the egg whites, salt, and cream of tartar (if using) and beat on medium-high speed until medium peaks form, about 3 minutes.

3 Turn the mixer speed to medium-low and drizzle in the water. Slowly sprinkle in the sugar a little at a time; this may take a minute or so. Turn the speed to high and whip until very stiff, glossy peaks form, about 5 minutes.

4 Using the whisk attachment or a rubber spatula, gently fold the cornstarch, vanilla, and vinegar into the egg whites.

CONTINUED

PAVLOVA,
CONTINUED

5   Mound the egg foam into the circle on the prepared parchment paper. Using a metal spatula, smooth the mound, then swipe grooves in the foam, creating curls at the top. Very gently create a crater at the top, like a volcano, where the grooves meet.

6   Bake until the pavlova starts to turn a very pale tan color, about 1 hour 15 minutes. If after about 45 minutes, the pavlova is darkening too fast, lower the oven temperature to 250°F / 120°C. Turn off the oven (don't open the door), turn on the oven light (if your oven doesn't have a light, bake 15 minutes more), and let the pavlova sit in the cooling oven for at least 3 hours, but it can be stored like this overnight or even up to 24 hours. Leaving the light on ensures it will stay dry.

7   The center of the pavlova will collapse—that's just the nature of the beast and the place where you will put your filling. If it doesn't fall into the cavity completely, use a paring knife to carefully open up a hole in the top. The outer edge may crack a touch, too, but I've made this shape several times, and it cracks far less if you do not open the oven door.

8   Run a metal spatula under the pavlova to release it from the paper and carefully transfer to a serving plate.

9   Fold half of the whipped cream into ½ cup / 130g of the lemon curd. Fit a pastry bag with a large round tip and fill with the cream-curd mixture. Alternatively, carefully spoon in the mixture. Fill the pavlova with half of the cream-curd mixture. Spoon ¼ cup / 65g of the remaining lemon curd over it, then sprinkle with some of the berries. Repeat with the remaining cream-curd mixture and then the remaining lemon curd. Finish with the remaining berries and whipped cream and then dust with confectioners' sugar.

10 Refrigerate the pavlova for about 1 hour before serving to make it easier to cut.

This is a pavlova with more attitude. If the original Pavlova (page 161) is named for a graceful ballerina, then this one is more Bob Fosse jazz hands. I layered the center of this with whipped milk-chocolate mascarpone, caramel, cream, and toasted nuts. If that doesn't make you want to dance, I'm not sure what will.

chocolate pavlova

This pavlova doesn't bake up as tall as the ballerina version, and the surface tends to crack more, but that's all part of the wabi-sabi charm. It will be helpful to read the headnote for the Pavlova recipe before diving into the chocolate version.

Makes about 8 servings

cake academy review

LIGHT-AS-AIR
EGG FOAM → page 36
PEAKS → page 38

5 egg whites,
at room temperature

1 pinch kosher salt

⅛ tsp cream of tartar

1¼ cups / 250g
superfine sugar

1 Tbsp plus 1 tsp Dutch-
processed cocoa powder

1 tsp vanilla extract
(see page 12)

1 tsp vinegar (white wine,
cider, or distilled)

½ recipe Whipped Milk
Chocolate Mascarpone
(page 237)

1 recipe Thick Caramel Sauce
(page 218)

¾ cup / 90g toasted, salted
nuts (peanuts, pecans,
macadamias, or your
favorite)

½ recipe Perfect Whipped
Cream (page 227)

1   Preheat the oven to 275°F / 135°C and place a rack in the bottom third of the oven. Trace a 6-inch / 15cm circle on a piece of parchment paper and set it, upside down, on a baking sheet.

2   In a stand mixer fitted with the whisk attachment, combine the egg whites, salt, and cream of tartar and beat on medium-high speed until medium peaks form, about 3 minutes.

3   Turn the mixer speed to medium-low and slowly sprinkle in the sugar a little at a time; this may take a minute or so. Turn the speed to high and whip until very stiff, glossy peaks form, about 5 minutes.

4   Using the whisk attachment or a rubber spatula, gently fold the cocoa powder, vanilla, and vinegar into the egg foam.

5   Mound the egg foam into the circle on the prepared parchment paper. Using a metal spatula, smooth the mound, then swipe grooves in the meringue, creating curls at the top. Very gently create a crater at the top, like a volcano, where the grooves meet.

6   Bake until the pavlova starts to turn a slightly darker brown color, about 1 hour 15 minutes. If after about 45 minutes, the pavlova is darkening too fast, turn the oven temperature to 250°F / 120°C. Turn off the oven (don't open the door), turn on the oven light

(if your oven doesn't have a light, continue baking for 15 minutes more), and let the pavlova sit in the cooling oven for at least 2 hours; it can be stored like this overnight or even up to 24 hours. Leaving the light on ensures it will stay dry.

7   The center of the pavlova will collapse—that's just the nature of the beast and the place where you will put your filling. If it doesn't fall into the cavity completely, use a paring knife to carefully open up a hole in the top. The outer edge may crack a touch, too, but I've made this shape several times, and it cracks far less if you do not open the oven door.

8   Run a metal spatula under the pavlova to release it from the paper and carefully transfer to a serving plate.

9   Fill the pavlova with half of the chocolate mascarpone, drizzle with one-third of the caramel sauce, sprinkle with one-third of the nuts, and then top with half of the whipped cream. Repeat with the remaining chocolate mascarpone, one-third caramel sauce, one-third nuts, and the remaining whipped cream. Finish by drizzling with the last of the caramel and sprinkling with the last of the nuts.

10 Refrigerate the pavlova for about 1 hour before serving to make it easier to cut.

6 the layered cakes

This is the fun part, putting all the pieces together in layers of delicious beauty. There are no rules here, just creative interpretation. You can pick any cake layers and match them with any filling and topping that reflect your mood or occasion. If you want to take a simple, understated cake to a sensational centerpiece, top it with a flourish, like Carrot Peel Candy (page 248) or Candied Hazelnuts (page 247).

Here are some cakes that I put together to inspire your cake journey. Some are classics, like Boston Cream Pie (page 168). Others I made up, like Chocolate–Peanut Butter Cake (page 171, and pictured opposite), after being inspired by something special. You be you, and please post them on Instagram and tag/mention me @zoebakes, so I can see your creations.

Let's get this party started!

It's a cake with a curious name. These soft buttery cakes were once baked in pie tins, then sandwiched around a thick layer of vanilla pudding and draped in deep, dark chocolate. According to history, the dessert was first created during the nineteenth century at Boston's Parker House by the hotel's French pastry chef, who wanted a cake but only had access to pie tins. It's likely it was those pie tins that created the confusing name. This story may be a myth, since there are other origins for this misnomer of a dessert, but the deliciousness of the cake is no lie; that is why it has endured as an American treasure.

boston cream pie

I bake this cake in cake pans, so there is no mistaking what it is. If you are not a stickler for tradition, you can really create this cake/pie with any cake layers you like, but a yellow cake is likely the closest to the original. A hot milk sponge or even chocolate cake makes an excellent choice as well.

Makes about 12 servings

cake academy review

PEAKS → page 38

FOLDING → page 42

POURED GANACHE → page 52

2 layers Yellow Cake (page 122), Hot Milk Sponge (page 140), or Hot Chocolate Cake (page 126)

1 recipe Pastry Cream (page 231)

⅓ cup / 80ml heavy whipping cream, whipped to stiff peaks

1 cup / 240g Dark Chocolate Ganache (page 221; thick enough to coat but still pourable, warm slightly over a double boiler if it has set)

1 Place one cake layer on a serving plate.

2 Stir the pastry cream to loosen, then mix in one-third of the whipped cream to lighten. Fold in the remaining whipped cream.

3 Using an offset spatula, spread all of the pastry cream over the cake; making sure not to go quite to the edge. Place the next cake layer over the pastry cream. Gently press down on the cake to make sure it is sitting snugly on the pastry cream. If the pastry cream goes beyond the edge, clean it up with a metal decorating spatula. Cover with plastic wrap and refrigerate for about 1 hour to set the pastry cream in place.

4 Pour the ganache over the top of the cake, starting in the center and stopping just as it drips over the edge.

5 Refrigerate the cake until the ganache sets, about 30 minutes, then serve right away.

chocolate–peanut butter cake

Like coffee with cream, bacon with eggs, and Hall with Oates, chocolate and peanut butter are just better together. That little bit of saltiness from peanuts enhances all the deep dark decadence of the devil's food cake.

This ideal everyday cake (pictured on page 166) is a sweet treat for kids hopping off the bus after an exciting day at school, although those who wander in, ragged from a long day of adulting, may appreciate this cake even more.

Makes about 10 servings

1 recipe Chocolate Devil's Food Cake (page 125), baked in a loaf pan

1 recipe Peanut Butter Whipped Cream (see variation, page 227)

1 cup / 240g Dark Chocolate Ganache (page 221; thick enough to coat but still pourable, warm slightly over a double boiler if it has set)

⅓ cup / 40g crushed salted peanuts

1   Place the cake on a serving plate.

2   Pile the whipped cream evenly on top of the cake and, using a metal decorating spatula, smooth, swiping the sides with the blade to create right angles, so it creates a tall rectangle.

3   Pour the ganache over the top of the cake, starting in the center and stopping just as it drips over the edge. Sprinkle the peanuts over the top while the ganache is still wet.

4   Refrigerate the cake until the ganache sets, about 30 minutes, then serve right away.

Baking stretches back through the centuries; and in every set of hands, it changes, creating a narrative of time and place. Recipes, techniques, and flavors are handed from cook to baker across generations, creating a tapestry that evolves and is added to over time.

Black Forest Cake is one of those recipes that seems downright ancient. Its classic combination of chocolate cake, cherries cooked in kirschwasser (a cherry liquor), and whipped cream is forever satisfying and has required few changes over the years.

black forest cake

Makes about 12 servings

cake academy review

PEAKS → page 38

2 layers Hot Chocolate Cake (page 126) or Chocolate Devil's Food Cake (page 125)

1 recipe Perfect Whipped Cream (page 227), whipped to stiff peaks

1 recipe Cherry Filling (page 234)

Chocolate shavings (see page 8) for topping

1   Place one cake layer on a serving plate.

2   Using an offset spatula, spread half of the whipped cream over the top of the cake. Distribute half the cherry filling over the cream. Repeat with the remaining cake, whipped cream, and filling. Finish by topping with chocolate shavings.

3   Serve the cake immediately or store in the refrigerator, covered, for up to 24 hours.

"german" chocolate coconut cake

Turns out we have Texas to thank for this wonderful combination—there's absolutely nothing German about a coconut-covered cake. In the 1850s, Sam German created a brand of dark baking chocolate for Baker's Chocolate Company. About a hundred years later, a home baker from the Lone Star State created this cake and named it German's Chocolate Cake, after the type of chocolate she used, Baker's German's Sweet Chocolate. Mystery solved. Since then, it's a confection that has endured with its rich and moist chocolate base that's gussied up with a gooey coconut frosting.

Makes about 12 servings

1 recipe Hot Chocolate Cake (page 126)

1 recipe Sticky Coconut Filling (page 233)

1   Place one cake layer on a serving plate.

2   Using an offset spatula, spread one-third of the filling over the top of the cake, making sure it goes all the way to the edge. Place the next cake layer over the filling and top with another one-third filling. Repeat with the final cake layer and the remaining filling.

3   Serve the cake at room temperature.

This is a delight on a cake stand, with all the party presence of Phyllis Diller. If this cake could laugh, it would cackle. Long before we, as a people, were using coconut oil, coconut milk, and coconut water for just about everything, it was a taste of the tropics. Those giant nuts filled with creamy, exotic flavor dress up this cake into something downright fancy.

The exterior doesn't have to be quite this extra, but—trust me—go with it. You'll find yourself laughing out loud. Then it's time to reach for the blowtorch. Don't be timid here—torch with purpose and empowerment. This tropical taste of whimsy is a blast to make.

coconut cream cake

Makes about 16 servings

cake academy review

PEAKS → page 38

1 recipe Coconut Cake (see page 131)

1 recipe Coconut Pastry Cream (page 232)

⅓ cup / 80ml heavy whipping cream, whipped to stiff peaks

1 recipe Fluffy Swiss Meringue Topping (page 217)

1   Place one cake layer on a serving plate.

2   Stir the pastry cream to loosen, then mix in one-third of the whipped cream to lighten. Fold in the remaining whipped cream.

3   Using an offset spatula, spread half of the pastry cream over the cake; making sure not to go quite to the edge. Top with the next cake layer. Gently press down on the cake to make sure it is sitting snugly on the pastry cream. Spread with the remaining pastry cream and top with the final cake layer. If the pastry cream goes beyond the edge, clean it up with a metal decorating spatula. Make sure the layers are straight.

4   Cover with plastic wrap and refrigerate for about 1 hour to set the pastry cream.

5   Reserve 1 cup / 60g of the meringue topping. Use a metal spatula to spread a thick layer of the remaining meringue evenly over the cake.

6   Take a blob—yes, a blob—of the reserved meringue between your fingers and press it against the meringue on the cake. Pull the blob away from the cake, it will break off in a wispy curl. The thicker the blob you lay down as a foundation on the cake, the bigger the curls will be. It may take a few times to get the hang of it, but then you'll be off and running. Plus, it's fun.

7   Once you have the cake fully set with curls, hold a kitchen blowtorch about 3 inches / 7.5cm from the cake, so just the tip of the flame is hovering over the cake. Keep the torch moving so it doesn't burn the meringue. The tip of the curls will set fire, which is not as scary as that sounds but you need to blow them out as you go. The burnt tips are a lovely contrast and add a wonderful flavor.

8   Serve the cake immediately or store in the refrigerator, covered, for up to 48 hours.

turtle cake

For decades, the turtle cake at Cafe Latte was voted the favorite cake in St. Paul, Minnesota. As a pastry chef, I couldn't deny its appeal and secretly wished I'd thought of it. Who doesn't love deep, dark chocolate cake with gooey caramel, ganache, and toasted pecans? It is a messy cake that will make everyone super-happy!

Makes about 16 servings

cake academy review

TRIMMING THE TOP →
page 47

1 recipe Chocolate Devil's Food Cake (page 125), baked in three 8-inch / 20cm rounds

1 recipe Thick Caramel Sauce (page 218), slightly warm

1 cup / 120g chopped toasted pecans, plus 18 whole toasted pecans

1 cup / 240g Dark Chocolate Ganache (page 221), slightly warm

Coarse sea salt

1   If the cake layers are domed, trim them to be flat. Place one cake layer on a serving plate.

2   Drizzle ⅓ cup / 80ml of the caramel sauce over the cake and sprinkle with ½ cup / 60g of the chopped pecans. Drizzle ⅓ cup / 80g of the ganache over the nuts. Repeat with a second layer of cake, caramel, chopped pecans, and ganache. Top with the final layer of cake, caramel, and ganache. Finish with the whole pecans and a sprinkle of salt on top.

3   Serve the cake immediately or store in the refrigerator, covered, for up to 24 hours.

chocolate hazelnut torte

These gorgeous hazelnut praline teardrops are pure kitchen magic with their long caramel spires reaching skyward. It's an impressive technique that's so much fun to pull off. This otherwise simple design is perfect for a festive table, with its elegant hazelnut garnish. Plus, the rich chocolate cake pairs beautifully with the meringue buttercream that's studded with praline. I feel like a good jazz riff is the playlist for this cake.

Makes about 16 servings

cake academy review

CRUMB-COATING →
page 49

PUTTING ON THE
FINAL LAYER OF
FROSTING → page 49

1 recipe Hot Chocolate Cake (page 126) or Chocolate Devil's Food Cake (page 125), baked in three 8-inch / 20cm rounds

1 recipe Crushed Praline (page 244; made with hazelnuts)

1 recipe Swiss Meringue Buttercream (page 216)

1 cup Nutella

Candied Hazelnuts (page 247) for garnishing

1 Place one cake layer on a serving plate.

2 In a food processor fitted with the metal blade, pulverize the praline until there are small bits about the size of pine nuts or smaller—but not as fine as powder.

3 In a medium bowl, combine the buttercream with the praline and mix until soft and spreadable. The buttercream won't be perfectly smooth because of the pieces of praline, but it should spread easily.

4 Using an offset spatula, spread one-third of the Nutella over the cake, then spread about one-third of the praline buttercream over it, making sure the buttercream goes all the way to the edge. Place the second cake layer over the buttercream, spread with another one-third of the Nutella and then another one-third of the buttercream. Top with the final cake layer and the remaining Nutella.

5 If desired, at this point, you could crumb-coat the cake with some of the buttercream.

6 Decorate the cake with a smooth layer of the remaining praline buttercream.

7 Garnish the cake with candied hazelnuts before serving.

7 rolled and fancy cakes

These are the cakes that have just a little extra something, either in the way of technique, like the roulades, or a touch of posh and worthy of a party, like Beehive Cake (page 194, and pictured opposite). There is nothing difficult about these cakes; they just look fancy and may have more components than the layered party cakes in chapter 6.

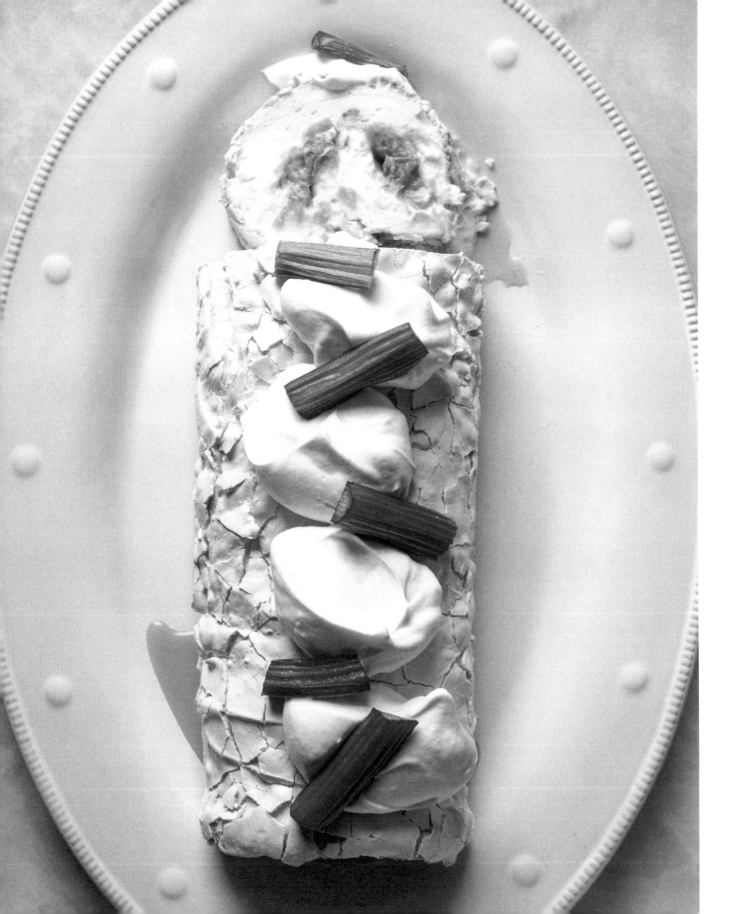

This recipe is simple to make, but it creates a huge impression when served. It is both rustic and elegant, perfect for a picnic in the park or that formal dinner you have twice a year in the otherwise unused dining room. Or is that just me? No matter where, it is always met with amazed glee. The meringue bakes up crisp on the outside and delicately soft on the inside. I like to pair it with barely sweetened cream and rhubarb, because the tartness is a match made in heaven for the sweet pavlova. When it is all rolled up, the textures, flavors, and beauty of this gluten-free cake make it a total winner.

pavlova roulade

This pavlova can go in so many tasty directions. You can toss in some berries, layer it with Coconut Pastry Cream (Page 232) and Dark Chocolate Ganache (page 221), or replace the cooked rhubarb with two fresh sliced peaches or substitute the Perfect Whipped Cream with Caramel Whipped Cream (page 229) and top with Crushed Praline (page 244) before serving.

Makes about 8 servings

1 recipe Pavlova batter
(see page 161)

RHUBARB FILLING

4 cups / 480g fresh or frozen rhubarb, cut into 1-inch / 2.5cm-long pieces

½ cup / 100g granulated sugar

Confectioners' sugar
for dusting

1 recipe Perfect Whipping
Cream (page 227)

1 Preheat the oven to 350°F / 175°C. Generously grease a 15 by 11-inch / 40 by 28cm sheet pan, then line it with greased parchment paper.

2 Evenly spread the pavlova batter in the prepared pan.

3 Bake until the pavlova starts to turn a light caramel color, about 25 minutes. It will puff considerably while it bakes but will settle once it is out of the oven. Let the pavlova cool completely. (Just leave it in the pan, dust with confectioners' sugar, and cover with a clean kitchen towel for up to 1 day.)

4 To make the filling: In a medium saucepan over low heat, combine the rhubarb and granulated sugar and cook, stirring gently, until the juices thicken and the rhubarb becomes very tender.

5 Dust a clean kitchen towel with confectioners' sugar. Invert the pavlova onto the prepared towel and carefully peel off the parchment paper.

CONTINUED

6 Cover the cake with half of the whipped cream, then top with half of the rhubarb.

7 Using the towel to get started, roll the cake, starting at the short end, into as tight a log as you can manage. Transfer the log to a serving platter. Cover with plastic wrap and refrigerate for 1 hour.

8 Remove the log from the refrigerator, then top with the remaining whipped cream and rhubarb. Dust with confectioners' sugar before serving.

This is a cake I had often marveled at in magazines and fancy cookbooks. It looked so majestic and unattainable with its many swirls, and I just couldn't wrap my mind around how to create its shape. A month into culinary school, a Charlotte Royale appeared on my syllabus, and the magic tricks (there are a few in this recipe) were revealed. Now I make these cakes without a care, and so I'm here to guide you through it, so you, too, can impress your unknowing guests.

I use raspberries because I love their flavor and bright pink color. You can use any berry, but don't stop there; you could replace the berry puree with peach, pear, quince, guava, cherry, rhubarb, or any other fruit puree. Go wild. You do need to avoid using straight juice, since the amount of gelatin I call for won't set a super-thin liquid.

raspberry charlotte royale

Makes about 8 servings

cake academy review

PEAKS → page 38

Confectioners' sugar for dusting

1 recipe Genoise Jelly-Roll Cake (see variation, page 146, omitting the butter), still in the baking pan

1 cup / 300g Berry Quick Jam (see page 236) or store-bought preserves; strain before measuring

RASPBERRY FILLING

3 cups / 360g fresh or frozen raspberries, divided

½ cup / 100g granulated sugar

One ¼-oz / 7g envelope unflavored gelatin

2 Tbsp cold water

1¼ cups / 300ml heavy whipping cream, whipped to stiff peaks

1   Dust a clean, dry kitchen towel generously with confectioners' sugar.

2   Invert the hot cake onto the prepared towel. Carefully peel the parchment paper from the bottom of the cake, dust the surface with more confectioners' sugar, drape the peeled parchment back onto the cake, and tightly roll up the cake, starting at the short end. Let the cake cool completely.

3   Unroll the cooled cake and cover it with a thin layer of the jam. Starting at the short end, roll the cake into a tight spiral that goes halfway up the sheet of cake. Cut off the spiral log at the midpoint, then wrap it tightly in plastic wrap to hold its round shape. Continue to roll the remaining cake, then wrap it in plastic wrap. Once the cakes are rolled and wrapped, place in the freezer for at least 1 hour or up to 1 day.

4   Using a serrated knife, cut the frozen cakes into ¼-inch / 6mm-thick disks. If the knife gets sticky from the jam, wash it off so you get a nice clean cut.

5   Line a 7-inch / 18cm sphere mold or bowl with plastic wrap, then line the mold with the disks of cake. Make sure they are positioned tightly together, so the filling can't seep between the disks and be seen when the cake is inverted from the mold.

6   Cover the lined mold with plastic wrap and set aside. There should be plenty of cake disks left; these will be used for the bottom.

7   To make the filling: In a medium saucepan over medium heat, combine 2 cups / 240g of the raspberries and the sugar and cook, stirring, until the fruit breaks down and the sugar is dissolved. If using fresh berries, you may need to break them down with the back of a spoon.

8   While the berries are cooking, put the gelatin in a small bowl, pour in the water, and let sit until the gelatin thickens, about 5 minutes.

CONTINUED

9   Put the cooked raspberries in a blender and puree until smooth. Return the puree to the saucepan, turn the heat to low, and add the gelatin, stirring until the gelatin dissolves. Transfer the raspberry mixture to a bowl, cover, and let cool to room temperature. (You can put the bowl in the freezer for 10 to 15 minutes to speed things up a bit; just don't forget it's in there or it will set too hard and wreck havoc with the gelatin.)

10 Fold the whipped cream into the cooled puree, then fold in the remaining 1 cup / 120g raspberries. Spoon the raspberry mixture into the cake-lined mold. Spread the filling so it is level and then use the last of the cake disks to cover the filling. Trim off any cake along the edge to be flush with the top. Cover with plastic wrap and put in the refrigerator to chill for several hours, or up to 2 days.

11 Invert the cake onto a cake plate, use a knife dipped in hot water to cut the cake, and serve immediately.

BAKER'S NOTE

Omitting the butter from the cake batter will make the structure of the cake a bit stronger and more flexible, which you'll need when rolling the cake into a tight log.

It has become a tradition to bring a Bûche de Noël to my folks' Christmas Eve party every year. Sometimes I go super-traditional with the aesthetics and flavor combinations, and other times I mix it up and create something a bit more modern. One year, Christmas and Hanukkah overlapped, so I wanted to honor the two holidays, since I have both traditions in my family. This cake may look like the traditional Christmas log, but the filling is flavored with halva, which borrows from my Jewish grandma, Sarah Berkowitz, who always kept a block of the sesame fudge in her refrigerator for me to nibble on.

You can use any flavors you want, cover the outside in buttercream instead of ganache for a snowy white version of the cake, or try my Mod Yule Log (page 192) for a modern twist.

bûche de noël (christmas yule log)

Makes about 12 servings

Confectioners' sugar for dusting

1 recipe Joconde (Almond Sponge Cake, page 145) or Chocolate Sponge Jelly-Roll Cake (see variation, page 144), still in the baking pan

¼ recipe Tahini Buttercream (see variation, page 213)

1 recipe Dark Chocolate Ganache (page 221), at room temperature

Chocolate sprinkles; silver, black, and steel-colored dragees; and Meringue Mushrooms (page 243) for decorating

2 oz / 55g halva, broken up

1   Dust a clean, dry kitchen towel generously with confectioners' sugar.

2   Invert the hot cake onto the prepared towel. Carefully peel the parchment paper from the bottom of the cake, dust the surface with more confectioners' sugar, drape the peeled parchment back onto the cake, and tightly roll up the cake, starting at the short end. Let the cake cool completely.

3   Unroll the cooled cake and spread the buttercream over it in an even layer. Then roll the cake back up into a log.

4   Using a serrated knife, cut off one-fourth of the log at an angle. Place the larger section of the log on a serving plate and place the cut portion on top, to create the illusion of a branch.

5   Spread the ganache over the entire cake and drag the top of a metal spatula through the ganache to give it the appearance of wood. Using the tip of metal decorating spatula, create a loose spiral on the cut ends to mimic the rings of a log. Decorate with chocolate sprinkles, dragees, and meringue mushrooms. Sprinkle the halva over all.

6   Serve the cake at room temperature.

mod yule log

This Yule log is for the next generation, who may want to go for a sleeker, less-fussy finish, one that is not quite so stuffy but still sharp. Despite the super-impressive spires of chocolate bark on the outside of this cake, it is so simple to make. The cake underneath can be whatever your mood suggests. Every year when my best friend throws a holiday party, I bring her favorite peanut butter–chocolate cake. It always makes quite a splash as I walk through the house.

Makes about 12 servings

cake academy review

CRUMB-COATING →
page 49

1 recipe Chocolate Devil's Food Cake (page 125), baked in four 6-inch / 15cm cake pans

1 cup / 240g Dark Chocolate Ganache (page 221), at room temperature

1 cup / 120g crushed, roasted salted peanuts

1 recipe Ultra-Rich Buttercream (page 210, flavored with peanut butter)

2 recipes Chocolate Bark (page 239)

Meringue Mushrooms (page 243) for decorating

1 Place one cake layer on a serving plate.

2 Spread one-third of the ganache over the cake, sprinkle 2 Tbsp of the peanuts over the ganache, and, using an offset spatula, cover in a ¼-inch / 6mm-thick layer of the buttercream. Set the next cake layer over the buttercream and repeat with the ganache, peanuts, and buttercream. Repeat this again with the third layer and then top with the final cake.

3 If desired, at this point, you could crumb-coat the cake with some of the buttercream.

4 Decorate the cake with a smooth layer of the remaining buttercream. Using the tip of a metal decorating spatula, create a loose spiral on the top of the cake to mimic the rings of a log. While the buttercream is still soft, add the chocolate bark to the sides, overlapping the pieces slightly and gently pressing them into the buttercream to resemble tree bark. (At this point, you can store the cake, covered, in the refrigerator for up to 1 day.)

5 When ready to serve, put a small pile of the remaining peanuts along the base of the cake and decorate with the meringue mushrooms. Serve at room temperature.

BAKER'S NOTE

If you have leftover chocolate from your bark, spread it out on a piece of parchment paper and let harden. It can be used for your next project.

My dad has always been ahead of his time. He ate local and kept honeybees way back in the 1970s, long before it was cool to have rooftop hives in Brooklyn. I only wish I'd paid closer attention when I was a kid, but, back then, I just looked forward to the honey. I created this cake (pictured on page 182) in the shape of a skep (which is an ancient dome-shaped beehive made of twisted straw) for his birthday. The cake is made of layers of banana cake, topped with honey buttercream, walnut praline for crunch, and marzipan bees. Eccentric beekeepers, like my dad, and little kids will all love this one.

beehive cake

Makes about 16 servings

cake academy review

TRIMMING THE TOP →
page 47

CRUMB-COATING →
page 49

1 recipe Banana Cake batter (see page 132)

MARZIPAN BEES

¼ cup / 55g marzipan

Black gel food coloring (see page 11)

Gold luster dust

¼ cup / 25g raw sliced almonds

1 recipe Crushed Praline (page 244; made with walnuts)

2 recipes Honey Buttercream (page 211)

Yellow paste food coloring

1   Preheat the oven to 350°F / 175°C. Generously grease two 8-inch / 20cm round cake pans, then line them with greased parchment paper. Grease and flour an 8-inch / 20cm metal mixing bowl.

2   Evenly divide the cake batter among the prepared pans and bowl.

3   Bake until a tester comes out clean, 35 to 40 minutes. The cake in the bowl may take several minutes more. Let the cakes cool completely.

4   To make the marzipan bees: Meanwhile, take twelve small pieces of the marzipan and roll between your fingers, until they are a ½-inch / 1.3cm-long narrow cylinder or capsule shape. Taper one end slightly to become the back of the bee.

5   Using a food-safe paintbrush or a toothpick and black food coloring, paint stripes on the marzipan. Let the stripes dry. Then, using a small, clean paintbrush, paint gold luster dust between the black stripes.

6   Press the sliced almonds into the sides of the marzipan to create the bees' wings. Put the finished bees on toothpicks and set aside.

7   In a food processor fitted with the metal blade, pulverize the praline until there are small bits about the size of pine nuts or smaller—but not as fine as powder.

8   In two separate bowls, divide the buttercream in half and add the praline to one batch and stir a few drops of yellow food coloring into the other.

9   Invert one of the cake rounds onto a serving plate.

10 Using an offset spatula, spread half of the praline buttercream over the cake, making sure it goes all the way to the edge. Place the second cake round over the frosting and spread with the remaining praline buttercream. Top with the cake baked in the bowl (trim the bottom flat) as the final layer.

11 If desired, at this point, you could crumb-coat the cake with some of the yellow buttercream.

12 Put a thick layer of yellow buttercream over the cake. Using a small icing spatula, and starting at the top of the cake, create a spiral by slowly spinning the cake turner and moving the spatula downward.

13 Place the bees' toothpicks into the cake to create the illusion of bees buzzing around. Serve the cake immediately.

This beauty just demands a spotlight at center stage. In culinary school, the opera torte is an exercise in creating multiple layers of perfectly balanced flavors and proportions, so that the stripes are bold to the eye and the palate. But that seems a wee bit stodgy, so I wanted to make an updated, brighter version. Much like an opera torte, the elegantly orchestrated layers of this cake also result in a showstopper. This cake still has some of the old elements, and the technique is similar, but now it's a real diva.

This recipe is also a fun opportunity to stretch those baking skills, baking a Joconde, making a downy buttercream, and mixing a chocolate ganache with its glinting sheen. But the grand finale happens when we break out a cook's best friend: the kitchen blowtorch. Seriously, nothing outside of my darling family gives me the unadulterated joy of sparking up and torching something sweet.

blackberry diva cake

Makes about 16 servings

1 recipe Ultra-Rich Buttercream (page 210)

¾ cup / 225g blackberry preserves

1 recipe Joconde (Almond Sponge Cake; page 145), still in the baking pan

½ recipe Dark Chocolate Ganache (page 221; see Baker's Note)

2 pints / 240g fresh blackberries

½ recipe Fluffy Swiss Meringue Topping (page 217; see Baker's Note)

1 In a medium bowl, combine the buttercream and preserves and stir until very smooth.

2 Using an offset metal spatula, spread the buttercream evenly over the cake. Transfer to the refrigerator and let set until solid, about 20 minutes.

3 Remove the cake from the refrigerator, pour the ganache over the chilled buttercream, and spread it evenly. Refrigerate the cake again until all the layers are solid, about 45 minutes.

4 Remove the cake from the refrigerator, run a knife all the way around the edges of the cake to loosen from the pan, cover with plastic wrap (this will protect the ganache when the cake is inverted), and invert the cake onto the back of a second baking sheet. Peel the parchment from the bottom of the cake and invert again onto a large cutting board.

5 Using a chef's knife, cut the cake in half on the long side and then in three equal sections from the short side, so you have six identical rectangles. Stack the six sections so you have a tall cake with many layers, making sure the layers are straight. Using a knife dipped in hot water, trim any uneven cake. (At this point, you can store in the refrigerator, covered, for up to 48 hours.)

6 When ready to serve, cover the top of the cake with the fresh blackberries.

7 Take a blob of the meringue topping between your fingers and press it against a blackberry. Pull the blob away, it will break off in a wispy curl. Repeat with the remaining meringue and blackberries. Using a kitchen blowtorch, toast the tops of the meringue.

BAKER'S NOTES

You want the ganache to be a pourable consistency but not so warm that it will melt the buttercream.

Prepare the topping just before decorating and serving the cake.

My mother's best friend, Barbara Mckeon, made one of my wedding cakes. Barbara is many, many things, but she's not a professional baker, so it was a true act of love and a sense of adventure that inspired her to make the cake for my big day. Now that I've been to culinary school and made dozens of wedding cakes myself, I'm even more impressed with Barbara for baking my cake, which perfectly represented (including a big dose of wabi-sabi) the sweetest day of my life.

I love making wedding cakes, and there are a few tricks I can share that will make your endeavor more fun and ensure the special cake will stand tall (and straight). Following are the nuts and bolts of assembling a wedding cake. Give yourself plenty of time, so you're not feeling rushed (I'll let you know what can be done ahead), and put on some good music. Something relaxing. The most important thing is to put love and joy into this cake!

I use a super-classic genoise cake, but you can make a wedding cake with just about any of the layer cakes from chapters 4 and 5. The bride and groom will determine the flavor, but no matter what they choose, you'll know how to set it up by following these directions.

Assembling and decorating this cake is best done at the wedding site. Trust me, driving with a stacked cake is a level of stress no one needs. You will need the following supports: six straws or wooden dowels, cut to the exact height of the 10-inch / 25cm bottom layer, and four straws, cut to the exact height of the 8-inch / 20cm layer. The goal is to have the straws bear the weight of the cake above, without being seen. Position them so they will be directly under the cardboard round and support the layer above as you assemble the whole cake.

wedding cake

The yield for this three-tiered wedding cake does not include the top layer, because some couples like to freeze that top piece for their first anniversary. (The tradition of eating year-old cake is a mystery to me, but that's for them to decide.)

Makes about 60 servings

cake academy review

TRIMMING THE TOP → page 47

CRUMB-COATING → page 49

PUTTING ON THE FINAL LAYER OF FROSTING → page 49

BASIC PIPING DESIGNS → page 56

CAKES

4 recipes Brown Butter Genoise batter (see page 146)

STRAWBERRY BUTTERCREAM FILLING

2 recipes Swiss Meringue Buttercream (page 216), divided

1 cup / 300g strawberry Quick Jam (see page 236) or preserves, divided

1½ cups / 210g finely chopped fresh strawberries, divided

1 Tbsp vanilla extract (see page 12), divided

2 cups / 480ml flavored Simple Syrup (see page 226; I use Pink Hibiscus Rose Syrup, but choose any flavor you want)

ICING

3 recipes Swiss Meringue Buttercream (page 216; see Baker's Note)

Scraped seeds from 1 vanilla bean (see Baker's Note)

CONTINUED

1   To prepare the cakes: Preheat the oven to 375°F / 190°C. Generously grease the bottoms of two 6-inch / 15cm (small), two 8-inch / 20cm (medium), and two 10-inch / 25cm (large) round cake pans, then line them with greased parchment paper.

2   Pour the batter into the prepared pans. Don't fill the pans more than halfway but, most important, do fill them all the same height, so they look even when cutting. Set the pans on baking sheets.

3   Bake until the cakes are golden and a tester comes out clean: about 18 minutes for the small, about 20 minutes for the medium, and about 25 minutes for the large. Let the cakes cool completely, then remove from pans, transfer to a baking sheet, and refrigerate for about 1 hour (or freeze for 30 minutes). Chilled cake is easier to cut, fill, trim, and frost. Trim the tops and cut the chilled cakes horizontally in half to make two layers each. Remove the parchment paper from the bottoms of the cakes.

4   To make the strawberry filling: In the bowl of a stand mixer fitted with the paddle attachment, combine 1 recipe of the buttercream, ½ cup / 150g of the jam, ¾ cup / 105g of the strawberries, and 1½ tsp of the vanilla and mix on low speed until incorporated and very smooth, about 5 minutes. Repeat with the remaining 1 recipe buttercream, ½ cup / 150g jam, ¾ cup / 105g strawberries, and 1½ tsp vanilla.

5   Set one of the large cakes on a 10-inch / 25cm cardboard round. Using a pastry brush, lightly brush with the simple syrup. It should not be sopping wet but should have just a thin layer of the soak across the whole cake. Using an offset metal decorating spatula, evenly spread some of the strawberry filling over the soaked cake, so it is about ¼ inch / 6mm thick.

6   Place the next large cake layer over the strawberry filling, brush with the simple syrup, and spread more of the filling over the soaked cake.

7   Repeat with a third large cake layer and more filling and then top with the final large cake layer, brushing with simple syrup. Cover this bottom layer of the wedding cake with plastic wrap and store in the refrigerator for up to 12 hours.

8   Repeat this entire process with the medium and small cake layers. Using a serrated knife, trim off any dark edges from the cakes and make sure all the sides are even.

9   To make the icing: In a large bowl, combine the 3 recipes buttercream with the vanilla seeds and stir until smooth.

10 Using a metal decorating spatula and a thin layer of the icing, crumb-coat one of the filled cake layers. Repeat with the remaining cake layers. Freeze the cake layers for about 20 minutes until set hard.

11 Put a large blob of icing on the top of one of the cake layers. Using the spatula, spread the icing flat on top and push it ever so slightly beyond the edge of the cake.

12 Spackle the sides with icing, trying not to smooth it out yet. Once the whole layer is well covered, smooth out the sides. Once the sides are straight and smooth, use your metal decorating spatula to smooth the top. Repeat with the remaining cake layers.

13 Push the supportive dowels or straws, straight down, through the top of the large cake layer until they hit the cardboard under the cake. The dowels should be positioned evenly around the cake within the 8-inch / 20cm circle of the next tier, so they will not show once the medium cake is placed over them. Mark the dowels where the line of buttercream hits, then remove them and cut so they are exactly the same height as the cake. Repeat this process with the dowels or straws in the medium cake layer.

14 Transfer the doweled but not stacked cake layers to the refrigerator. Once solidly chilled, you can wrap in plastic wrap for up to 1 day.

15 Be sure the cake stand or serving platter is stable and able to withstand the weight of the cake. Position the large, bottom cake layer in the center of the cake stand. Carefully position the medium, middle cake layer in the center of the layer below it. Then stack the small cake layer on top.

16 Fit a pastry bag with a decorating tip (I use Ateco star tip #820) and fill with the remaining icing. Pipe a simple border along the base of each of the layers to hide the cardboard rounds that are supporting them and to give the presentation some bling. Decorate to your heart's desire. (If the bride and groom want to use fresh flowers, make sure they aren't poisonous.)

17 Let the cake come to room temperature before cutting. The buttercream is luscious when served at room temperature, but it becomes too firm and loses its smooth texture when served cold. This isn't typically an issue, since the cake is usually on display.

BAKER'S NOTES

If you need to figure out the proper size to cut for each serving, there is a good cutting guide at wilton.com.

If you've made the buttercream ahead and chilled it, you will need to put each batch in a stand mixer fitted with the paddle attachment, mix on low speed until smooth, and then combine them.

You may have extra buttercream after icing the exterior of the cake. Use it to make flowers, or freeze it for another project.

Adding the vanilla seeds to the butter will give it a boost of flavor, but also adds a speckled finish. If you prefer a pure white, add 1 Tbsp vanilla extract instead.

Supports

Stacking

Finishing touches

ROLLED AND FANCY CAKES

8 icing, frostings, buttercreams, and ganaches

This chapter is literally the icing on the cakes. The loving touch can be anything from a sleek finish with glitz and glam or just a comfy sweater of a covering. But first, what's the difference between frosting and icing? Frosting is thick and is spread onto a cake with a spatula, and you really want to run your finger through it. Icing is thinner and clings to the cake, like an elegant gown. Ganache is a CHOCOLATE covering that can be poured or spread like frosting, depending on its temperature, and your mood.

You'll notice that I've included several "buttercreams" in this chapter. Each one has a unique consistency. You may want to try them all eventually to land on your favorite. I tend to use them for different occasions and cakes. Go with super-familiar American Buttercream (page 213) or bust a move and try one you've never had before. The Italian meringue version (see page 215) is similar, just a touch lighter and fluffier, but it requires a candy thermometer to make. German Buttercream (page 214) is based on custard, so it's super-rich and creamy. Then there is also Ultra-Rich Buttercream (page 210), which is silky smooth and may be my family's favorite.

confectioners' sugar icing

It doesn't get any easier than this; just two ingredients stirred together in a bowl and you have a sweet and decorative finish to a cake. It is also a blank canvas for other flavors, so you can dress it up to match any cake you bake. This icing will set up with a sugary crust, so use it as soon as you make it.

Makes about ½ cup / 120ml

1 cup / 120g confectioners' sugar, sifted

3 Tbsp heavy whipping cream, plus more as needed

1 In a small bowl, combine the confectioners' sugar and cream, then stir with a spoon to mix into a thick paste.

2 Add additional cream, 1 Tbsp at a time, to achieve a consistency that can be drizzled over your cake. You should be able to draw a line through the icing with the back of a spoon.

3 Use immediately.

VARIATION: FLAVORED ICING

The sugar icing is just sweet, without much flavor on its own, which means you can add all the personality you want by adding zest, spices, or just about anything you can dream up. Start slow with the flavor, and you can always add more to build more intensity. Proceed as directed and mix in any of the following.

Cardamom—¼ tsp ground cardamom

Citrus—½ tsp lemon, lime, orange, or grapefruit zest

Cranberries—2 Tbsp pulverized cranberries (pulse whole cranberries in a food processor)

Espresso—1 tsp espresso powder

Ginger—½ tsp freshly grated ginger

Maple syrup—1 to 2 Tbsp pure maple syrup

Pumpkin spice—½ tsp pumpkin pie spice

Raspberries—3 crushed raspberries, or more for brighter pink color and additional flavor

chocolate frosting

This is the ultimate chocolate frosting, nothing less. It will pair with anything from White Cake (page 119) to Chocolate Devil's Food Cake (page 125), for a chocolate lover's dream come true.

This fudgy covering (pictured on page 202) will set with a sugar crust, so spread it just after mixing.

Makes enough to cover one 8-inch / 20cm triple-layer cake or two 9 by 13-inch / 23 by 33cm sheet cakes

½ cup / 120ml heavy whipping cream, plus more as needed

1 cup / 220g unsalted butter

1 tsp espresso powder

1 pinch kosher salt

16 oz / 450g bittersweet chocolate, coarsely chopped

2½ cups / 300g confectioners' sugar (sifted if lumpy)

1 In a medium saucepan over low heat, combine the cream, butter, espresso powder, and salt and bring to a gentle simmer, stirring often until the butter is melted. Add the chocolate and swirl the pan until the chocolate is submerged in the hot cream. Let the mixture sit for about 3 minutes, then whisk until smooth.

2 Pour the mixture into the bowl of a stand mixer fitted with the paddle attachment. Let the mixture cool to room temperature; it will become quite thick as the butter and chocolate set.

3 Turn the mixer speed to low, add the confectioners' sugar, a little at a time, and beat until smooth and spreadable. If the frosting is at all grainy, add additional cream, 1 Tbsp at a time, until it's smooth. The frosting will be quite soft but firm enough to cling to the cake and spread evenly.

4 Use immediately.

BAKER'S NOTE

On a hot day, the mixture may not thicken adequately. Don't despair! You can just pop the bowl into the refrigerator for several minutes before adding the confectioners' sugar.

ICING, FROSTINGS, BUTTERCREAMS, AND GANACHES

ermine frosting

This frosting is pure, homemade joy! When I made it, my boys said it tasted just like the stuff you buy in the can from the grocery store. That may seem like a strange compliment, but I was thrilled. It has that smooth, lusciously thick texture, and it's sweet but not quite as sweet as those cans. You can add your own flavors and make it match your vision for your cake; see American Buttercream (page 213) for ideas.

Makes enough to cover
one 8-inch / 20cm triple-layer
cake or two 9 by 13-inch /
23 by 33cm sheet cakes

cake academy review

CREAMING → page 33

2 cups / 480ml
whole milk

1¾ cups / 350g
granulated sugar

⅔ cup / 80g
all-purpose flour

½ tsp kosher salt

Seeds scraped from
1 vanilla bean or 1 Tbsp
vanilla extract (see page 12)

1 tsp almond, orange, or
other naturally flavored
extract

2 cups / 450g unsalted
butter, at room temperature

1   In a large saucepan over medium heat, whisk together the milk, sugar, flour, salt, vanilla, and almond extract and bring to a boil, whisking continuously. Once the mixture boils, continue to cook and whisk for about 3 minutes; it will become quite thick and glossy, like pudding.

2   Pour the mixture into a shallow container and cover with plastic wrap, pressed directly onto the surface. Let cool to room temperature, or freeze for about 20 minutes until just cool to the touch but not frozen.

3   In a stand mixer fitted with the paddle attachment, beat the butter on high speed until light and fluffy, about 1 minute. Turn the speed to medium-high, add the cooled mixture, and beat until smooth and light in texture and color.

4   Use immediately.

BAKER'S NOTES

Make sure your butter is soft but still firm enough to handle without your fingers squishing into it. If the butter is too soft, the frosting won't have enough body to cover the cake.

This frosting really absorbs flavors, so taste it once it is finished and smooth to see if you need another splash of vanilla.

I shouldn't have favorites, but, really, I'd eat this icing on just about anything, including toast. It's just the right amount of sweet, without being cloying, so it goes perfectly with super-rich Chocolate Devil's Food Cake (page 125), Ultimate Carrot Cake (page 136), or Hummingbird Cake (page 135). You can even pair it with Olive Oil–Chiffon Cake (page 153) or Pumpkin-Mocha Swirl Bundt Cake (page 78). I think you get the picture of its versatility. There are no rules, so whatever you want to slather it on will be made all the better for it.

Because this frosting is so soft, it is hard to pipe decoratively, unless you chill it first.

cream cheese frosting

Makes enough to cover one 8-inch / 20cm triple-layer cake or two 9 by 13-inch / 23 by 33cm sheet cakes

1½ lb / 680g cream cheese, at room temperature

1½ cups / 330g unsalted butter, at room temperature

2 tsp vanilla extract (see page 12)

¼ tsp lemon extract (optional)

2 tsp freshly squeezed lemon juice

5 cups / 600g confectioners' sugar

2 Tbsp Lyle's Golden Syrup (see Baker's Note; optional)

1   In the bowl of a stand mixer fitted with the paddle attachment, beat the cream cheese on low speed until it's smooth and there are no lumps. Scrape down the bowl and paddle often.

2   Add the butter to the cream cheese and continue mixing until smooth, scraping often. You want to make sure none of the cream cheese or butter is sticking to the paddle, or it may end up creating lumps. Mix in the vanilla, lemon extract (if using), and lemon juice.

3   Slowly add the confectioners' sugar and then the golden syrup (if using) and continue mixing until smooth.

4   If the frosting is thin and soft, you may want to chill it to give it more body and allow you to fill and decorate with more ease. Just cover the bowl and refrigerate until the frosting is firm, up to 24 hours, then return to the stand mixer fitted with the paddle attachment and mix on low speed until smooth.

5   Use immediately.

BAKER'S NOTE

Golden syrup is like a light caramel but not as overpowering a flavor; it just adds a nuance that is exquisite. Golden syrup is a staple in most British kitchens, but if you happen to find it in your own grocery in the United States, give it a try.

ICING, FROSTINGS, BUTTERCREAMS, AND GANACHES

This is one of my favorite buttercreams because it is rich, luscious, and goes with just about any cake for any occasion, like Espresso Sponge Cake (page 144) or simple Yellow Cake (page 122). It also uses up all the egg yolks I tend to hoard from my angel food, pavlova and other egg white–only recipes. This recipe is inspired by one of my baking mentors, Flo Braker, from her book *The Simple Art of Perfect Baking*. Flo's recipe required cooking a hot sugar syrup and pouring it carefully into whipping egg yolks, which required a candy thermometer and a sense of adventure that some home bakers may feel intimidated by. I simply cook the yolks and sugar over a double boiler (as I do with the Swiss Meringue Buttercream on page 216), whip the cooked yolk mixture, and add butter. Much simpler, and the results are what cake dreams are made of. See American Buttercream (page 213) for flavor ideas.

ultra-rich buttercream

Makes enough to cover one 8-inch / 20cm triple-layer cake or two 9 by 13-inch / 23 by 33cm sheet cakes

cake academy review

LIGHT-AS-AIR EGG FOAM → page 36

1 cup / 200g granulated sugar

8 egg yolks, at room temperature

2 cups / 440g unsalted butter, at room temperature

1 Tbsp vanilla extract (see page 12)

¼ tsp kosher salt

1 In the bowl of a stand mixer fitted with the whisk attachment, combine the sugar and egg yolks and beat on medium speed to mix. The mixture will be very thick and grainy.

2 Put 1 inch / 2.5cm of water in the bottom of a double boiler or a medium saucepan and bring to a gentle simmer over medium-low heat. Place the bowl with the yolk mixture over the simmering water and stir the mixture with a rubber spatula until the sugar is completely melted. Brush down the sides of the bowl with the spatula to make sure all the sugar is melted. Feel the mixture between your fingers to check for graininess. Once all the sugar has melted and the mixture is smooth, the syrup is hot enough (140°F / 60°C) to be safe to consume.

3 Return the bowl to the stand mixer fitted with a clean whisk attachment and beat on medium-high speed until the egg foam is light, fluffy, and glossy and the bowl feels just about room temperature. (If the egg foam isn't cooled sufficiently, the butter will melt when you add it.)

4 Once the egg foam is whipped and cooled, turn the mixer speed to medium, add the butter, 2 Tbsp at a time, and beat until incorporated. Turn the speed to low, add the vanilla and salt, and mix until incorporated.

5 Use immediately or transfer to an airtight container and store in the refrigerator for up to 7 days or in the freezer for up to 1 month.

BAKER'S NOTE

Be sure to clean the whisk attachment after combining the sugar and eggs to prevent getting any undissolved sugar crystals in your smooth buttercream.

honey buttercream

This is Swiss Meringue Buttercream (page 216) made with honey instead of sugar, so you have the lovely scent and flavor of whatever honey you pick. There are more assertive honeys that will have a strong flavor and be a real personality in your cake, as well as mellow varieties that will just create elegant, easy undertones. This buttercream is a natural fit for Beehive Cake (page 194).

Makes enough to cover one 8-inch / 20cm triple-layer cake or two 9 by 13-inch / 23 by 33cm sheet cakes

cake academy review

LIGHT-AS-AIR
EGG FOAM → page 36

¾ cup / 255g honey

½ cup / 120ml egg whites (from about 3 eggs), at room temperature

1½ cups / 330g unsalted butter, at room temperature

2 Tbsp very strong espresso, or 2 tsp espresso powder diluted in 1 Tbsp water (optional)

1 tsp vanilla extract (see page 12)

¼ tsp kosher salt

1   In the bowl of a stand mixer, combine the honey and egg whites.

2   Put 1 inch / 2.5cm of water in the bottom of a double boiler or a medium saucepan and bring to a gentle simmer over medium-low heat. Place the bowl with the egg mixture over the simmering water and stir the mixture with a rubber spatula until melted, hot (140°F / 60°C), and thin.

3   Place the bowl on the stand mixer fitted with the whisk attachment and beat on medium-high speed until the egg foam is light, fluffy, and glossy and the bowl feels just about room temperature. (If the egg foam isn't cooled sufficiently, the butter will melt when you add it.)

4   Once the egg foam is whipped and cooled, turn the mixer speed to medium, add the butter, 2 Tbsp at a time, and beat until incorporated. Once you have finished adding the butter and it has mixed for about 1 minute, the buttercream will be creamy and glossy looking again. Turn the speed to low; add the espresso (if using), vanilla, and salt; and mix until well blended.

5   Use immediately or transfer to an airtight container and store in the refrigerator for up to 7 days or in the freezer for up to 1 month.

BAKER'S NOTE

After you have added about half of the butter, it may look curdled and runny. This is normal, and you should continue adding the rest of the butter.

ICING, FROSTINGS, BUTTERCREAMS, AND GANACHES

roasted chestnut buttercream

Roasted chestnuts evoke the holidays and classic Christmas songs playing on the radio. The richness of the nuts makes for a decadent addition to chocolate, but is especially delicious on a dacquoise (see page 157).

Makes enough to cover one 8-inch / 20cm triple-layer cake or two 9 by 13-inch / 23 by 33cm sheet cakes

1½ cups / 360ml whole milk

8 oz / 225g roasted chestnuts

3 Tbsp granulated sugar

Seeds scraped from 1 vanilla bean, or 2 tsp vanilla extract (see page 12)

1 recipe Swiss Meringue Buttercream (page 216)

1 In a medium saucepan over medium heat, combine the milk, chestnuts, sugar, and vanilla; stir to mix; and bring to a simmer. Let simmer until the milk reduces to about ½ cup / 120ml.

2 Transfer the nuts and cooking liquid to a blender and puree until they form a smooth paste. Let cool to room temperature.

3 In a stand mixer fitted with the paddle attachment, combine the puree and buttercream and mix at medium-low speed until smooth.

4 Use immediately or transfer to an airtight container and store in the refrigerator for up to 7 days or in the freezer for up to 1 month.

american buttercream

This is the buttery frosting most of us grew up loving. It is by far the easiest and fastest buttercream to make. It comes together in a snap and is a blank canvas for whatever flavor you can imagine. I've made some tasty suggestions in the variation, but you can get super-creative. Oh, the places you'll go!

This creamy covering will set with a sugary crust as it sits, so spread it just after mixing.

Makes enough to cover one 8-inch / 20cm triple-layer cake or two 9 by 13-inch / 23 by 33cm sheet cakes

6 cups / 720g confectioners' sugar

1½ cups / 330g unsalted butter, at room temperature

1½ Tbsp vanilla extract (see page 12)

1 tsp almond extract

¼ tsp kosher salt

¼ to ½ cup / 60 to 120ml heavy whipping cream

1   In a stand mixer fitted with the paddle attachment, combine the confectioners' sugar and butter and beat on low speed until combined.

2   Turn the mixer speed to medium and beat until a thick paste forms. Scrape down the bowl and paddle, then add the vanilla, almond extract and salt and beat for a few seconds more.

3   With the mixer on low speed, add enough of the cream, 1 Tbsp at a time, to make the frosting spreadable.

4   Use immediately.

VARIATION: FLAVORED BUTTERCREAM

Buttercream is just waiting for you to add color and flavor. Here are some of my favorite options. Be careful not to add too much liquid or you may change the consistency of the buttercream and make it hard to spread or pipe. Proceed as directed, adding one of the following flavorings, and stir or beat until incorporated.

Berry Buttercream—Add ⅓ cup / 35g of your favorite thick berry preserves.

Caramel Buttercream—Add ⅓ cup / 115g Thick Caramel Sauce (page 218).

Chocolate Buttercream—Add 4 oz / 115g semisweet bittersweet, milk, or white chocolate, melted and cooled to room temperature, with the vanilla and almond extract.

Citrus Buttercream—Add 2 tsp lemon, lime, orange, or grapefruit zest.

Espresso Buttercream—Add 1 tsp espresso powder mixed with 1 tsp water.

Nutella Buttercream—Add ½ cup / 140g Nutella.

Peanut Butter Buttercream—Add ½ cup / 140g peanut butter.

Spice Buttercream—Add 2 tsp cinnamon or pumpkin pie spice.

Tahini Buttercream—Add 4 oz / 115g bittersweet chocolate, melted and cooled to room temperature, and ⅓ cup / 95g tahini, plus 4 oz / 115g chopped halva pieces (optional).

BAKER'S NOTE

If you have leftover buttercream, you can freeze it. Just wrap it in plastic, so it doesn't absorb the smells and flavors of your freezer. To defrost, leave it wrapped and bring it fully to room temperature before using. Cold buttercream will have a hard time emulsifying. If you are close to room temp but it still looks "broken" while you're mixing, wave the metal bowl over the heat of your stove or a pan of simmering water. You can also wave your kitchen blowtorch over the metal bowl a few times, just to warm the bowl slightly—another reason to have a blowtorch.

german buttercream

This recipe combines two of my favorite things, luscious pastry cream and butter. Part pudding and part frosting, the texture of this buttercream is sublime—it's like velvet and is super-rich. The flavor profile can be made to match whatever cake creation you are making. See American Buttercream (page 213) for flavor ideas.

Makes enough to cover one 8-inch / 20cm triple-layer cake or two 9 by 13-inch / 23 by 33cm sheet cakes

2 cups / 440g unsalted butter, at room temperature

2 cups / 240g confectioners' sugar

1 Tbsp vanilla extract (see page 12)

1 recipe Pastry Cream (page 231), chilled

1 pinch kosher salt

1. In the bowl of a stand mixer fitted with the paddle attachment, combine the butter and confectioners' sugar and beat on medium-low speed until very soft. Mix in the vanilla.

2. Using a rubber spatula, stir the pastry cream until very smooth.

3. Turn the mixer speed to medium, add the pastry cream and salt to the butter mixture, and beat until light and smooth.

4. Use immediately or transfer to an airtight container and store in the refrigerator for up to 7 days or in the freezer for up to 1 month.

italian meringue buttercream

Italian meringue buttercream has a reputation for being the strongest of the buttercreams, in terms of holding up on a cake, but I feel its real strength is in its texture. This buttercream is made from pouring boiling sugar syrup, brought to just the right temperature on a candy thermometer, into whipping egg whites, thereby cooking them and making them safe to eat. This whips up into an incredibly light meringue. See American Buttercream (page 213) for flavor ideas.

Makes enough to cover one 8-inch / 20cm triple-layer cake or two 9 by 13-inch / 23 by 33cm sheet cakes

cake academy review

ITALIAN MERINGUE → page 40

PEAKS → page 38

¾ cup / 175ml water

2¼ cups / 450g granulated sugar

1 Tbsp light corn syrup

1 cup / 240ml egg whites (from about 6 eggs), at room temperature

3 cups / 680g unsalted butter, at room temperature

2 tsp vanilla extract (see page 12)

1 pinch kosher salt

1 Pour the water into a medium saucepan and clip a candy thermometer to the side. Add the sugar and corn syrup to the center of the pan, trying to keep the sugar from hitting the sides. Set the pan over high heat. Do not stir.

2 When the sugar mixture reaches 230°F / 110°C on the thermometer, add the egg whites to the bowl of a stand mixer fitted with the whisk attachment. Beat the egg whites on high speed, until medium peaks form, then turn the speed to low.

3 Remove the sugar from the heat when it reaches 248°F / 120°C and then slowly add to the egg whites, avoiding the whisk attachment so that the sugar doesn't spray and become spun sugar. Once all the sugar is added, turn the speed to high and whip until a glossy meringue is formed and it has cooled to room temperature, about 8 minutes.

4 Add the butter, 1 Tbsp at a time, to the meringue. The mixture will become soupy after a bit of butter has been added but will come back together once all the butter has been added.

5 Once you have finished adding the butter and it has mixed for about 1 minute, the buttercream will be creamy and glossy looking again. Turn the speed to low, add the vanilla and salt, and mix until well blended.

6 Use immediately or transfer to an airtight container and store in the refrigerator for up to 7 days or in the freezer for up to 1 month.

ICING, FROSTINGS, BUTTERCREAMS, AND GANACHES

This is my go-to buttercream, because it is fast, easy, and never fails me. The flavor is all about the butter, so use a good variety. If you go with something such as Kerrygold, just realize the buttercream will come out a romantic antique off-white color, as opposed to a bright white.

This buttercream goes through an awkward phase about midway through the addition of the butter. It will look soupy and as if it might never regain its composure, but it will, I promise. As long as you whip those eggs until they are room temperature and add room-temperature butter, it should snap back into shape; it may just take the very last tablespoon of butter to get it in line. See American Buttercream (page 213) for flavor ideas.

swiss meringue buttercream

Makes enough to cover one 8-inch / 20cm triple-layer cake or two 9 by 13-inch / 23 by 33cm sheet cakes

cake academy review

SWISS MERINGUE →
page 39

2 cups / 400g
granulated sugar

1 cup / 240ml egg whites
(from about 5 eggs),
at room temperature

3 cups / 660g unsalted
butter, at room temperature

1 tsp vanilla extract
(see page 12)

1 pinch kosher salt

1 In the bowl of a stand mixer fitted with the whisk attachment, combine the sugar and egg whites and beat on medium speed to mix. The mixture will be very thick and grainy.

2 Put 1 inch / 2.5cm of water in the bottom of a double boiler or a medium saucepan and bring to a gentle simmer over medium-low heat. Place the bowl with the sugar mixture over the simmering water and stir the mixture with a rubber spatula until the sugar is completely melted. Brush down the sides of the bowl with the spatula to make sure all the sugar is melted. Feel the mixture between your fingers to check for graininess. Once all the sugar has melted and the mixture is smooth, the syrup is hot enough (140°F / 60°C) to be safe to consume.

3 Return the bowl to the stand mixer fitted with a clean whisk attachment and beat on medium-high speed until the egg foam is light, fluffy, and glossy and the bowl feels just about room temperature. (If the egg foam isn't cooled sufficiently, the butter will melt when you add it.)

4 Once the egg foam is whipped and cooled, turn the mixer speed to medium, add the butter, 2 Tbsp at a time, and beat until incorporated. Turn the speed to low, add the vanilla and salt, and mix until incorporated.

5 Use immediately.

BAKER'S NOTE

After you have added about half of the butter, the mixture may look curdled and runny; this is normal, and you should continue adding the rest of the butter. Once you have finished adding the butter and it has mixed on medium speed for about a minute, the buttercream will be creamy and glossy looking again.

If you've ever been to my Instagram page, you KNOW how much I love a good meringue. I'm not only in love with its texture but also with how it takes on flavor, with its ability to achieve that Dr. Seuss look, with its light-as-air quality, and last, but certainly not least, that you can blowtorch it and make it toasty. Because I am so mad about meringue, I want you to be as well. You can use a spatula to cover the cake with an even layer of this topping and/or pipe the meringue into designs. It will become stiff and unspreadable if it sits after mixing.

You can use this meringue to top cakes or pipe it to make Meringue Mushrooms (page 243) to accompany Bûche de Noël (page 191) or Mod Yule Log (page 192).

fluffy swiss meringue topping

Makes enough to cover one 8-inch / 20cm triple-layer cake or two 9 by 13-inch / 23 by 33cm sheet cakes

cake academy review

SWISS MERINGUE →
page 39

PEAKS → page 38

1½ cups / 360ml egg whites (from about 7 eggs), at room temperature

3 cups / 600g granulated sugar

1 pinch kosher salt

2 tsp vanilla extract (see page 12)

1   In a medium saucepan over medium-low heat, bring 1 inch / 2.5cm of water to a simmer.

2   In the bowl of a stand mixer, combine the egg whites, sugar, and salt; place over the simmering water; and stir with a rubber spatula until the mixture is hot and all of the sugar has dissolved, about 5 minutes.

3   Remove the bowl from the heat and place onto the stand mixer fitted with the whisk attachment, then beat on high speed until very thick and glossy and stiff peaks form, about 5 minutes. If the meringue is not stiff enough, your spikes will slouch and lose the drama. Add the vanilla and mix well.

4   Use immediately.

ICING, FROSTINGS, BUTTERCREAMS, AND GANACHES

thick caramel sauce

This caramel sauce is thick enough to cling to cakes, like Turtle Cake (page 179), and sets up but not so much that it is hard. The beauty of this sauce comes from the complex flavor achieved by a perfectly cooked caramel. I like a really dark, smoky flavor in my caramel, but you may prefer something lighter and more delicate. What is perfect to you is all that matters. Just add the cream when the caramel turns the right hue of amber to lock in your perfect flavor. If you aren't sure what your caramel shade is, you may need to do some experimenting.

Makes about ¾ cup / 255g

cake academy review

CARAMELIZATION MAGIC
→ page 50

1 cup / 200g
granulated sugar

1 tsp corn syrup

¼ cup / 60ml water

⅓ cup / 80ml heavy
whipping cream (see
Baker's Note, page 229)

2 Tbsp unsalted butter

1 pinch kosher salt

1   Carefully place the sugar and corn syrup in the center of a medium saucepan, being careful not to get the sugar on the sides of the pan.

2   Add the water by gently running it down the sides of the pan, washing any rogue sugar back into the center. Do not stir, but gently run your finger through any dry spots of sugar, allowing the water to flow into it.

3   Once the mixture is all wet, set over high heat and bring to a boil, without stirring.

4   Allow the mixture to boil until the sugar just starts to turn amber along the edge. You can now stir without fear of crystallizing.

5   Continue cooking until the caramel just starts to smoke; be careful not to let it go too far.

6   Using a whisk with a long handle, carefully and slowly whisk the cream into the saucepan. The caramel will sputter. (If you add the cream too fast, the caramel may seize and become hard.)

7   Continue to cook and stir the mixture, until it eventually melts and becomes smooth. Add the butter and salt and whisk until smooth. Remove from the heat.

8   Let the caramel cool for 15 to 20 minutes, until it becomes thick. Transfer to an airtight container and store in the refrigerator for up to 4 days. Before using, microwave for 20 seconds to loosen to a pourable consistency.

BAKER'S NOTE

Once the caramel is cooled to room temperature, and thicker but pourable, drizzle it over a cake to add caramel flavor. You can swipe the sides with a spatula to get a softer look.

There is no simpler chocolate covering for a cake—just two ingredients that become something special when blended together. Ganache can be poured over a cake while still liquid to create the smoothest, cleanest finish you can get.

white chocolate ganache

Anywhere you use Dark Chocolate Ganache (page 221), you can replace it with this white chocolate version. I like my chocolate dark and a wee bit bitter, but I know there are white-chocolate fans out there, so this is for you.

Makes about 2 cups / 550g

cake academy review

POURED GANACHE →
page 52

½ cup / 120ml heavy whipping cream

16 oz / 450g white chocolate, coarsely chopped

½ tsp lemon or orange zest (optional)

1 In a medium saucepan over low heat, warm the cream until just simmering. Turn off the heat and add the chocolate and lemon zest (if using). Swirl the pan to make sure all the chocolate is submerged in the hot cream. Let sit for 3 minutes and then stir gently until smooth.

2 Transfer the ganache to an airtight container and store at room temperature for up to 2 days, or in the refrigerator for up to 1 week.

3 Gently warm the ganache over a pan of simmering water, forming a double boiler, to a pourable or spreadable consistency, depending on your needs.

ICING, FROSTINGS, BUTTERCREAMS, AND GANACHES

dark chocolate ganache

This ratio of chocolate to cream is meant for bittersweet or semisweet chocolate, so don't go using milk chocolate, which behaves more like White Chocolate Ganache (page 219). Use a really fine chocolate to get the best pour and sheen (see page 8 for my recommendations).

Makes about 3 cups / 780g

cake academy review

POURED GANACHE →
page 52

2 cups / 480ml heavy whipping cream

16 oz / 450g bittersweet chocolate, finely chopped

1 In a medium saucepan over low heat, warm the cream until just simmering. Turn off the heat and add the chocolate. Swirl the pan to make sure all of the chocolate is submerged in the hot cream. Let sit for 3 minutes and then gently stir until smooth.

2 Transfer the ganache to an airtight container and store at room temperature for up to 2 days, or in the refrigerator for up to 1 week.

3 Gently warm the ganache over a pan of simmering water, forming a double boiler, to a pourable or spreadable consistency, depending on your needs.

VARIATION: GANACHE FROSTING

Firm, fudgy ganache can be spread just like chocolate frosting, but it is even more decadently chocolatey. Let the ganache set to room temperature, it will be quite thick. Use a decorating spatula to put it on like buttercream or even pipe it to decorate a cake.

BAKER'S NOTE

All chocolate behaves differently, so if you are having any trouble achieving a smooth, glossy ganache, see "Zoë's Ganache SOS" on page 52.

fondant

I love the sleek elegance that fondant can add to a cake. It has the look of porcelain when left white, but it can be tinted any color you desire. I've never met anyone who truly loves the flavor of fondant, but making your own certainly makes it taste better than the store-bought varieties. Getting that taste comes at a slight cost, in that homemade fondant is a little more temperamental to use than commercial varieties. The called-for glycerin can be found online.

Makes enough to cover one
8-inch / 20cm triple-layer cake

cake academy review

ROLLED FONDANT →
page 53

2½ lb / 1.1kg
confectioners' sugar, divided

3 Tbsp cold water

1 Tbsp unflavored gelatin

½ cup / 120ml
light corn syrup

1½ Tbsp glycerin

1 Tbsp vanilla extract
(see page 12 and
Baker's Note)

Paste food coloring
(optional; see Baker's Note)

1   In the bowl of a stand mixer fitted with the paddle attachment, sift 1½ lb / 680g of the confectioners' sugar. Set aside.

2   In a separate metal bowl, stir together the water and gelatin. Allow to bloom for about 5 minutes.

3   Put 1 inch / 2.5cm of water in the bottom of a double boiler or a medium saucepan and bring to a gentle simmer over medium-low heat. Place the bowl of bloomed gelatin over the simmering water and warm until the gelatin is dissolved.

4   Remove the gelatin from the heat and stir in the corn syrup, glycerin, and vanilla.

5   Turn the mixer speed to low and slowly pour the gelatin mixture into the confectioners' sugar. Stop the mixer and scrape down the sides of the bowl with a rubber spatula, then turn the speed to medium and continue beating until well combined and very sticky, about 1 minute.

6   Scrape the sticky fondant onto a silicone pastry mat or a sheet of vinyl.

7   Sprinkle the remaining 16 oz / 450g confectioners' sugar over the fondant a little at a time. Using the palm of your hand, knead the sugar into the dough, then fold it over while continuing to work in the sugar. Using a plastic bowl scraper, continue to knead and work in the sugar until all of the sugar has been added and the fondant is smooth and forms a uniform ball.

8   Wrap the ball twice in plastic wrap and let it rest in a dry, cool spot for at least 12 hours, or up to 2 weeks. DO NOT REFRIGERATE! The fondant will get tacky and be impossible to work with if it is refrigerated. (If you unwrap it and it feels too hard, heat it in the microwave for 10 seconds at a time until it's workable.)

9   When you are ready to work with the fondant, unwrap it and knead it to make it smooth and pliable. If using food coloring, add it and then knead until the color is uniform throughout. (To prevent getting food coloring all over your hands, wear a pair of latex gloves.)

BAKER'S NOTES

If you want a PURE white fondant, then use clear vanilla extract. I used pure vanilla extract, and you can see that my fondant is a creamy porcelain color, which I really love. You can add other extract flavors as well but stick to those with an alcohol base, and not an oil extract. You don't want to add any fat to the recipe.

For coloring, use paste colors, which are thicker and more intense than liquids, so you don't need as much to achieve the color you desire.

9 fillings and flourishes

Sure, you can eat cake all by itself, with nothing more than a glass of milk. Sound familiar? But if you want to create a layered cake, you'll need something to put between those stacks of cake. In this chapter, you'll find everything from a simple berry jam that's perfect for Victory (Victoria) Sponge Cake (page 141) to a coconut pastry cream for Coconut Cream Cake (page 176), plus many more. You can also return to chapter 8 to view myriad choices for frostings, buttercreams, and ganaches, which are delicious options to sandwich between your layers.

Even with these fillings, sometimes you just want to go a bit extra with your cakes. The last part of this chapter includes flourishes, ideas to give you some creative ways to take a simple cake from rustic to showstopper.

This syrup is used to soak cakes to give them moisture and an infusion of flavor. You can create just about any flavor by steeping aromatic flowers, herbs, spices, zest, or teas in the syrup. Go bold with the flavor, since this should be used as just a light soak; you're not dousing the cake. The addition of corn syrup in the recipe prevents simple syrup from forming crystals as it cools.

The longer you let the lavender, flowers, herbs, spices, or zest steep in the simple syrup, the stronger the flavor will be. (I store it with the aromatics still in the syrup and strain it when I need it in a recipe.) Simple syrup can also be used to candy fruit, nuts, and even carrot peels (see page 248) for garnishes.

simple syrup

Makes 1 cup / 240ml

1 cup / 240ml water

1 cup / 200g granulated sugar

1 Tbsp light corn syrup

3 Tbsp dried or fresh lavender flowers (optional)

1 In a small saucepan over medium-high heat, combine the water, sugar, and corn syrup; bring to a simmer; and allow to simmer until the sugar is completely dissolved, about 10 minutes.

2 Add the lavender (if using) to the syrup and let simmer for 1 minute, then turn off the heat and let cool to room temperature.

3 Use immediately, or store in an airtight container in the refrigerator for up to 1 month.

VARIATION: FLAVORED SIMPLE SYRUP

The syrup you make gives the cake it's personality, so be adventurous with the flavors. I have listed a few of my favorites, but be bold and create your own. Any leftovers are great in a cocktail! Prepare as directed but in place of the lavender, use one of the following.

Cinnamon—Add two 3-inch / 7.5cm-long cinnamon sticks.

Citrus—Add the zest of 1 lemon, lime, orange, or grapefruit.

Espresso—Add 1 tsp instant espresso powder.

Ginger—Add one 1-inch / 2.5cm piece of ginger, peeled and cut into coins.

Mixed flowers—Add 2 Tbsp fresh or dried chopped rose, hibiscus, geranium, chamomile, or any edible-grade flower/petals (if using fresh, you may need more to get a strong flavor).

Pink hibiscus—Add 1 Tbsp rose petals plus 3 whole hibiscus flowers

Pink peppercorn—Add 1 Tbsp of these sweet peppercorns (gives a wonderful hint of heat to a pound cake).

Rhubarb—Add one bright-red stalk of rhubarb, cut into 1-inch / 2.5cm pieces (cook until the syrup turns pink).

Tea—Add 1 Tbsp loose tea; use a strainer or a tea ball and then strain before using.

Whole spices—Add 6 to 12 whole spices, such as cloves, star anise, and/or cardamom pods (the more you add, the stronger the flavor).

There is no better complement to a cake than perfectly whipped cream. It should be full of body but light and creamy. We all have had whipped cream that is over-whipped to the point of looking curdled and feeling greasy on the tongue, or a sadly deflated pile on top of an otherwise perfect slice of cake. There's a trick to getting cream to behave perfectly, and it's super-simple: go low and slow. Whipping on high speed may go faster, but you'll have huge air bubbles in your cream that aren't as strong; and they will pop, leaving you with weeping cream and a sad dessert. By whisking slowly, the cream will create tiny bubbles that are much more stable. You can achieve the perfect whipped cream by using a stand mixer, with a handheld mixer, or even whipping it by hand (a real workout, but then you'll feel as if you earned it!). A cake made with a perfectly whipped cream should last for a couple of days in the refrigerator.

Using confectioners' sugar not only sweetens the cream but you also don't have to whip it as long, because confectioners' sugar melts faster than granulated sugar. The tiny amount of starch that is added to most confectioners' sugar may also help with the stability, but the real power comes from how you whip it. Some like it sweet and others just want the cream to shine through, so use as much of the sugar as needed to suit your taste.

perfect whipped cream

| Makes about 3 cups / 720ml | 2 cups / 480ml heavy whipping cream | 1 to 2 Tbsp confectioners' sugar | 1 tsp vanilla extract (see page 12) |

1 In a stand mixer fitted with the whisk attachment, combine the cream, confectioners' sugar, and vanilla and beat on medium speed (you read that right) until just thick—it will start to leave marks from the whisk in the cream.

2 Remove the bowl from the mixer and, using the whisk attachment, continue whipping by hand for several seconds until the cream reaches the desired consistency; this way, you can ensure the mixer won't take it too far. Whipped cream is best used right away.

VARIATION: FLAVORED WHIPPED CREAM

Whipped cream is such a great place to add flavor to your cake, so by all means don't let this list be exhaustive. You should be bold and try new combinations to fit your mood.

Coffee Whipped Cream—Crush ½ cup / 40g coffee beans with a mortar and pestle. In a small saucepan over medium heat, bring 1 cup / 240ml of the whipping cream to a simmer. Add the coffee beans and let steep for about 20 minutes (the longer they sit, the stronger the flavor). Strain the mixture through a fine-mesh sieve and let chill thoroughly, at least 2 hours, then mix as directed.

Jammy Whipped Cream—Add ½ cup / 100g quick jam (see page 236) or any store-bought preserves to the whipping cream and mix as directed.

Peanut Butter or Nutella Whipped Cream—In a small saucepan over low heat, melt ½ cup / 130g peanut butter or ½ cup / 140g Nutella with ½ cup / 120ml of the whipping cream. Pour into a container, mix in the remaining 1½ cups / 360ml whipping cream, and refrigerate for 1 hour. Once the mixture is thoroughly chilled, mix as directed.

Raspberry Whipped Cream—Using a fork, gently smash ½ cup / 60g fresh raspberries until a few berries have broken up; leave some large pieces. Add the raspberries and any juice to the whipping cream and mix as directed.

FILLINGS AND FLOURISHES

caramel whipped cream

This is a decadent and rather sophisticated take on whipped cream. The trick is to cook the caramel as dark as possible, without burning it, so the flavor is intense and has that wonderful sweet and bitter balance, which pairs perfectly with whipped heavy cream.

Makes about 4 cups / 950ml

cake academy review

CARAMELIZATION
MAGIC → page 50

½ cup / 100g
granulated sugar

1 tsp corn syrup

3 Tbsp water

2 cups / 480ml heavy
whipping cream, divided
(see Baker's Note)

1 tsp vanilla extract
(see page 12)

1 Carefully place the sugar and corn syrup in the center of a medium saucepan, being careful not to get the sugar on the sides of the pan.

2 Add the water by gently running it down the sides of the pan, washing any rogue sugar back into the center. Do not stir, but gently run your finger through any dry spots of sugar, allowing the water to flow into it.

3 Once the mixture is all wet, set over high heat and bring to a boil, without stirring.

4 Allow the mixture to boil until the sugar just starts to turn amber along the edge.

5 When the caramel is dark amber in color, turn off the heat and slowly drizzle in 1 cup / 240 ml of the cream. The caramel will sputter and may seize up, which is normal. If it seizes, whisk gently until the caramelized sugar dissolves, which may take several minutes. Then whisk in the vanilla and remaining 1 cup / 240ml cream.

6 Strain the caramel cream through a fine-mesh sieve into a shallow container. Cover and refrigerate until well chilled, at least 2 hours or up to 1 day. (The cream needs to be thoroughly chilled and thick before whipping. You can throw it into the freezer for 15 minutes before refrigerating to speed this up a bit, but make sure it is chilled throughout).

7 In a stand mixer fitted with the whisk attachment, beat the chilled cream on medium speed (you read that right) until just thick—it will start to leave marks from the whisk in the cream.

8 Remove the bowl from the mixer and, using the whisk attachment, continue whipping by hand for several seconds until the cream reaches the desired consistency; this way, you can ensure the mixer won't take it too far. Whipped cream is best used right away.

BAKER'S NOTE

Warming the cream slightly before adding it to the hot caramel will decrease the chances of the caramel seizing.

pastry cream

Pastry cream is rich, luscious pudding that's used in all kinds of cakes, a true staple in the pastry kitchen. To flavor this silky custard, you can use pure vanilla extract or a scraped vanilla bean, which will give the most intense and satisfying flavor. If you have never tried baking with a real vanilla bean, try it now and you'll be hooked. The seeds will add a fragrant aroma and flecks of real vanilla. You can replace the vanilla bean with other flavors, like cinnamon sticks, star anise, ginger, instant espresso, or anything else you think up.

Makes about 3 cups / 730g

2 cups / 480ml whole milk

½ cup / 100g granulated sugar

¼ cup / 55g unsalted butter

1 pinch kosher salt

Seeds scraped from ½ vanilla bean, or 2 tsp vanilla extract (see page 12)

3 Tbsp cornstarch

1 egg, at room temperature

4 egg yolks, at room temperature

1 In a medium saucepan over medium heat, combine the milk, ¼ cup / 50g of the sugar, butter, salt, and vanilla; bring to a gentle boil; and then remove from the heat.

2 In a medium bowl, whisk together the cornstarch and remaining ¼ cup / 50g sugar. Add the egg and egg yolks and whisk into a smooth paste.

3 Whisk enough of the hot milk, a little at a time, into the egg mixture until it is warm to the touch. Once the eggs are tempered, pour the mixture back into the remaining milk in the pan.

4 Return the saucepan to medium-high heat and bring the mixture to a boil; continuously whisk for 3 minutes more or the pastry cream will separate once it cools.

5 If there are any lumps in the pastry cream, strain it through a fine-mesh sieve into a shallow container and cover with plastic wrap, pressed directly onto the surface, to prevent a skin from forming.

6 In a large bowl, add enough ice cubes and cold water to create a bath for the container to sit in without the water breaching the sides.

7 Set the container in the ice bath or place in the freezer until chilled, about 15 minutes before using. Or transfer to an airtight container and store in the refrigerator for up to 3 days.

coconut pastry cream

This creamy coconut pudding is good enough to eat straight out of the bowl with a spoon, but it's even better when paired with layers of Coconut Cream Cake (page 176). Three kinds of coconut are used to give the custard a mellow tropical flavor. Try to avoid artificial coconut extract, or this sublime treat can turn to something reminiscent of tanning lotion.

Makes about 2½ cups / 650g

1 cup / 100g loosely packed sweetened coconut flakes

One 13.5-oz / 400ml can unsweetened coconut milk

½ cup / 100g granulated sugar, divided

1 pinch kosher salt

Seeds scraped from ½ vanilla bean, or 1 tsp vanilla extract (see page 12)

¼ tsp coconut or almond extract

2 Tbsp cornstarch

3 egg yolks, at room temperature

2 Tbsp unsalted butter

1   In a food processor, pulse the coconut flakes ten times to slightly break up the strands. Set aside.

2   In a medium saucepan over medium heat, combine the coconut milk, ¼ cup / 50g of the sugar, salt, vanilla, and coconut extract and cook, stirring, until it simmers.

3   In a medium bowl, whisk together the cornstarch and remaining ¼ cup / 50g sugar. Add the egg yolks and whisk into a smooth paste.

4   Whisk enough of the hot milk, a little at a time, into the egg mixture until it is warm to the touch. Once the eggs are tempered, pour the mixture back into the remaining milk in the pan.

5   Return the saucepan to medium-high heat and bring the mixture to a boil; continuously whisk for 3 minutes more or the pastry cream will separate once it cools. After the 3 minutes, whisk in the butter and coconut flakes.

6   Pour the pastry cream into a shallow container and cover with plastic wrap, pressed directly onto the surface, to prevent a skin from forming.

7   In a large bowl, add enough ice cubes and cold water to create a bath for the container to sit in without the water breaching the sides.

8   Set the container in the ice bath or place in the freezer until chilled, about 15 minutes before using. Or transfer to an airtight container and store in the refrigerator for up to 3 days.

BAKER'S NOTE

For added depth of flavor, place the coconut flakes on a baking sheet and toast in a 350°F / 175°C oven until golden, about 15 minutes. Let cool completely before using.

sticky coconut filling

This sticky filling is most closely associated with "German" Chocolate Coconut Cake (page 175), but why not put it between layers of Banana Cream Cake (page 132) or over a sheet of Yellow Cake (page 122)?

Makes about 3 cups / 710g

2 cups / 200g loosely packed sweetened coconut flakes

1 cup / 200g loosely packed brown sugar

½ cup / 110g unsalted butter

2 tsp vanilla extract (see page 12)

½ cup / 120ml evaporated milk

½ tsp kosher salt

1½ cups / 180g pecan pieces, lightly toasted

1 In a food processor, pulse the coconut flakes ten times to slightly break up the strands. Set aside.

2 In a medium saucepan over medium-low heat, combine the brown sugar, butter, evaporated milk, vanilla, and salt and cook, stirring, until smooth, about 3 minutes.

3 Remove from the heat and stir in the coconut and pecans, then let cool for about 10 minutes.

4 Use immediately or transfer to an airtight container and store in the refrigerator for up to 1 week. Warm slightly before using so it will spread easily.

This is the classic filling for Black Forest Cake (page 172), but don't stop there. It is also great between layers of dacquoise (see page 157) or sponge cakes (see pages 140 to 145), rolled up into a Pavlova (page 161), or served warm with a slice of Vanilla-Bean Pound Cake (page 63). Feel free to swap out the cherries with any berry or stone fruit, like peaches, apricots, pluots, or plums.

cherry filling

Makes about 2½ cups / 590g

4 cups / 550g fresh or frozen sweet dark cherries, pitted

¼ cup / 60ml water

2 Tbsp kirschwasser or brandy

½ cup / 100g granulated sugar

1½ Tbsp cornstarch

1 In a medium saucepan over medium heat, stir together the cherries, water, and kirschwasser. Cover and cook until the cherries are tender, about 10 minutes (for frozen cherries), or 15 minutes (for fresh cherries).

2 In a small bowl, whisk together the sugar and cornstarch.

3 Strain the cherries through a fine-mesh sieve and return the juice to the pan; reserve the fruit.

4 Add the sugar mixture to the juice, turn the heat to medium, and cook until it comes to a boil and the liquid thickens and is transparent, about 3 minutes. Add the reserved fruit back to the pan and cook for another 30 seconds. Transfer to a bowl and let cool to room temperature.

5 Transfer the filling to an airtight container and store in the refrigerator for up to 3 days.

This bright, tart, super-delicious citrus curd is perfect for slathering on Victory (Victoria) Sponge (page 141) or swirled into Lemon-Curd Pound Cake (page 69). It can also be folded into Perfect Whipped Cream (page 227) and used with any number of other cakes, so mix up a batch and let it inspire you. It's also a great way to use up egg yolks left over from Angel Food Cake (page 150) or Fluffy Swiss Meringue Topping (page 217).

The key to a clean, bright lemon curd that has no hint of egg is to cook it low and slow in a nonreactive bowl on a double boiler. Eggs are sensitive to heat and certain metals, so we need to be gentle with them, or they can give off a sulfur smell and taste that will shift our sublime curd to something that tastes metallic. For the best results, use a stainless-steel or glass bowl (glass takes longer, because it doesn't conduct heat as quickly). The bowl should fit snugly within the pan, so it traps the steam.

lemon curd

Makes about 2 cups / 520g

6 egg yolks, at room temperature	½ cup / 120ml freshly squeezed lemon juice	½ cup / 110g unsalted butter, cut into 8 pieces
1 cup / 200g granulated sugar	Zest of 2 lemons	1 pinch kosher salt

1   In a medium stainless-steel bowl, whisk together the egg yolks, sugar, lemon juice, lemon zest, butter, and salt.

2   Put 1 inch / 2.5cm of water in the bottom of a double boiler or a medium saucepan and bring to a gentle simmer over medium heat. Place the bowl with the lemon mixture over the simmering water.

3   Using a rubber spatula, stir the mixture constantly, making sure to clean the sides of the bowl as you go, until the lemon curd begins to thicken, about 10 minutes; it will be the consistency of smooth pudding.

4   If there are any lumps in the curd, strain it through a fine-mesh sieve into a shallow container and cover with plastic wrap, pressed directly onto the surface, to prevent a skin from forming.

5   In a large bowl, add enough ice cubes and cold water to create a bath for the container to sit in without the water breaching the sides.

6   Set the container in the ice bath or place in the freezer until chilled, about 15 minutes, then transfer to the refrigerator for up to 5 days.

VARIATION: CITRUS CURD

Try the curd with lime, grapefruit, or passion fruit for a different taste sensation. Prepare as directed but swap out the lemon for another type of juice and zest. Or try an orange-lemon curd, using ¼ cup / 60ml orange juice and ¼ cup / 60ml lemon juice, plus the zest of ½ orange. (Oranges on their own will be too sweet.)

berry quick jam

This is a simple, super-fast way to make homemade jam. The flavor is pure and the color vibrant, since it is made with nothing more than fruit and a bit of sugar. Because it relies on the natural pectin in the fruit, it will be looser than a store-bought jam. But if cooked as directed, it will be plenty thick enough to use as a filling in a cake such as Victory (Victoria) Sponge (page 141) or swirled into whipped cream or buttercream.

Makes about 1 cup / 290g

16 oz / 450g fresh or frozen raspberries, strawberries, or other berries

½ cup / 100g granulated sugar

1 Tbsp freshly squeezed lemon juice

1 In a medium saucepan, combine the raspberries, sugar, and lemon juice and use a fork to break up the raspberries just enough to produce a bit of juice. Set over medium-low heat and simmer for about 30 minutes, stirring often.

2 The jam is ready when it clings to a spoon and you can draw a line through the jam that doesn't immediately fill in. Remove from the heat and let cool thoroughly.

3 Transfer to an airtight container and store in the refrigerator for up to 10 days.

VARIATION: ASSORTED FRUIT QUICK JAM AND APPLESAUCE

This method works for just about any fruit that catches your eye. You'll want to adjust the sugar, or you can use honey, depending on your taste and the sweetness of the fruit you pick. The amount of time needed to reduce the liquid in the fruit will depend on the fruit, so it may take more or less time to make—just use your best judgment and the cling test (it runs off a spoon in a glob instead of drops). Try equal amounts of any of the following fruit in place of the raspberries.

Apples—Peel, core, and chop first; decrease the amount of sugar by about half to make applesauce. The type of apples you pick may require adjusting the sugar, so taste before adding it all.

Concord grapes—Use more sugar; these grapes are pretty tart.

Peaches or other stone fruits—Blanch and peel them first.

Sweet or sour cherries—Stem and pit them.

whipped milk chocolate mascarpone

This is both a filling and a topping, but honestly, you may just want to eat it as a dessert all on its own. Milk chocolate has a mellow sweetness that can be a little too cloying for my taste, BUT marry it with mascarpone cheese and it is nothing short of perfection. My youngest son declared this his new favorite icing, and, believe me, that kid has a discerning palate and quickness of opinion. Slather this mascarpone in and/or on just about any cake, like my classic Yellow Cake (page 122), and you'll have yourself a real crowd-pleaser.

Makes about 4½ cups / 1kg

1½ cups / 360ml heavy whipping cream

1 tsp vanilla extract (see page 12)

1 pinch kosher salt

12 oz / 340g milk chocolate, finely chopped

1½ cups / 340g mascarpone cheese

1   In a small saucepan over medium-low heat, stir together the cream, vanilla, and salt and warm until simmering. Turn off the heat, add the chocolate, and then swirl the pan until the chocolate is submerged in the hot cream. Let sit for about 3 minutes, then whisk gently until smooth. Add the mascarpone and whisk until smooth.

2   Pour the mixture into a bowl, cover, and refrigerate until chilled, at least 1 hour or up to 1 day. It won't whip up well if it's not fully chilled.

3   In a stand mixer fitted with the whisk attachment, beat the mixture on medium speed until it just starts to thicken and turns a bit paler, about 30 seconds. Remove the bowl from the mixer and continue to whip by hand, using the whisk attachment. Once the mascarpone is thick enough to spread, stop mixing.

4   Use immediately.

chocolate bark

Chocolate bark is a simple but stunning way to cover a cake and create the illusion of a much taller cake. For an impressive Christmas centerpiece, use the bark to decorate my Mod Yule Log (page 192). Or you can make feathers, since the method for making feathers is essentially the same as it is for bark and can be done in either white, milk, semisweet, or bittersweet chocolate. Use a good-quality chocolate and not a "coating" chocolate, which has a waxy mouthfeel.

Makes about 12 pieces

8 oz / 225g white or dark chocolate, melted

1 Line a baking sheet with parchment paper.

2 Using a large spoon with about 2 Tbsp of the melted chocolate, pour a ½-inch / 1.3cm-wide by 4-inch / 10cm-long line, on the parchment.

3 Using a pastry brush, gently paint the line of chocolate so it is about 1 inch / 2.5cm wide by 6 inches / 15cm long. Repeat with the remaining chocolate, making sure to leave plenty of space between each one. You should end up with about twelve lines.

4 Transfer the chocolate to the refrigerator until set, 15 to 20 minutes, before using. Or, loosely cover, and store for up to 24 hours.

5 When ready to place on a cake, using a small offset spatula, ease the chocolate off the paper.

VARIATION: CHOCOLATE FEATHERS

Follow steps 1 through 3 of the method, but after painting each line, use a toothpick to draw through the edges to create a feathered look. Chill and attach the feathers in the same way as the bark but don't overlap so you can see the details.

BAKER'S NOTE

The bark is easily attached with soft buttercream. If the frosting on the cake is still soft, the bark will easily stick to the cake, just overlap the pieces slightly to create a solid bark texture. If the buttercream is chilled, you'll need to "glue" them on with some soft buttercream.

Even people who claim they don't care for marshmallows (yes, that person exists) love these. I like to use a bit of extract (mint, ginger, cardamom, almond, orange, lemon, or anything really, but make sure it is an extract, NOT an oil) to add a tasty element of surprise. These are perfect for Hot Chocolate Cake (page 126), but you'll end up with extra to add to your own cup of hot chocolate—or to toast and squeeze between two graham crackers. These make large squares that add plenty of drama to the cake, but you can cut the marshmallows to any size you desire.

marshmallows

Makes about forty 2-inch / 5cm marshmallows

1 cup / 240ml cold water, divided

Three ¼-oz / 7g envelopes unflavored gelatin

1¾ cups / 350g granulated sugar

¾ cup / 240g light corn syrup

1 pinch kosher salt

2 tsp vanilla extract (see page 12)

1 tsp flavored extract (see headnote)

Paste food coloring (optional)

1 cup / 120g confectioners' sugar

1 Lightly grease a 9 by 13-inch / 23 by 33cm baking dish. Set aside.

2 In the bowl of a stand mixer fitted with the whisk attachment, add ½ cup / 120ml of the water and sprinkle in the gelatin to bloom. Make sure there is no dry gelatin remaining in the packets.

3 In a small saucepan, fitted with a candy thermometer, over medium-high heat, combine the granulated sugar, corn syrup, and remaining ½ cup / 120ml water and cook until the temperature reads 245°F / 118°C on the thermometer. Remove the pan from the heat.

4 Carefully pour the hot sugar syrup along the side of the mixer bowl into the bloomed gelatin, being careful that it doesn't hit the whisk attachment.

5 Once you have all the syrup in the bowl, add the salt, turn the mixer speed to high, and let mix for 10 to 12 minutes, until very thick, sticky, and just warmer than room temperature. Add the vanilla and flavored extract and/or food coloring (if using) and mix until thoroughly incorporated.

6 Using a rubber spatula, spread the marshmallow mixture into the prepared dish. Let set, uncovered, for 3 hours.

7 Generously dust a work surface with the confectioners' sugar. Ease the (giant) marshmallow out of the pan; it should fall out with a bit of coaxing. Dust the top of the marshmallow with confectioners' sugar to prevent the knife from sticking as you cut. Grease a chef's knife and cut the marshmallow into squares, cutting five even rows along the short end and eight rows along the long end. Dust the cut ends of the marshmallows with confectioners' sugar.

8 Transfer the marshmallows to an airtight container and store at room temperature for up to 1 week.

BAKER'S NOTE

To toast the marshmallows, place them on a metal baking sheet and use a kitchen blowtorch to achieve a crispy exterior, or put them on a stick and toast them the old-fashioned campsite way over a live fire.

meringue mushrooms

These little woodland gems are a perfect accompaniment to Christmas Yule logs, either classic Bûche de Noël (page 191) or my more modern take, the Mod Yule Log (page 192).

Makes 12 to 24 mushrooms, depending on the size

cake academy review

BASIC PIPING DESIGNS → page 56

¼ recipe Fluffy Swiss Meringue Topping (page 217)

1 oz / 30g bittersweet or semisweet chocolate, melted

1   Preheat the oven to 275°F / 135°C. Line a baking sheet with parchment paper.

2   Place three-fourths of the meringue into a piping bag fitted with a medium round tip (I use Ateco #803). Pipe the meringue into dime-size mounds on the prepared baking sheet. Using the same tip, pipe the remaining meringue into the same number of squat stems that come to a point; this is done by forming a mound that is half the size of the mushroom cap. But instead of a round top, keep squeezing and then lift the bag ¼ inch / 6mm off the paper to form a point before releasing pressure.

3   Bake for 30 minutes, then turn off the oven and let the meringues sit in the cooling oven for about 1 hour. Leave in the oven or transfer to another dry spot for up to 1 day.

4   Poke a small hole in the bottom of each mounded meringue mushroom cap. Dip a stem in the melted chocolate and place the stem into the hole to create the mushroom. Repeat with the remaining meringue pieces and chocolate.

5   Allow the chocolate to set, which will secure the stem to the mushroom cap, about 1 hour (you can pop them in the refrigerator to set faster). Store in a dry, cool spot for up to 48 hours.

VARIATION: SESAME MUSHROOMS

I use sesame mushrooms for my Bûche de Noel. Proceed as directed but just before baking, sprinkle each mounded meringue mushroom cap with a pinch of sesame seeds.

crushed praline

Burnt (in the best way) sugar and nuts create a candy that, when crushed, makes a great addition to whipped cream or buttercream. Or, when pressed against the sides of a cake, adds a beautiful garnish that provides flavor and texture. Depending on your cake, try making this simple recipe with different nuts and seeds.

Makes about 1 cup / 170g

cake academy review

CARAMELIZATION
MAGIC → page 50

½ cup / 100g
granulated sugar

2 Tbsp water

1 tsp light corn syrup

½ cup / 60g whole or
chopped pecans

1 pinch sea salt

1   Line a baking sheet with lightly greased parchment paper or a silicone mat.

2   In a medium saucepan over high heat, combine the sugar, water, and corn syrup and let melt, without stirring.

3   Allow the mixture to boil until the sugar just starts to turn amber along the edge. You can now stir without fear of crystallizing.

4   When the caramel is evenly deep amber throughout and just starting to smoke, turn off the heat and stir in the pecans and salt. Immediately pour the nut mixture in a thin layer onto the prepared baking sheet.

5   Let the mixture cool completely, then transfer to a food processor and pulse until the praline is pulverized and there are no pieces larger than a pine nut.

6   Transfer the praline in an airtight container and store in a cool, dry spot for up to 3 days.

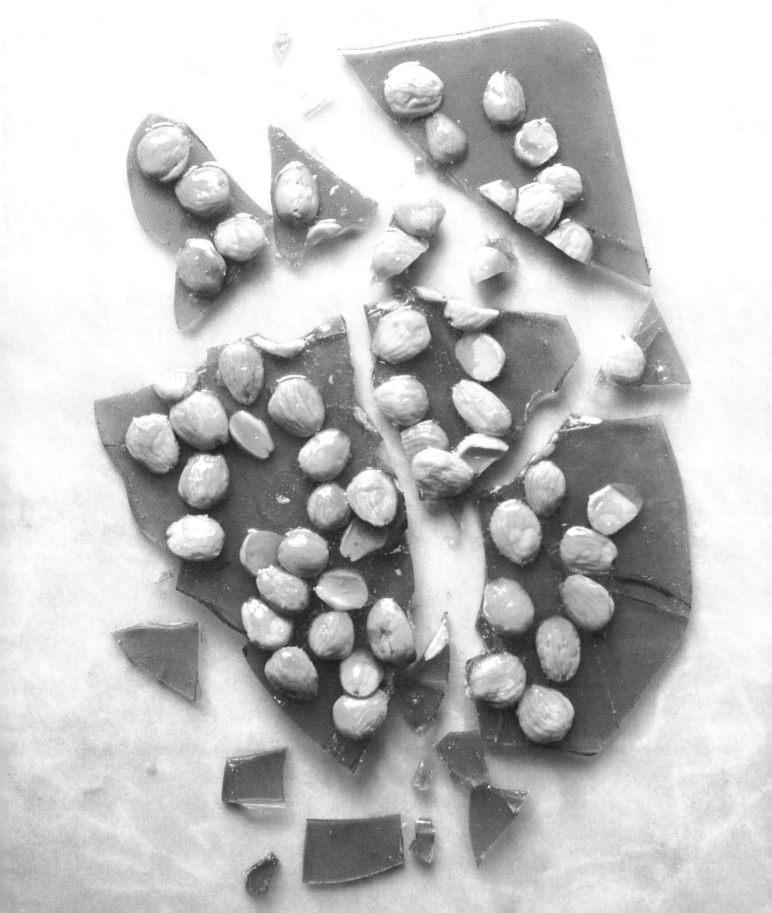

candied hazelnuts

This is an exquisite garnish on a cake that needs a bit of drama. I recommend you save this activity for the winter months, since it doesn't play well with humidity. The tall spires of delicate caramel will wilt if they are left out on a sultry day. You will need eighteen wooden skewers as well as a 6 by 6-inch / 15 by 15cm Styrofoam block in which to set them.

Makes 12 candied hazelnuts

cake academy review

CARAMELIZATION
MAGIC → page 50

18 blanched hazelnuts
(see Baker's Note)

2 cups / 400g
granulated sugar

1 Tbsp light corn syrup

¼ cup / 60ml water

1 In a medium skillet over medium heat, warm the hazelnuts for 1 minute, to soften them, shaking the pan so they don't burn; this will make it easier to skewer them. Stick the skewers into the hazelnuts. Set aside.

2 Place a piece of parchment paper or newspaper on the work surface and set the Styrofoam onto something tall and sturdy (I use a cookie jar to get it up and off the work surface) that won't interfere with the dripping caramel. Place a heavy can on top of the Styrofoam to weight it down. In a large bowl, add enough ice cubes and cold water to create a bath for a medium saucepan to sit in without the water breaching the sides.

3 Carefully place the sugar and corn syrup in the center of the medium saucepan, being careful not to get the sugar on the sides of the pan.

4 Add the water by gently running it down the sides of the pan, washing any rogue sugar back into the center. Do not stir, but gently run your finger through any dry spots of sugar, allowing the water to flow into it.

5 Once the mixture is all wet, set over high heat and bring to a boil, without stirring.

6 Allow the mixture to boil until the sugar just starts to turn amber along the edge. You can now stir without fear of crystallizing.

7 Continue cooking until the caramel just starts to smoke; be careful not to let it go too far.

8 Immediately set the pan in the ice bath to stop the cooking and aid in thickening the caramel. Stir the caramel until it thickens enough to cling to the hazelnuts and drip down in a thin stream. (You'll have to test it out a few times to know when it is ready. If the caramel starts to get too hard before you have dipped all the hazelnuts, return it to low heat until it is the right consistency.)

9 Dip each hazelnut in the caramel, trying not to dip the skewer. Then stick the skewer into the side of the Styrofoam, so the excess caramel drips onto the parchment paper. Repeat with the rest of the hazelnuts, making sure they have plenty of room, so the caramel from one hazelnut doesn't cross sticky paths with another.

10 Allow the hazelnuts to set up, at least 20 minutes or up to 1 hour before using, so the caramel is hard. Very carefully twist the hazelnut loose from the skewer. If the caramel is stuck to the skewer, it is easiest to dislodge it by cutting it away with a pair of kitchen shears.

BAKER'S NOTE

Because these are delicate and can break as you're working, I call for 18 hazelnuts, so you have some extra.

FILLINGS AND FLOURISHES

This is an easy way to add serious drama to a simple cake. It also uses up all the carrot scraps you'd just be wasting. This garnish doesn't care for humidity, so if it's a sticky summer day and you don't have air-conditioning, you may want to cover your cake with shredded sweetened coconut instead.

carrot peel candy

You want to make sure you get a nice thick peel; if they are too thin, they will fall apart while you candy them. When peeling the carrots, you may need to press a bit harder to get a thick enough peel.

Makes about 36 peels	1 cup / 240ml Simple Syrup (page 226)	1 Tbsp orange blossom water, or ½ tsp orange extract	1 pinch kosher salt
			Peels from 2 lb / 900g organic carrots, washed

1 Preheat the oven to 200°F / 95°C. Line a baking sheet with a silicone baking mat.

2 In a saucepan over medium-low heat, stir together the simple syrup, orange blossom water, and salt and warm to a gentle simmer. Add the carrot peels and cook just until the peels are turning translucent.

3 Strain the peels in a fine-mesh sieve and then lay them out on the prepared baking sheet.

4 Bake until the carrot peels start to curl up, anywhere from 30 to 60 minutes, depending on their thickness. Then turn the oven temperature to 100°F / 40°C and bake until completely dry; this can take several hours.

5 Transfer to an airtight container and store in a cool, dry place for up to 48 hours.

VARIATIONS

You can make dehydrated chips out of just about anything (although stone fruits are too juicy to dry nicely), so use a mandoline to slice your produce paper-thin and dry them in the oven. Apples, pears, and pineapples are particularly beautiful when dried.

Apple or Pear Chips—Thinly slice whole, unpeeled apples or pears, from top to bottom (no more than ¹⁄₁₆-inch / 2mm-thick). Bake as directed until dry.

Pineapple Flowers—Thinly slice peeled pineapple disks (no more than ¹⁄₁₆-inch / 2mm-thick). Bake as directed until dry.

BAKER'S NOTE

Once you put the peels on the cake, you want to serve it immediately. Refrigerating the carrot peel candy will cause them to wilt.

SOURCES

You will find links to all the products I use for my cakes on my website, zoebakes.com.

Ateco: nycake.com/ateco-usa
Cake turners and decorating supplies

Bob's Red Mill: bobsredmill.com
Specialty flours and other dry ingredients

Breville: breville.com
Mixers and other small appliances

Driscoll's: driscolls.com
Year-round source of berries

Emile Henry Cookware: emilehenryusa.com
Cookware and ceramic dinnerware

Kerrygold: kerrygoldusa.com
European-style butter

King Arthur Flour: kingarthurflour.com
Flour, specialty cake ingredients, and baking supplies

KitchenAid: kitchenaid.com
Mixers and small appliances

Magnolia Market: shop.magnolia.com
Cake plates and tableware

Maryfrances Carter: maryfrancescarter.com
Cake stands

Mauviel: mauvielusa.com
Cookware

Nordic Ware: nordicware.com
Bundt pans and other baking equipment

Penzeys Spices: penzeys.com
Spices

Seed+Mill: seedandmill.com
Halva and tahini

S.O.S.: sos-chefs.com
Spices

Vermont Creamery: vermontcreamery.com
Butter and other fine dairy products

Valrhona Chocolate: valrhona-chocolate.com
Chocolate and cocoa powder

Wilton: wilton.com
Baking and decorating supplies

ACKNOWLEDGMENTS

Any gratitude I express for the love, support, guidance, and help that my husband, Graham, has provided needs to be multiplied a million times over. Thank you, Graham, this book would simply not exist without your constant, steady hand and head. Henri and Charlie, my sons, thank you for always eating the cake and being so damn honest about what you think of my bakes. I know this book is good because it has your stamp on it! Rafman and Miles (the poodles), thank you for leaving me just a little butter to play with and for keeping me company in the kitchen. Thank you, my family, I know the sacrifice was real, but at least there was cake!

Thank you, Jane Dystel, for believing in me and having my back during the past fifteen years of creating books. I have such peace of mind knowing that you, along with Miriam Goderich and Lauren Abramo, are there to guide and represent me through this not always intuitive process.

I got off my first phone call with my new team from Ten Speed Press and I told my husband that something special was going to be created with them. They instantly got it; it was as if I was talking to old friends about my dreams. They understand what this book means to me as an author, a photographer, and baker. They know that it is written from my heart and soul; and from the outset, they wanted to help me create my vision. I am so grateful to have them as a part of this project. Thank you Kelly Snowden, Betsy Stromberg, Doug Ogan, Emma Campion, Jane Chinn, and Dolores York, for helping me create the book of which I've always dreamed.

Jen Sommerness, thank you for being my cheese, and eating more cake than you've ever wanted. Thanks for opening the door when I carried the hundredth cake across the street to your smiling face. Heather, Jason, and Rowan, thank you for taking cake off my hands with such enthusiasm. Craig and Patricia Neal, my folks, thank you for enthusiastically eating cake and more cake. Lorrain Neal, my mom, thank you for everything, including all the stressed-out dog walks, recipe testing, and loving book edits. Leslie Bazzett; Jay, Tracey, Gavin, Natalie, and Megan Berkowitz, and Leila Quinn; the late Sarah Berkowitz; the late Barbara Neal; Marion and John Callahan; Adam Cohn, thank you for taking all my calls, graciously guiding me through all my contracts and even testing the occasional recipe. Barb and Fran Davis, thank you for always supporting me and running over last-minute props. Todd France, thank you for patiently guiding me through the technical side of my camera and being my birthday-cake muse. Anna and Ewart François, thank you for inspiring me with hazelnut cake. Mathew, Jen, Madison,

Dylan, and Sydney François; Maxine and Bob Kelly; Kathy and Lyonel Norris; Kristin Neal and Bill Freeman; Carey, Heather, Victoria, and Bennett Neal; Sally Simmons and David van de Sande, thank you for all the love and support, always. Stephen Tedesco, thank you for being the trusted navigator on my cake walk. And Amy Vang, thank you for making my work space shine.

Thank you to Joanna and Chip Gaines for giving me a home at Magnolia where I can play in my kitchen and share my love of sweets.

Gratitude to colleagues in our baking and culinary adventures past and present: Steven Brown of Tilia and St. Genevieve; Stephen Durfee of the Culinary Institute of America; Bill Hanes, Kelly Olson, and Linda Nelson of Red Star Yeast; Ragavan Iyer, who explained how the publishing world really works; Riad Nasr of Frenchette; Karl Benson, Marie, and the team at Cooks of Crocus Hill; the entire family at Quang; Suvir Saran and Charlie Burd; Tara Steffen and Susan Jardon of Emile Henry & Mauviel; Madeline Hill, Dusti Kugler, Kelly Lainsbury, Patrick McMahill, Patrick Weiland, Andrew Zimmern, and the entire team at Intuitive Content/Food Works for believing in my cake walk and taking it beyond; Eliza and Ann from Blue Star; and Brian and Ali from Kerrygold.

Thanks to Randee Zarth and Jennifer Burkholder, my first teachers; Stephen Durfee, Thomas Gumpel, and Stacy Radin from the Culinary Institute of America; Michelle Gayer, my friend and mentor; Dorie Greenspan, my baking hero; Abby Dodge, my cookbook mentor; Kevin Masse, a baking fast friend; Manuela, encouraging me from afar; Thank you to Stephanie Meyer, Stephanie March, Kim Kolina, Molly Hermann, Kellee O'Reilly, Ali Kaplan, and Eliesa Johnson, for pushing me to be my best self; Judy Kim, for always being there to support; Brian Hart Hoffman and the incredible team at Bake from Scratch; Julie Jones, pastry artist; and Helen Goh, for being an inspiration.

Appreciation to David Lebovitz, for being a constant source of inspiration in the kitchen and on the page; Candace Nelson, for making cupcakes cool and all the sage advice; Molly Yeh, for being so smart and generous and talented.

Jeff Hertzberg has been my coauthor and friend for well over a decade. I really missed our collaboration while I was working on this book, but he was there for me when I needed a dose of encouragement and a bowl of pho.

Stephani Johnson, thank you for helping me build ZoëBakes into a better, smarter, more fun place to work and freeing me up to bake more cakes. Thank you, Joy Summers, for helping me get words to paper and push past the fear, such a gift. And all my gratitude to Sarah Kieffer, for always sending just the right text to make me laugh and for being my creative sounding board. Thank you also for taking photographs that tell the story I wanted to convey, not to mention being the wizard of Lightroom.

I had several people test recipes for me, but Sara Bartus baked them ALL! I am so grateful for her honest insight, and masterful attention to detail. This book is better by her testing, and she taught me the phrase "Hot Bottom Cake!"

ABOUT THE AUTHOR

Zoë François studied art at the University of Vermont while also founding a cookie company as a way to earn extra money. She then traveled throughout Europe, tasting pastries along the way, and later studied at the Culinary Institute of America in New York. Since then she has been a pastry chef at several Twin Cities restaurants and has worked repeatedly with Andrew Zimmern. Together with Jeff Hertzberg she wrote the book *Artisan Bread in Five Minutes a Day*, which turned into a bestselling series. She created the Zoë Bakes website in order to share her passion for pastry. She lives in Minneapolis with her husband, Graham, and two sons, her best creations yet!

INDEX

All rights reserved.
Published in the United States by Ten Speed Press, an imprint of Random House, a division of Penguin Random House LLC, New York.
www.tenspeed.com

Ten Speed Press and the Ten Speed Press colophon are registered trademarks of Penguin Random House LLC.

Library of Congress Cataloging-in-Publication Data is on file with the publisher.

Hardcover ISBN: 978-1-9848-5736-1
eBook ISBN: 978-1-9848-5737-8

Printed in Canada

Editor: Kelly Snowden | Production editor: Doug Ogan
Designer: Betsy Stromberg | Production designer: Mari Gill
Production manager and prepress color manager: Jane Chinn
Copyeditor: Dolores York | Proofreader: Amy Bauman |
  Indexer: Ken DellaPenta
Publicist: Erica Gelbard | Marketer: Andrea Portanova

10 9 8 7 6 5 4

First Edition